Parliamentary reform at Westminster

MANCHESTER
1824

Manchester University Press

Parliamentary reform at Westminster

Alexandra Kelso

Manchester University Press
Manchester and New York
distributed exclusively in the USA by Palgrave Macmillan

Published by Manchester University Press
Oxford Road, Manchester M13 9NR, UK
and Room 400, 175 Fifth Avenue, New York, NY 10010, USA
www.manchesteruniversitypress.co.uk

Distributed in the United States exclusively by
Palgrave Macmillan, 175 Fifth Avenue,
New York, NY 10010, USA

Distributed in Canada exclusively by
UBC Press, University of British Columbia, 2029 West Mall,
Vancouver, BC, Canada V6T 1Z2

British Library Cataloguing-in-Publication Data is available

Library of Congress Cataloging-in-Publication Data is available

ISBN 978 0 7190 9118 6 paperback

First published by Manchester University Press in hardback 2009

This paperback edition first published 2013

Printed by Lightning Source

Contents

Dedicated to my mother
Rona Brooks
(1955–2002)

Preface

I had better recall before someone else does, that I said on one occasion that all was fair in love, war and parliamentary procedure. (Michael Foot)

It is a common call, perhaps even a prosaic one: 'parliament must be reformed.' There cannot surely be a day that goes by in the life of British politics when these words are not uttered by someone, somewhere. Parliament is perceived to be never quite living up to expectations, to be never quite fulfilling its role properly, to be never quite the institution that it could and should be. It is an issue over which some politicians obsess, on which various think tanks report regularly, and about which some political scientists can get themselves rather worked up (a sight indeed). Schemes for parliamentary reform pop up regularly, and from time to time even parliament itself manages to take a sustained interest in the topic.

Yet, while much has been written about parliament and its various roles and functions, and while countless journal articles have been produced documenting reform schemes and their progress, there has never been a monograph dedicated to the topic, which seeks to map out the history of parliamentary reform and also analyse that reform in a conceptually informed and analytically rigorous way. This book seeks to fill this significant gap in the literature. It emerged from my interest in the topic as a doctoral student, when I was still naïve enough to imagine that dedicating several years of study to a subject might answer all my questions. This, I discovered, was not the case: at the end of my doctoral thesis, I had generated more questions than I had answered, which is, I understand, something you just have to get used to as an academic. Writing this book helped me to tackle (if not conclusively answer) some of the new questions that were posed during that process.

The book explores the history of parliamentary reform and procedural development from the start of the twentieth century until the end of the Blair era in 2007. It aims to do more than talk simply about 'parliamentary reform', as if this were a self-explanatory term. Reform means lots of different things to lots of different people, and the book seeks to explore those definitions in detail. It examines the goals of reforms as they are explained by those who propose them, and how they fit into broader conceptions of the role of parliament in the political system. It maps out the successes and failures of different kinds of reform projects, and pays particularly close attention to the post-1997 era, when the New Labour government took a keen interest in constitutional and parliamentary issues.

However, the book aims to be more than a description of the history of reform. It seeks also to analyse parliamentary reform through the lens of historical institutional theory. This perspective has been used extensively to analyse public policy, but has not been regularly applied to the analysis of formal political institutions. Such a framework involves utilisation of the language of institutional norms and values, of path dependency, and of structured institutional contexts, all of which help in the analytical work of the book. Yet, there are also problems with the historical institutional approach: consequently, the book aims to examine the utility of this perspective, and to examine some of the problems associated with it.

This book seeks to contribute to the academic goal of taking the study of the Westminster parliament beyond simple description. It is not an introduction to parliament, although it does map out some of the historical development of relevance. It explores notions about some of the key principles which underpin the operation of parliament and of parliamentary government, which are informed by contemporary understanding of the Westminster Model, and which help us to understand the institutional context in which parliamentary reform does (or does not) occur. The book is located within an institutional approach to the study of British politics: if it is true, as some scholars of British politics have long argued, that parliament matters, then so too does an analytical approach to understanding how parliament is changed and reformed over time.

Acknowledgements

In any project such as this, there is always a long list of people to thank, so here goes. I would like to acknowledge the support of the Economic and Social Research Council, which funded my PhD and postdoctoral fellowship: the former provided the time to conduct the research on which this book is based, and the latter provided the opportunity to convince a publisher to take it on. I spent my doctoral and postdoctoral years in the Department of Government at the University of Strathclyde, and owe special thanks to everyone there for their support and encouragement. The reason I became absorbed in this topic in the first place is entirely the fault of David Judge: his interest in parliament was infectious, and without his excellent supervision and guidance, this book would never have existed.

Thanks are also due to my colleagues in the division of Politics and International Relations at the University of Southampton, all of whom have offered much encouragement as I completed the manuscript, and who tolerated without complaint my anti-social behaviour in the final weeks of compiling the manuscript. In addition to the financial support of the ESRC, the last months of writing were aided by the award of a University of Southampton School of Social Sciences Small Research Grant for the purposes of completing a few additional interviews in London.

I am grateful to Tony Mason at Manchester University Press, for answering my (many) questions and guiding me through the publication process with patience and courtesy. My thanks also go to those many MPs and peers who kindly found the time to talk to me through the years about this project, and without whom this book would be much the poorer. I owe special thanks to Matthew Flinders, for his comments and advice throughout the writing of this book, and for his support and attention more generally. Thanks also to the many other people who have taken an interest in this book, and in me, and offered words of support just when they were needed. Special mention goes to Philip Cowley, Mark Shephard and Michael Rush for their helpful feedback on very early versions of this work. Naturally, while the advice I've received from everyone has much improved this book, it goes without saying that all errors and misinterpretations are, sadly, mine alone.

Finally, I must thank my family, who are of course the people who put up with all the wailing and despair which inevitably accompanies the writing of any book. Eternal gratitude goes to my grandparents, May and William Cowan, for their unswerving support in what I'm sure must seem to them to be a strange career choice. Much thanks also goes to my sister, Elizabeth Kelso, for looking at the world the same way as I do. And love and thanks to my husband, David Deady, for putting up with me, and for always being there for me.

1
Parliament and parliamentary reform

For some time, there has been a sense that something is wrong with politics. Declining electoral turnout across many liberal democracies in recent decades has prompted concerns that the public has become disaffected about, and disengaged from, political processes and political institutions. As Stoker (2006: 7) notes, 'there appears to be a considerable amount of discontent and disenchantment about the operation of democracy both in those countries that have practiced democracy for decades and those that are more recent converts'. Hay (2007: 1) comments that '[n]owhere, it seems, does politics animate electorates consistently and *en masse* to enthusiastic participation in the democratic process'. In the United Kingdom, the 2001 general election, in which turnout was just 59.6 per cent, occasioned much introspection about why the public did not feel sufficiently motivated to participate, and induced the notion that the massive Labour party landslide secured at the election had been won on the back of political apathy (Harrop 2001). Formal political institutions seem to be in trouble, not least because the public does not apparently trust them. In the autumn 2007 Eurobarometer survey, for example, just 30 per cent of UK respondents said they tended to trust the UK government, and just 34 per cent said they tended to trust the UK parliament (Eurobarometer 68, 2007). Low levels of trust as reported by the public, coupled with what are, for many, unsatisfactory levels of participation in and engagement with democratic processes, raise questions about the health of representative democracy, and necessarily prompt analysis of the condition of national political institutions, and what might be done to 'improve' them.

Consequently, the Westminster parliament has attracted attention in recent years in terms of how it can be changed and reformed so as to improve the role it plays in the British political system. Think tanks, public commissions and even parliament itself have all examined the way in which it functions as a political institution and how changes might lead to enhanced public engagement with politics and thus to more robust representative democracy

(Kelso 2007a). The Hansard Society Commission on the Communication of Parliamentary Democracy, for example, outlined a comprehensive plan geared towards enabling parliament, as a holistic institution, to better inform the public about its work (Hansard Society 2005). The Power Commission inquiry into the condition of British democracy recommended a range of solutions aimed at changing the basis on which parliament operates, and making it into a different kind of representative institution (Power Commission 2006). Various House of Commons select committees have explored ways of making communication between parliament and the public more meaningful and more useful, so as to better engage the public with the work that parliament does (e.g. HC 368, 2003–4; HC 1248, 2003–4; HC 513, 2006–7).

However, if we presently look at the Westminster parliament through a lens which refracts popular concerns about the health of representative democracy, then it is worth noting that this is a very contemporary lens indeed. These concerns prompt a range of specific responses aimed at improving how parliament works as an institution of representation. Yet, parliament has long been subject to a broad range of calls for reform, for a great many different reasons. Throughout its history, parliament has provided a forum both for conducting government and for recalibrating power within the political system, and has been the arena where the legislative and executive capacities of the state interact and intermesh. There has always been debate about the institution of parliament, about its composition, power and function, and much of this has centred on the perceived need to reform parliament in one way or another. Controversies have hinged on the purpose of parliamentary reform, on the specific characteristics of parliament with which reform would engage, and on the merits of various reform proposals in addressing different problems. Ultimately, these debates have been concerned with the fundamental nature of executive-legislative relations at Westminster, how that relationship might be transformed, and the ideal role of parliament within the political system. Key to any plan for parliamentary reform is the existence of a clear understanding of what is specifically wrong with parliament. However, one of the lessons of parliamentary history is that 'there is little agreement on what, if anything, is wrong with parliament, let alone what, if anything, can be done about it' (Judge 1983a: 1).

This book aims to explore some of the history of parliamentary reform, and, in so doing, pursue answers to three key questions. First, why are calls for reform heard in the first place? Calls to reform parliament in any substantive way always have a motivating reason, and are always informed by particular interpretations of the functions of parliament, and how it can better perform those functions. Second, why are they heard at particular times? While there are almost always committed parliamentary reformers attempting to be heard, the fact is that substantial efforts at markedly reforming the institutional infrastructure and power of parliament have come in waves, and this ebb and flow of the reform tide requires some explanation. And third, why are there are such uneven outcomes for reform initiatives in terms of their perceived 'success'? Naturally, not every reform proposal that is forwarded meets with implementation, and different kinds of reform have different kinds of support, and this invites analysis. What the book therefore seeks to do is to unpack a very vague argument that is too frequently put forward without sufficient examination: that is, the argument which states that 'parliament ought to be reformed'. Such a statement is very often heard on the lips of those who claim they have an idea of how parliament can be made to work better. But reform is a multi-faceted thing, and it is not value-free. What might seem like a good reform plan to one observer may well be a recipe for disaster to another. Consequently, the whole rationale for parliamentary reform, its timing and its outcomes require considerable investigation.

Parliamentary reform is essentially about the key principles that underpin the constitutional relationships on which the British political system is based, and so in examining parliamentary reform we are also examining some of the vital debates at the heart of British politics. Consequently, this book, while seeking to analyse one specific British political institution – the Westminster parliament – necessarily engages with many of the key controversies that characterise British politics and which also link into the debates about political engagement that opened this introduction. Where does political power lie? What should executive-legislative relations in Britain ideally look like? How can parliament best perform its scrutiny role and hold the government to account? In asking these kinds of questions, the book, while specific to Britain, also analyses a range of issues which have long occupied legislative scholars and, indeed, comparative political scientists. Institutional development and, indeed, renewal are themes which have had particular resonance in recent decades, and those who study Westminster-style democracies will find much of interest to them in the analysis and arguments presented in this volume.

Indeed, legislative scholars in particular will be interested in the in-depth study provided here of the course of parliamentary reform pursued following the election of the New Labour government in 1997. There was, at that time, renewed interest in the prospects for parliamentary reform, mainly, although not exclusively, due to the party's commitment to reforming the House of Lords, and to its stated desire to 'modernise' parliament more broadly. More than ten years into the New Labour government's term of office, and with the Blair era at a close, it is possible to examine the recent parliamentary reform 'episodes' with the benefit of some perspective. Yet, while we can study contemporary events and dissect them in order to extract meaning and understanding, we cannot really study parliamentary reform without reference to the political context in which it takes place, nor can we attempt to understand it without placing it in the historical context of what has gone before. So, while there has been a decade of substantial parliamentary reform activity since 1997, and much written about it, such reform is perhaps best understood and most usefully analysed when it is contextualised with an understanding of the parliamentary reform which preceded it.

Consequently, this book adopts both a historical and a contemporary approach to the issues it explores. The historical aspect involves an analysis of various kinds of parliamentary reform discussed and implemented since 1900. Naturally, we could go back further still, but parameters must be set somewhere: while the pleasing aesthetic of the turn of the century is appealing, so too is its ability to provide some preface to the substantial reforms that happened in the first decade of the twentieth century. The contemporary aspect of the book examines parliamentary reform pursued by the New Labour government since its election in 1997, and while it seeks to set it in the context of reform history, it also seeks to provide structure and narrative to the post-1997 reform 'story' with the benefit of ten years of development.

The book is guided by the three fundamental questions noted earlier. The first two questions are intimately related: why reform and why now? Both of these very broad questions break down into many other smaller lines of enquiry. Why do various people want to reform parliament in the first place? What is it that they think is wrong with parliament? What kind of solutions do they offer to these problems? Is there a reason why certain kinds of parliamentary reform seem to command more interest or attention at particular times? What do reform proposals suggest about the constitutional outlook of those who propose them?

The third question is more complex, and more controversial: why have certain kinds of parliamentary reform had differing degrees of 'success'? This necessarily leads us to make a clear distinction between different kinds of reform, a distinction which permeates the arguments made throughout this book. That distinction is predicated on the argument that some reforms are designed to make parliament more effective, while others are designed to make it more efficient. Efficiency reforms are those which seek to streamline the workings of parliament, to ensure that the government's legislative programme is secured expeditiously, and to maximise the use made of scarce parliamentary resources, such as time. Effectiveness reforms are those which seek to enhance the ability of parliament to hold the government to account, and to rebalance executive-legislative relations at Westminster. The definitions used here of effectiveness and efficiency are explored fully in Chapter 2, and play a crucial role in helping us better to understand parliamentary reform when it does, and does not, happen.

While his book is geared towards answering the three questions just outlined, it aims to do so through the employment of a particular conceptual framework. On the one hand, we seek to explore and analyse reform with reference to the historical context in which it takes place. Adopting a relatively expansive time frame facilitates an analysis that can be relatively holistic in terms of the conclusions it attempts to draw. On the other, we also seek to understand reform with reference to the institutional context in which it takes place. Consequently, a historical institutional framework is utilised throughout as a way of providing more analytical muscle to the accounts provided of reform 'success' and 'failure'. The narrative and description of reform is of course essential, but if we also want to attempt to *explain* why things happen as they do, then we must employ a conceptual framework which can at least help us find those explanations. In adopting the approach of historical institutional theory, we therefore not only *acknowledge* the role of the political context in affecting reform, but also try to *explain* why and how institutional norms and values impact on reform in the way that they do. Crucially, while it is often easy to be sceptical about the extent to which things ever do change at Westminster, the fact remains that change does take place, and we must be able to account for it. Traditionally, observers refer to the essentially 'evolutionary' nature of change at Westminster, yet this is by itself neither particularly accurate from a descriptive perspective nor helpful from an explanatory perspective. In utilising historical institutional theory as a way to underpin the description and narrative, it cannot provide an answer to every question we may ask, but it at least provides a basis on which we can begin to analyse parliament in a conceptually grounded way.

Yet, while an institutional approach can help us assess the norms and values of parliament, and their role in structuring reform, we must also remain aware of the role of the individuals who collectively comprise an institution and confer meaning on it. Consequently, this book pays considerable attention to some of the key political actors (or agents, in institutional-speak) who have influenced the reform agenda, particularly after 1997. It also draws on a series of interviews conducted by the author with some of these key actors, particularly MPs, who have been interested in and involved with parliamentary reform in the post-1997 era. The individual analyses they offer provide interesting insights into how they understand the reform mechanisms in operation, and how they conceptualise the parliament of which they are a part.

This book therefore attempts to make an original contribution to the wider literature on the Westminster parliament in a number of key ways. First, it seeks to study in depth a particular aspect of the Westminster parliament – that is, its reform – which has not previously enjoyed the dedication of an entire volume. This affords the opportunity to provide detailed, specialised analysis of what is a particularly controversial issue at Westminster. There are many scattered examinations of various examples and episodes of parliamentary reform, but there has not until now been a broad analysis of them in monograph format. Second, the empirical study provided is also couched in a conceptual framework – historical institutional theory – in order to lend analytical vigour to the project. This helps the volume make an original contribution to the field because few other studies have attempted to do this. Although many reviews of and commentaries on parliamentary reform have been written, few, if any, have attempted to utilise one particular conceptual framework for the purposes of explanation. Consequently, while this book contains a great deal of description in terms of reform, that description is underpinned by historical institutional theory for the purposes of providing a more sophisticated analysis of both the institutional persistence and change that are described. Furthermore, much of the historical institutional literature has been dedicated to the study of public policy; far less attention has been devoted to applying the perspective to formal political institutions, and so the book is attempting something relatively innovative in that regard. In addition, the book seeks to tackle some of the difficulties inherent in the historical institutional literature, with respect to its ability to explain change. It does not attempt to offer definitive answers to this problem, but, in actually examining this problem of explanation by way of empirical analysis, it does provide discussion that is derived from the evidence of change experienced by a real political institution. Finally, the volume benefits from the inclusion of interview material collected from 2001 onwards, and which is of use in helping to frame the contemporary reform debates, and the perceptions of those individual actors involved with them. The book does not, therefore, simply provide historical and documentary analysis: it also offers an insight into how recent reform episodes have been understood and negotiated by parliamentarians themselves.

The book adopts a particular approach to examining this broad subject of Westminster parliamentary reform. Chapter 2 begins the process of analysing Westminster parliamentary reform by setting out the conceptual framework in which the study is embedded. It maps out the content and arguments of historical institutional theory, and explores how these arguments and ideas can help us in terms of explaining parliamentary reform. It also examines what is perhaps the key weakness in historical institutional theory – how to explain change when it happens. This is of key importance in a study such as this which has at its heart a focus on parliamentary reform. Institutional theory might be good at explaining institutional persistence, but when change does happen, we must be equipped to explain it. This book seeks to contribute to this debate by doing just that. Chapter 2, in addition to mapping out the conceptual framework adopted by the book, also discusses the historical context which we must acknowledge if we want to understand the contemporary Westminster parliament. The British political system has, over time, produced a legislature and executive which are tightly fused

together, and it is the existence of the government inside parliament which
conditions much of the parliamentary reform 'story'. The way in which the
executive and legislature are fused together is the consequence of the key
principles on which the British political system is based: parliamentary sovereignty, ministerial responsibility, and party government. The institution of
parliament is conditioned by these principles, and so an approach which
stems from the implications of institutional theory must therefore acknowledge them and their continued impact on parliament as an institution.
Chapter 2 therefore seeks to fulfil the twin aims of explaining the utility of
historical institutional theory for this book, and also setting out the political
context in which parliament operates, a context which institutional theory
states to be of supreme importance in understanding development and
change.

Chapters 3 to 8 then take this institutional framework and political
context and use them as lenses through which we can view parliamentary
reform empirically. Chapter 3 examines the course of House of Commons
reform from 1900 to 1997 in terms of efficiency reforms – those designed
to streamline the functioning of the House and ensure that government
secures its legislation expeditiously – and particularly charts the development
of the Commons as a 'legislative machine'. Chapter 4 takes this focus into the
post-1997 era, and examines how the Labour government delivered its
manifesto commitment to 'modernise' the Commons, with a particular focus
on how this process of modernisation impacted on the legislative process.
Chapter 5 then pursues the second aspect of the parliamentary reform discussion by examining the course of House of Commons effectiveness in the
1900 to 1997 era: that is, how the Commons attempted to improve its ability
to hold the executive to account. Chapter 6 takes this study into the post-
1997 era, by analysing how the Labour government's modernisation
programme accommodated issues of effectiveness, and the various successes
and failures experienced. Chapters 7 and 8 move to the other end of
Westminster to examine the House of Lords. The second chamber experienced several important changes in the pre-1997 era, in terms of efforts to
curb its powers and reform its composition, all of which are explored in
Chapter 7. Chapter 8 then proceeds to examine the course of House of Lords
reform since 1997, in the context of the Labour government's manifesto
pledge to reform its composition, and so unpacks the various difficulties that
have impeded this process. Chapter 9 seeks to draw conclusions from the
empirical analysis of the history of parliamentary reform, and to offer
answers to the three key questions that guided the study.

Positioned at the core of the British political system, parliament is the
forum for, and a partner in, a number of different kinds of political relationships, each of which are structured by the institutional context in which it
exists. The story of parliamentary reform is a compelling one, marked by high

political drama, partisan manoeuvring, individual determination and institutional complexity. It is a story which can only be fully appreciated if we first understand the political context in which parliament exists, and how that context has developed over time. We therefore begin by exploring how institutional theory can be used as a useful conceptual framework here, and how it might enhance our understanding and explanations of parliamentary reform.

2

Historical institutionalism and parliament

Introduction

To understand why parliamentary reform does or does not take place requires a prior understanding of the context in which it does or does not occur. The characteristics of the institution of parliament are a product of its historical development, and that development has fostered the emergence of particular norms and values that continue to shape its functioning and capabilities. Crucially, parliament cannot be understood in isolation from government and, consequently, parliamentary reform cannot be understood separately from its likely impact on government.

Parliamentary reform can most usefully be analysed with reference to the norms and values that structure the institutional context in which parliament exists. It is necessary, therefore, to explore those norms and values, and the specific ways that they regulate and restrict parliamentary capabilities. These norms and values, and the nature of the institutional development of parliament, are very usefully analysed with reference to the historical institutionalist perspective.

Institutional theory and historical institutionalism

Clearly, the Westminster parliament can be classed as a formal institution. Peters (1999: 18–19) explains that an institution is characterised by four features: it is a structural component of the society of which it is a part; it displays a level of stability over time; it affects individual behaviour; and it is possible to perceive a sense of shared values and meaning among its members. The new institutional approach that emerged in the 1980s (DiMaggio and Powell 1991; Koelble 1995; Hall and Taylor 1996) spawned a number of variations, historical institutionalism being one, each of which conceptualises institutions in slightly different ways.

The benchmark work within new institutionalism is that of March and Olsen (1984, 1989), which has subsequently been described as 'normative institutionalism' (Peters 1999). March and Olsen emphasise the role of norms and values within institutions in explaining the actions of actors within them. Institutions are 'collections of standard operating procedures and structures that define and defend values, norms, interests, identities and beliefs' (March and Olsen 1989: 17). The approach underscores the impact of forces endogenous to the institution in shaping the preferences of actors within it (March and Olsen 1986), so that '[i]nstitutions thus to a great extent mold their own participants, and supply systems of meaning for the participants in politics' (Peters 1999: 26). There is also a 'logic of appropriateness', whereby,

> Political actors associate specific actions with specific situations by rules of appropriateness. What is appropriate for a particular person in a particular situation is defined by political and social institutions and transmitted through socialisation. Search involves an inquiry into the characteristics of a particular situation, and choice involves matching a situation with behaviour that fits it. (March and Olsen 1989: 23)

This logic ensures that actors can correctly interpret the dominant value system of an institution and act accordingly (Peters 1999: 29). Furthermore, this logic of appropriateness permits institutions to maintain order and stability while also ensuring flexibility and adaptability (March and Olsen 1989: 160).

These ideas fundamentally inform the historical institutionalist perspective, which has its roots in the work of Skocpol (1985) and Hall (1986), and which was subsequently developed by Steinmo and Thelen (1992) for the purposes of conducting comparative political analysis. A key theme of the historical institutionalist approach is that 'institutions provide the context in which political actors define their strategies and pursue their interests' (Thelen and Steinmo 1992: 7). The institutional framework provides a set of rules to structure the political game (Aspinwall and Schneider 2000: 6). In the context of policymaking, Hall (1986: 19, quoted in Thelen and Steinmo 1992: 2–3) observes that:

> Institutional factors play two fundamental roles in the model [historical institutionalism]. One the one hand, the organisation of policy-making affects the degree of power that any one set of actors has over the policy outcomes ... On the other hand, organisational position also influences an actor's definition of his own interests, by establishing his institutional responsibilities and relationship to other actors. In this way, organisational factors affect both the degree of pressure an actor can bring to bear on policy and the likely direction of that pressure.

From this perspective, institutions constrain politics and structure political battles, but the perspective does not advocate institutional determinism (Thelen and Steinmo 1992: 3). Institutions do not *cause* particular outcomes, but instead 'structure political interactions and in this way *affect* political outcomes' (Thelen and Steinmo 1992: 13; emphasis added). While institutions are able to 'shape and constrain political strategies in important ways, they are themselves also the outcome (conscious or unintended) of deliberate political strategies, of political conflict, and of choice' (Thelen and Steinmo 1992: 10). Human agency, therefore, has a part to play within historical institutionalism, and relates closely to the 'logic of appropriateness' outlined in normative institutionalism.

Historical institutionalists perceive political actors not as rational maximisers, but as rule-following satisficers (Simon 1985; March and Olsen 1984). These actors follow institutionally defined rules, and so will not always act in congruence with their best interests (Thelen and Steinmo 1992: 8). Historical institutionalists do not view preference formation as a straightforward matter. Instead, it is inherently problematical, because it is 'not just the strategies but also the goals actors pursue' that are shaped by the institutional environment (Thelen and Steinmo 1992: 8). Actors' preferences are politically and socially constructed, and are endogenous to the institutional setting in which actors operate (Thelen and Steinmo 1992: 8–9). Consequently, actors' attitudes towards institutional persistence are explained by their 'vested interests ... in preserving the institutional basis of their relative strength' (Torfing 2001: 287). The role and impact of institutions is therefore profound:

> By shaping not just actors' strategies (as in rational choice), but their goals as well, and by mediating their relations of cooperation and conflict, institutions structure political situations and leave their own imprint on political outcomes. Political actors of course are not unaware of the deep and fundamental impact of institutions, which is why battles over institutions are so hard fought. Reconfiguring institutions can save political actors the trouble of fighting the same battle over and over again. (Thelen and Steinmo 1992: 9)

Integral to the historical institutionalist perspective is the notion that 'policy choices made when an institution is being formed, or when a policy is initiated, will have a continuing and largely determinate influence over the policy far into the future' (Peters 1999: 63). Levi (1997: 28) notes that 'the entrenchment of certain institutional arrangements obstructs an easy reversal of the initial choice'. As Pierson (2000b: 493) explains:

> Actors do not inherit a blank slate that they can remake at will when their preferences shift or unintended consequences become visible. Instead, actors find that the dead weight of previous institutional choices seriously limits their room to manoeuvre.

This idea of 'path dependency' (Krasner 1984) has been utilised to explain the trajectory of public policy, and how initial choices can constrain subsequent evolution. As Pierson (2000a: 253) explains, '[t]he farther into [a] process we are, the harder it becomes to shift from one path to another'. Because of path dependency, historical institutionalism has been described as better placed to explain institutional continuity than to explain institutional change (Peters 1999: 68). This observation has implications here, given the aim of explaining not only those occasions when parliamentary reform attempts fail, but also those occasions when they are successful.

Crucially, however, path dependency does not necessarily preclude institutional change. Instead, the 'path may be altered, but it requires a good deal of political pressure to produce that change' (Peters 1999: 63). Historical institutionalism does not equate with institutional determinism. Thelen and Steinmo (1992: 16–17) prefer to discuss the concept of institutional dynamism, and Peters (1999: 65) remarks that path dependency need not be 'simple and straightforward [because] institutional rules and structures generate attempts to solve the problems that they themselves have caused'. Path dependency can accommodate evolution within the confines of the institutional pathway. Peters (1999: 65) concludes that '[t]here will be change and evolution, but the range of possibilities for that development will have been constrained by the formative period of the institution.'

The 'cynical wisdom' of political scientists is that, despite attempts to change things, 'everything tends to stay pretty much the same', and when actors do succeed in securing even marginal change, such change serves mainly to preserve the status quo (Torfing 2001: 277). However, Peters (1999: 68–70) has pinpointed a number of ways that change can be accounted for within the historical institutional perspective, each of which has varying degrees of explanatory capacity. Krasner's (1984) punctuated equilibrium approach, for example, assumes a natural state of equilibrium, which is occasionally punctuated by periods of change brought on by crisis, followed by a return to a level of institutional stability which incorporates the resultant change. The crisis faced by the institution is the result of exogenous changes, and this 'precipitates intense political conflict over the shape of the new institutional arrangements' (Thelen and Steinmo 1992: 15). Part of the power of this approach is its emphasis on the 'stickiness' of 'historically evolved institutional arrangements' (Thelen and Steinmo 1992: 15). In a similar vein is the critical junctures approach (Collier and Collier 1991), which assumes constancy or inertia until there is a confluence of circumstances that are together capable of provoking change into taking place. Institutional change may also occur as a result of learning, which impacts upon the state of equilibrium and leads to change. Such learning may be the result of responses to discoveries made within the institution, or to more exogenous discoveries (Peters 1999: 69). Pierson (1996) argues that the focus is much more on evolution and evolutionary change, as opposed to sudden exogenous jolts to the system, and is thus more in keeping with an incremental approach to institutional change. From this perspective, there should be less emphasis on change producing identifiable departures from past practice, and more attention to the ability of institutions to change more gradually. This evolutionary approach seems to preclude radical institutional change. Torfing (2001: 288) argues somewhat differently that change happens because of a destabilisation of the institutional framework concurrent with a weakening of the institutional barriers to change. Change may also be triggered by an imperfect integration of the institutional framework, which creates institutional pathway ambiguity. In this case, 'institutional reform is facilitated by a complex interplay of internal sources of instability and external events that dislocate the structured coherence of the policy path' (Torfing 2001: 288).

Yet, Peters (1999: 70–1) notes that the historical institutionalist perspective is not a 'fertile source' of explanations for institutional change, and that when they do offer explanations, they are largely reliant on events that are exogenous to the institution. Pierson (2000b: 476) similarly argues that '[p]olitical scientists have had much more to say about institutional effects than about institutional origins and change'. Gorges (2001: 137) is somewhat less delicate in his criticisms:

> By relying on such variables as critical junctures, path dependency, leadership, technological change and the role of ideas, new institutionalist analyses leave institutions behind and resort to a grab-bag of explanations that proponents of almost any theoretical perspective could use.

Gorges argues that, all too often, it is 'extra-institutional factors that really shape outcomes' and that institutional theory is of no use in explaining change. However, we should exercise caution when criticising institutional theory in this way. In one respect, there are certainly questions over whether factors that prompt institutional change are properly labelled exogenous in the first place (Lindner and Rittberger 2003). In addition, endogenous factors may help explain continuity, but that does not preclude the possibility that they may also prompt change to correct path dependent deficiencies, as Peters (1999: 69) suggests. Furthermore, institutional authors have always been at pains to stress, in line with Thelen and Steinmo (1992: 3) that 'institutions constrain and refract politics but are never the sole "cause" of outcomes'. Yet, for Peters, Pierre and King (2005), the problem is that historical institutionalism has not been applied in a way that takes sufficient account of agency and of the role of ideas, and that far more attention needs to be given to the politics of path dependency itself. At any rate, there is little question that historical institutionalism enjoys its most convincing explanatory utility when mapping the reasons why institutions can resist change in the face of compelling forces for change: it is disingenuous to discard it simply because it cannot explain absolutely everything, when, after all, no conceptual framework ever could.

Ultimately, historical institutionalism does have a perspective on change:

> Change is seen as the consequence (whether intended or unintended) of strategic action (whether intuitive or instrumental), filtered through perceptions (however informed or misinformed) of an institutional context that favours certain strategies, actors and perceptions over others. Actors then appropriate a structured institutional context which favours certain strategies over others and they do so by way of strategies they formulate or intuitively adopt. Such strategies are, in turn, selected on the basis of an always partial knowledge of the structures (the institutional context) within which the actors find themselves and the anticipated behaviour of others. (Hay and Wincott 1998: 955–6)

The key to understanding change within the historical institutional approach, therefore, lies in the idea of a *structured institutional context that favours certain strategies over others*. It is the norms and values of the institution that provide this structured context, and which thus constrain the opportunities for change. The path dependency set in motion by the existence of a particular institution creates difficulties for those who wish to see institutional change, because certain characteristics of the institution – its norms and values – become embedded and cannot easily be altered.

What, therefore, is the *structured institutional context* in which the Westminster parliament exists? What are the norms and values in operation there? If we accept one of the central tenets of historical institutional theory, that institutional origins have a lasting and substantial impact on institutional development, then it is necessary to examine the historical origins of the Westminster parliament in order to understand how its development has been shaped by them. The 'dead weight of previous institutional choices' described by Pierson (2000b: 493) will, from a historical institutional perspective, significantly shape the evolution of parliament, and, crucially, structure the context in which its reform does, or does not, occur. Actors do not inherit a blank slate in institutional terms, and nor do parliamentary reformers, who exist in a context in which some strategies for reform will be favoured over others, and where those strategies so favoured are the result of the norms and values that are embedded into the parliamentary landscape. Consequently, parliament's norms and values can only be fully appreciated by tracing their origins through the historical development of the Westminster parliament and of the system of parliamentary government. It is by mapping the historical origins of parliament that we can understand the structured institutional context in which it now operates, and thus begin to analyse the reforms proposed for it. Consequently, we must undertake a 'mini-tour' of some of the key highlights in the long history of the Westminster parliament.

The historical development of parliamentary government

Judge (1993: 6) explains that, '[t]he evolution of parliament as a legislative assembly – fusing legislative, judicial and executive functions in an exceptional constitutional mixture – is at the very centre of the British state tradition'. Since the beginning, this state tradition has placed the emphasis 'on *government* rather than parliament' (Judge 1993: 6; original emphasis). Parliament's fundamental role has been to facilitate legitimate government. Consequently, any notion that parliament exists primarily to promote democracy and democratic processes is historically inaccurate.

Barons and knights began meeting as a parliament in the thirteenth century, and their earliest function was 'to provide for consultation between successive English governments and those sections of the community, or their representatives, which have mattered in terms of political power' (Butt 1969: 31). The aim was not to approach policymaking in a 'democratic' manner: rather, consultation enabled the monarch legitimately to extract taxation from his subjects by meeting with the most important members of the 'political community' and hearing their grievances. This underlying principle of consultation as a means to legitimate executive actions became the foundation stone of parliamentary government. As Rush (1981: 21) notes, the principle of consultation 'reflect[s] on the one hand a desire to establish and maintain effective government and on the other, to impose limits on the exercise of political power'.

Concepts such as representation and legitimation are therefore intrinsically bound up in the system of parliamentary government, and accordingly frame the relationship between executive and legislature. The Tudor monarchs, for example, enjoyed parliamentary support, and this enhanced the status of parliament because monarchs became increasingly reliant on that support to govern effectively (Norton 2001: 42). Parliament therefore endured as the forum through which the monarch governed, and its importance was reinforced when Henry VIII used it as a means to legitimise the English reformation (Rush 1981: 28).

Nonetheless, scope for disagreement and conflict still persisted. James I, committed to the doctrine of the divine right of kings, caused destabilisation by attempting to raise taxation without parliamentary consent. Furthermore, the meeting of parliaments was erratic even until the time of Charles I: indeed, only near financial catastrophe compelled Charles to call parliaments to approve his taxes. One of those, known as the Long Parliament, used the opportunity to agree on a series of laws that secured regularity in the calling of parliaments, and which ensured that only parliament had the authority to dissolve itself. Yet parliamentarians remained unsure of parliament's ability legitimately to curb royal power and this, coupled with the continued refusal of Charles I to accept parliament as a part of the governing process, effectively led to the Civil War and the Protectorate (Rush 1981: 29). Despite Cromwell's professed commitment to parliament, government during the Protectorate operated on the authority of military rule. As Judge (1993: 19) remarks, '[w]ithout the consent and legitimacy conferred upon executive actions by a representative parliament – the quintessential feature and central problem of government since medieval times – the Protectorate was inherently unstable'. Once the move began to restore the monarchy in 1660, therefore, it was understood to be the restoration of legitimate government also, 'of government consented to by representatives of the political nation' (Judge 1993: 19). The Restoration also marked the beginning of a move towards constitutional monarchy (Rush 1981: 29). Charles II accepted the need to share power with his ministers and with parliamentary representatives, thus marking the early development of the Cabinet. Yet, with James II on the throne, parliament was once more forced to assert its political authority, and, as a result of the Glorious Revolution of 1688, 'acted to spell out precisely the conditions under which the monarch was to operate' (Judge 1993: 20).

Until parliament invited William and Mary to take the throne in 1689, the essential struggle between parliament and the executive concerned the nature and manner of exercising political power, and parliament's right to check or curb that power. By 1689, however, parliament was the established forum for political power in the nation, and had secured its freedom from the exercise of arbitrary monarchical power by means of the Bill of Rights. The essential purpose of the Bill of Rights 'was to assert the position of Parliament in relation to the Crown', and it became illegal for the Crown to raise taxes without the consent of parliament (Norton 2001: 43). The locus of authority had shifted towards parliament, which had successfully subordinated monarchical power to its own parliamentary sovereignty (Judge 1993: 20). This process was also consolidated by the financial repercussions of the Nine Years War (1689–97), which required unprecedented revenue raising powers from the state, and which forced William III to become ever more reliant on parliament to service that need (Harling 2001: 17). Parliament was called annually in order to extract the sums necessary for waging war, and MPs became adept at the machinations of financial control. Indeed, '[t]he debates on the estimate and the "supply" quickly became the main highlights of the annual session, serving as potent reminders that it was only through parliamentary consent that the machinery of the state would be paid for' (Harling 2001: 18). Despite the continued existence of numerous royal prerogatives, real decision-making power had shifted towards those influential and powerful individuals who sat in parliament, primarily by virtue of their aristocratic backgrounds. These individuals soon formed loose coalitions or factions with others of like-minded persuasion in order to guide governmental decision-making. Therefore, by the time George I came to the throne by parliamentary statute, royal power had been thoroughly cropped, and the King, and his successor George II, relaxed into a settled relationship with a parliament that had consolidated its power within the state (Harling 2001: 34). As Harling (2001: 37–8) summarises:

> It was indisputable that parliament now governed alongside the monarch, and parliamentary government throughout the eighteenth century was government of and by a fairly narrow propertied elite, if not exactly government for their behalf alone.

Parliamentary government is, therefore, deeply rooted within the political system. As Birch (1964: 13) explained, the debate over constitutional arrangements was always about the representation of valid interests and about securing strong and responsible government. Yet, once the authority of parliament had been asserted, a new fault line began to emerge within parliament itself, between the House of Commons and the House of Lords. This conflict is fundamentally about which House can legitimately claim superiority over the other, and it has helped delineate the norms and values in operation at Westminster.

The barons and knights who comprised the early parliaments very quickly met separately from each other (Norton 1981: 12). This separation fostered the practice of the Commons having sole control over financial matters (Shell 1988: 7), and the status of the House of Commons as the pre-eminent chamber consequently was consolidated. Prior to the Reform Act, and despite the existence of rudimentary forms of elections, membership of the Commons was largely decided by a small group within the aristocracy (Ostrogorski 1902). However, the limited expansion of the franchise in 1832 had serious repercussions for the role of the Commons within parliament, and for its relationship with the Lords, as did the subsequent electoral reforms of 1867. As the size of the electorate increased, political power was extended to such a degree that the aristocracy could no longer influence the political community as easily as it once had, and new forms of patronage were thus required. The new electoral climate proved conducive for the growth and emergence of modern parties, designed to act as conduits for political communication and as vote-gathering machines. Electoral reform laid the foundations for the notion that party was essential for the effective operation of parliamentary government (Butt 1969: 73).

As election was to the Commons, rather than to the Lords, the understanding emerged that government was a creature of the lower chamber. Consequently, the Lords became less able to challenge the Commons because of its electoral legitimacy (Norton 2001: 45). The reforms of 1832 and 1867 together consolidated the status of the Commons as the pre-eminent House with the legitimate authority to govern (Shell 1988: 8). Yet the 1867 reforms also stripped the House of Commons of two of its most important functions, as described by Bagehot (1867). The legislative function passed out of the hands of the Commons and upwards to cabinet ministers. The elective function, of choosing the personnel of government, passed downwards into the hands of the electorate. The increasing complexity of the business of government also contributed to the marginalisation of parliament in terms of its involvement in formulating legislation (Norton 2001: 46).

By the early decades of the twentieth century, then, the executive was dominant within the political system, and parliament's role was that of legitimating the actions of government. As Norton (2001: 47) explains, 'Britain retained a parliamentary form of government, but what that meant was not government by Parliament but government through parliament'. Parliamentary government bestows considerable power on the executive, but on the basis that the executive enjoys the confidence of the House of Commons, and that the government collectively, and ministers individually, are accountable to parliament for their actions (Rush 1981: 1). Accordingly, parliament is important not for the formal powers and procedures that it possesses, but because it facilitates responsible and legitimate government (Judge 1993: 2).

The historical development of parliamentary government at Westminster has fostered the development of norms and values that shape the structured institutional context in which parliament exists. Parliament's development has reinforced the centrality of strong and responsible government. So, what are the specific norms and values in operation at the Westminster parliament, and how can they be understood in light of the historical institutionalist perspective? These two questions are essentially linked together in one answer: the Westminster Model. This model emerged in the latter part of the nineteenth century as scholars sought to describe the political system in which politicians and institutions operated. Crucially, what has always been compelling about the Westminster Model is that it is not just a conceptual framework constructed by academics: it was also championed then, as it is now, as an ideal set of principles on which British government should operate (Judge 2005). In other words, the Westminster Model is not only descriptive, but also normative. And it is because the model describes not only how government *does* proceed, but also how it *should* proceed, that enables it to provide the link between the central principles of the British constitution and historical institutionalism. The main tenets of the Westminster Model were, and are, the fundamental norms and values that structure the institutional context in which parliament exists and in which its reform takes place. Crucially, three of those tenets are of integral importance here: parliamentary sovereignty, ministerial responsibility, and strong party government. It is these fundamental constitutional principles which are the norms and values that give structure to the institution of parliament, and which provide the parameters within which the path of parliamentary development and reform is constrained.

Parliamentary sovereignty

Parliamentary sovereignty is the constitutional principle at the heart of the Westminster Model and of the British political system. Yet the term 'sovereignty' has a straightforward legal meaning that exists in a more complex political reality. The clearest description of parliamentary sovereignty comes from the legal theorist A.V. Dicey ([1885] 1959: 39–40), who defined it to mean that 'Parliament has ... the right to make or unmake any law whatever' and that nobody could override parliamentary legislation. Although Dicey's ideas are more than a century old, 'his statement of the doctrine has retained a remarkable influence on both legal and political thinking about Parliament' (Bradley 2007: 28). What is perhaps most insightful about Dicey's definition is that it makes a distinction between legal sovereignty and political sovereignty: parliament may have no legal constraints on its actions, but it is constrained politically by what the electorate will tolerate. For Foley (1999: 25), Dicey's distinction between legal and political sovereignty rested on the existence of a mass electorate that the House of Commons 'was now progressively embodying rather than merely reflecting'. British constitutional thought has long accommodated a parliament that is considered 'both legally sovereign and subject to customary restraints' (Goldsworthy 1999: 190). In the words of Jennings (1957: 8), 'the fact that no Government could secure powers to kill all blue-eyed babies is not due to any legal limitations in the powers of Parliament but to the fact that both the Government and the House of Commons derive their authority from the people'.

The 'practice' of sovereignty therefore contributes to the way that norms and values are constructed and interpreted at Westminster. In theory, sovereignty is exercised as a result of the Commons making a collective decision, in which all MPs participate. However, parliament and its members are organised for the benefit of the executive, and it is therefore executive sovereignty that is in operation, underpinned by the medium of party. Yet executive sovereignty is still justified in terms of parliamentary sovereignty, because of the representative and democratic legitimacy of the House of Commons. In addition, the continued functioning of parliamentary sovereignty is defended even in the context of membership of the European Union and of devolution in the UK, despite, or perhaps because of, the impact such developments have on the political capabilities of Westminster. For example, the legislation which established the Scottish Parliament, the Scotland Act 1998, contained provisions which stipulated that Westminster would remain sovereign and retain its ability to legislate for Scotland. Yet the generally accepted view was that, despite this re-statement of Westminster sovereignty, the UK parliament would not thereafter legislate for Scotland on devolved matters without its express consent (Bradley 2007: 50–1). The almost mythical status of the principle of parliamentary sovereignty is therefore intrinsically bound up in the norms and values that shape the institutional structure in which Westminster exists.

Ministerial responsibility

Ministerial responsibility is the principle that breathes life into the functioning of British government, and is the key to understanding how the relationship between government and parliament is structured and mediated. It was the bedrock for the development of modern parliamentary government, and is a key component of the Westminster Model. As Judge (1993: 135) explains:

> [t]he belief that a minister alone is in some sense responsible for the performance of an administrative department is the principle around which the British central state has been organised and around which the relationship between elected representatives and non-elected bureaucrats has been defined.

Collective ministerial responsibility involves government ministers accepting responsibility for decisions reached at cabinet level, while individual ministerial responsibility involves ministers accepting responsibility for the policy of their departments (Blackburn and Kennon 2003: 28, 45). The whole notion that ministers are responsible and accountable to parliament for the actions and decisions of the departments of which they are in charge is a product of the development of the House of Commons in the mid-nineteenth century, when the House, in many respects (and very unusually), dominated government. The House was able to set the terms of this convention of ministerial responsibility in the context of the emergence of clearly identifiable ministerial departments, whereby the need for government to be able to govern effectively was conditioned by the desire to ensure that government would remain accountable to parliament. Crucially, these emerging government departments were, through the operation of the ministerial responsibility doctrine and the accountability processes to which it gave effect, supposed to be subservient to parliament. By the end of the nineteenth century, the executive was once more ascendant, and the Westminster Model thus privileged the principle of strong government (and increasingly powerful ministers), so long as it was also accountable government. The convention of individual ministerial responsibility supplied the bridge between these two constitutional norms of strong and accountable government, with parliament, and particularly the House of Commons, providing the institutional arena in which ministers were individually held to account.

The traditional interpretation of the individual ministerial responsibility convention is that ministers are answerable to parliament for the actions of their departments, and, more controversially, that they must resign when serious mistakes are made. The controversy stems from the relative dearth of instances of resignations on account of departmental failures. As Woodhouse (2001: 40–1) comments, 'it would seem that rather than being motivated to morality, ministers are motivated to distance themselves from any culpability and hence from the requirement of resignation'. Non-resignation has been defended on the grounds that it is impossible for one individual to be aware of all that occurs within a sprawling government department. Consequently, the distinction has been made between operational and policy responsibility (Drewry 2000), with ministers responsible for the latter and agency chief executives for the former. Governments have increasingly enhanced the responsibility-accountability distinction, resulting in a situation where 'the practical workings of ministerial responsibility are divorced from the theory' (Drewry 2000: 180). The concern is not a new one: in 1964, A.H. Birch observed that the power of parliament to bring about ministerial resignation was 'apparently nominal rather than real'. However, the absence of ministerial resignation on the grounds of departmental failure does not mean that the doctrine is irrelevant (Kam 2000: 380). The ministerial responsibility convention 'continues to affect state form and political relationships at the centre of government' (Judge 1993: 138). Gradients of responsibility exist at the level of application, and those gradations permit the operation of a range of accountability mechanisms, from simple explanatory accountability to resignation accountability (Judge 1993; Woodhouse 1994). Contemporary instances of ministerial resignations have also prompted some exploration of the factors that induce ministers to resign (Woodhouse 2004a).

Nonetheless, the convention remains problematic, and many of the concerns remain the same across the decades. Birch (1964: 140) claimed that it was used to prevent alternative scrutiny procedures from developing, and that the convention, 'far from ensuring that the departments are subservient to Parliament, actually serves to protect the departments from Parliamentary control'. The convention has, in fact, been inverted by ministers so as to control their relationship with the legislature and to enable them to dictate the terms of accountability and responsibility (Judge 1993). This enables ministers significantly to shape the structured institutional context in which parliament operates. Woodhouse (2004b: 325) explains that 'ministerial responsibility ... remains dependent on the integrity of ministers and on the co-operation of government for its operation'. Judge (1993: 152) argues that 'ministerial responsibility ... inverts the logic of the doctrine – of openness and accountability – precipitating a secret and closed process of decision making'.

This inversion of the convention is the result of historical development. The rise of the ministerial state is located in the context of Whig and Peelite theories of state functioning (Beattie 1995; Birch 1964). The former emphasises the representative element of the doctrine, and the need for government to be held responsible for state action. The latter focuses on limiting the encroachment of democracy so as to facilitate strong government. Both strands have shaped the evolution of the doctrine, and, therefore, it can be made as flexible as is required: it can act as a tool for enhanced accountability or as a tool to protect the perceived rights of the executive. Flinders (2000: 78) explains that both views have served, 'albeit from opposing standpoints, to rationalise and justify the ministerial state'. Yet problems with how the convention impacts on civil servants (Polidano 1999, 2000) has led to a 'responsibility gap' which the convention alone cannot fill (Flinders 2000: 80). For some, ministerial responsibility has become a serious curb on the effective operation of democratic accountability (Weir and Beetham 1999: 367). The convention remains central to political relationships, not because it provides for accountable government, but because it can be used 'by the executive as a legitimating tool to justify the refusal to introduce reforms' (Flinders 2000: 80).

In institutionalist discourse, the convention is used to structure political interactions between government and parliament and thus influence outcomes. The structured institutional context, of which the ministerial responsibility convention is a part, shapes preference formation regarding the potential for its reform. Parliament struggles to secure effective ministerial accountability, and as the executive benefits from that situation, it is unlikely to seek institutional changes which impact on the operation of the convention in a significant way.

Party government

The Westminster political system facilitates strong and responsible government, and it is through party that the executive asserts its dominance within parliament. Weir and Beetham (1999: 373) observe that, '[i]f it is the political executive's tripod of power in Whitehall, Westminster and party that creates the structure of its dominance over Parliament, then it is essentially party loyalty which holds it in place'. Party cohesion is integral to parliamentary government, because without it, 'the accountability of the executive to both legislature and voters falls flat' (Bowler et al. 1999: 3). The governing party's claim to work to a clear policy programme facilitates both democratic responsiveness and responsible government (Beer 1974: 19–21).

The institutional context in which modern parties emerged in the late eighteenth and early nineteenth centuries ensured that the party system was intimately intertwined with parliamentary development. This relationship can be seen 'as the institutional embodiment of the principles of representation, consent and legitimate government' (Judge 1993: 68). The electoral reforms that began in 1832 contributed significantly to the development of a two-party system. The emergence of party cohesion aided the ability of

governments to sustain majorities inside the House of Commons, a requirement for effective government recognised long before the move towards
representational reform (Evans 1985). Electoral reform consolidated the
position of party inside the Commons, and parties exploited this development by 'grafting on to the pre-1832 putative party system the essential
ingredients of discipline' (Judge 1993: 74, original emphasis). While party
organisation benefited from electoral expansion in the nineteenth century,
parliamentary independence was severely wounded by it (Ostrogorski
1902). By 1880, there was a clear 'polarisation of loyalties' between the
parties (Conservative and Liberal) and their leaders (Pugh 2002: 3).
Governments began losing fewer divisions as a result of increased party
voting cohesion in the Commons, aided by the growing influence of the
party whips and of the willingness of MPs to acknowledge their party
responsibilities (Self 2000: 34–5; Berrington 1968). The strengthened discipline within parties eventually led to parliamentary government, as it has
been traditionally understood, being superseded by party government.
Government governs through the institution of parliament, but the means by
which it governs is through party.

The evolutionary nature of the democratic process dovetailed with a
system that had 'long accommodated notions of representation' (Garrard
2002: 279). The democratisation process produced an electoral system based
on the plurality model, and which 'seeks to reconcile the idea of strong
government with the principle that everyone's vote should count equally,
though … it gives far more emphasis to the first objective and neglects the
second' (Weir and Beetham 1999: 46). The electoral system is geared towards
producing an outcome in which one party can clearly claim victory and the
right to govern, thereby ensuring strong government. The electoral system
also produces an adversary system, where parliamentary government is institutionalised into government and opposition, and characterised by conflict.
The parliamentary process is organised around the government and opposition front benches, and the 'usual channels' are the forum through which
parliamentary time is organised (Rush and Ettinghausen 2002: 5–8). Both
have an interest in a degree of collaboration: the government does not want
the opposition to use its weapon of time to interfere too much with the
legislative timetable, and the opposition does not want the government to
restrict its scrutiny opportunities (Blackburn and Kennon 2003: 407).

Internal party pressures generally encourage Members to accept the party
line, and this is particularly pronounced for MPs in the governing party. In
one respect, there is perhaps a degree of rational choice in operation here.
Those MPs who seek a ministerial career know that this will be more attain-
able if they demonstrate loyalty and support, and may adopt certain strategies
towards that end (Searing 1994: 100–08). Nonetheless, the overwhelming
fact remains that most MPs follow their party line because they are party

members and agree with that line (Cowley 2005). In this respect, party whips play a pivotal role in maintaining the norms and values that support the structured institutional context from which the executive benefits. However, when disagreements do occur, the role of the whips is vital. Their disciplinary strategies emphasise the 'conduction of loyalty simultaneously to the leadership of the party and the government' (Judge 1981). The whipping system operates on the basis of information, persuasion and authority (Searing 1994: 252), all of which are integral in ensuring MPs can do their jobs effectively. The dominant value system at Westminster, which is predicated on executive strength, is fundamentally underpinned by party loyalty and the role of the whips in maintaining that loyalty. The institutionalisation of party cohesion can be problematic for MPs, who may frequently find themselves torn between their party and parliamentarian roles. As the late Robin Cook, a former Leader of the House, noted:

> We are all parliamentarians, but we are also party politicians. We are deeply ambivalent as to whether we want Parliament reaching independent decisions or whether we want our party securing its own agenda. (Cook 2003a: 78)

The party system, and its attendant partisanship, thus significantly contribute to the norms and values in operation within parliament, and add to the structured institutional context in which Members operate. This context consequently structures the nature of demands for parliamentary reform, the nature of the proposals for such reform, and the responses to those proposals.

Approaches to parliamentary reform

In thus outlining the power of the executive at Westminster, and the crucial role played by party in facilitating that power, we necessarily also map out the specific role of parliament within the political system, and, indeed, of individual MPs. However, this particular view of the power of party has been challenged on the basis that this kind of institutional perspective attributes too much significance to structure and not enough to agency. This 'attitudinal' view (Kelso 2003), most forcefully championed by Philip Norton, argues that MPs have at their disposal the formidable power to vote against the government whenever they choose to, and that if MPs used this power more frequently, executive-legislative relations in the UK might be transformed (Norton 1983: 61). Essentially, the argument boils down to one of political will: MPs have the ability to vote against the government if they have the political will to do so (Norton 1981: 234).

This attitudinal approach has implications for the issue of parliamentary reform. Norton (1985: 143) argued that 'significant structural and procedural reforms are achievable, but only if the political will exists among MPs *as a whole* to ensure their implementation and sustenance' (emphasis added).

MPs must have the political will to own and control the parliamentary reform process itself, rather than let government dominate the issue (Norton 1982: 113). As Robson (1964: 194) observed, '[n]o government, whatever its political complexion, is going to make the first move towards enhancing the status of Parliament: the initiative must come from the House of Commons'. Furthermore, successful parliamentary reform requires a particular climate in which to operate, a climate characterised by three clement conditions (Norton 2000: 1–14). First, a window of opportunity must be present for reform to occur. That may appear at the beginning of a new parliament, 'but in general refers to fortuitous circumstances arising in which a climate for reform may brew' (Kelso 2003: 67). Second, there must be a coherent reform agenda, to provide a package behind which Members can unite. Third, there must be leadership to take the reform package through parliament. At the heart of these conditions, there must be political will for successful reform (Kelso 2003: 67). This idea about pre-requisite conditions for reform closely resembles Collier and Collier's (1991) 'critical junctures' approach to institutional change, where institutional inertia is destabilised by the emergence of a confluence of circumstances that enable change to occur.

The attitudinal approach to parliamentary reform has been challenged, however, by those who argue that it underestimates the political context in which MPs exist, and that the summoning of political will is insufficient to circumvent this context. This view echoes a historical institutionalist interpretation of parliament, emphasising as it does the norms and values in operation at Westminster, the argument that the structured institutional context of parliament has a highly significant degree of influence over those actors who operate there, and that parliament's path dependency substantially constrains the range of reform options that might be realistically contemplated. This 'contextual' approach (Kelso 2003) is most concerned with explaining why parliamentary reform does not occur, even when there is apparent support for it. Crick (1965), discussing the prospect of parliamentary reform, explained that '"the executive mind" on both sides of the House has little patience with even the existing opportunities of parliamentary participation'. Walkland (1976) argued that, because of the nature of the political system, parliamentary reform is an inherently political process, and cannot be divorced from its context. Judge (1993: 191) explains the reform predicament in these terms:

> Ultimately, the fact remains that the logic of parliamentary reform is that of 'Catch 22': the reassertion of Parliament's power is dependent upon the fragmentation of the executive's power, but the centralisation of power in the hands of the government effectively means that it alone has the capacity to sanction the diffusion of power necessary for the rejuvenation of the legislature.

Parliamentary norms and values 'reflect the interests of the most powerful actors therein, and so support the existing distribution of power and the status quo' (Judge 1989: 412). As a result, 'proposals for internal reform which fail to tackle the "structural underpinnings" of the norms at work inside the Commons, underpinnings which have party as a central girder, will be largely ineffectual' (Kelso 2003: 69).

The contextual approach points to the specific norms and values that are characteristics of the political system at Westminster as the serious stumbling blocks for parliamentary reform. Parliamentary sovereignty has been channelled into executive sovereignty in order to secure the executive's legislative goals. The ministerial responsibility convention has been inverted to undermine scrutiny and accountability. Partisanship has been used to marginalise the capabilities of individual MPs for the benefit of the executive. With these norms and values operating to the advantage of the government and party elites, it is unlikely that they would wish to recast them. It is equally unlikely that there would be sufficient political will in a partisan and executive-driven House of Commons to change the rules of the game and opt for serious parliamentary reform of a structural nature. As Flinders (2002: 30) points out:

> [c]ontrary to constitutional theory, the supremacy of parliament over the executive is thwarted by the latter's tight party management and procedural control of the House's timetable. In the face of executive obduracy, the impotence of the House is unequivocal.

From this perspective, the attitudinal approach is doomed to failure because 'parliament is largely a creature of the executive' (Flinders 2002: 31). The structured institutional context of Westminster, and its associated norms and values, are the determining factors with regards to parliamentary reform:

> The power of party as a paramount organisational factor within the House of Commons therefore limits the scope for mobilisation of parliamentary opinion in favour of fundamental reform. The parameters within which parliamentary reform occurs are drawn by the governing elites over whom parliamentarians would gain more control as a result. (Kelso 2003: 70)

Conclusion

For the remainder of this book, the historical institutionalist approach serves as a lens through which to view the course of Westminster parliamentary reform. The perspective illuminates the norms and values – parliamentary (executive) sovereignty, ministerial responsibility, and strong party government – that contribute to the structured institutional context in which strategies for institutional change must operate. The path dependency concept, as the following chapters demonstrate, can help account for why the parliamentary system maintains its various characteristics, and why changing them has been so particularly difficult. The idea of path dependency is not without its critics, as noted earlier, and the debate over the extent to which the historical institutionalist perspective can adequately deal with institutional change is one to which successive chapters will return. Crucially, however, the historical institutionalist perspective forces us to take account of parliament's history, and how that history frames what is and is not possible in the present. In so doing, the approach helps illuminate the reasons why reform does and does not take place, by grounding explanations in an understanding of the institutional context of parliament, and of the norms and values which structure it. The historical institutional approach also delineates the way we can conceptualise reform strategies themselves, to which the next chapter will turn.

3
Efficiency in the House of Commons 1900–97

Introduction

The previous chapter revealed how the historical development of the Westminster parliament has bestowed a pre-eminent position on the executive inside the House of Commons. The historical institutionalist perspective highlights the norms and values of the executive as the dominant actor at Westminster, and how these norms and values contribute to a structured institutional context in which institutional change does, or does not, take place. Through their position as the dominant actors at Westminster, successive executives have sought to bring about institutional change designed to consolidate and expand the ability of the government to govern without undue interference from parliament. Executives have used their position to engineer a House of Commons that is a procedural reflection of their commitment to strong government. Consequently, reforms intended to improve the efficiency of the House of Commons are qualitatively different from those that are intended to improve its effectiveness. The distinction is derived from the historical development of the executive and legislature at Westminster, and has a direct bearing both upon the content of reform and the likelihood of its success. Both effectiveness reforms and efficiency reforms are concerned with the nature of the relationship between the executive and the legislature. Effectiveness reforms are based on the premise that the balance in the executive-legislative relationship requires adjustment. Somewhat differently, efficiency reforms are based on the premise that the outputs of parliament should be maximised using the minimum of resources. The notion of effectiveness will be explored in Chapter 5: the question of parliamentary efficiency will be the focus of this chapter and the next.

The two different kinds of reform – efficiency and effectiveness – do not occupy categories such as 'good' or 'bad'. No such judgements are intended here. Furthermore, the pursuit of particular kinds of efficiency reform may even contribute to an increase in the perceived effectiveness of the chamber. The two categories are not necessarily mutually exclusive. Yet, the two different types of reform are ultimately indicators of how different individuals or groups perceive the purpose of parliament in general, and the House of Commons in particular. Those who predominantly advocate effectiveness reforms seek to encourage parliament in having a more proactive role than at present. Those who predominantly advocate efficiency reforms seek to ensure that elected governments can successfully secure their legislative programmes in a parliament that is unencumbered by procedural complexities.

Efficiency in the House of Commons

The idea that the output of parliament must be maximised, while the resources expended in generating those outputs are minimised, suggests two rather different dimensions to the notion of efficiency, which neatly intertwine. First, efficiency reforms may be concerned with streamlining the workings of the House of Commons. This streamlining might involve changes to the sitting hours of the House and other similar procedural reforms. This dimension of reform seeks to secure an efficient functioning of the House as a whole, and to ensure that MPs manage available resources efficiently. Such changes fit well under the rubric of the current term 'modernisation' (see Chapter 4), as opposed to the much broader term 'reform'.

Second, efficiency reforms may also be taken forward for the specific purpose of ensuring that government business progresses through the Commons as quickly as possible. The aim is to expedite the business of government and remove any perceived undue hindrance to the progress of legislation. So, for example, the trend of moving more business off the floor of the House and into committees is predicated on the assumption that it will therefore proceed faster through the legislative process and facilitate the introduction of a greater volume of business in general.

These two strands of efficiency reform – streamlining and expediting – neatly intertwine. Governments that wish to ensure that their legislative programme is approved by parliament expeditiously will also be interested in ensuring that the Commons is a streamlined chamber. Similarly, many types of reform that are concerned with securing a streamlined chamber may also complement the goal of securing government business expeditiously.

Expediting government business 1900–30

Although our study has chosen to begin its analysis at the start of the last century, parliamentary procedure actually underwent considerable change in the final decades preceding 1900, change which was insightfully discussed by Josef Redlich in 1908. His key observation was that parliamentary procedure was highly political, the result of the nature of House of Commons development in the nineteenth century. As he explained:

> The fundamental notion underlying the change was … the endeavour to adapt the regulation and carrying out of parliamentary work to the fully matured system of party government. Both the original impulse in the direction of procedure reform and the continuous driving power which forced it on came from the universal recognition of the fact that democratisation of the House of Commons called for a rearrangement of its work. (Redlich 1908, vol. 1: xxxii)

Parliamentary procedure had become an intensely political problem, as well as a political resource, in the years after the 1867 Reform Act, when parties came to more clearly structure life in the House of Commons. Procedural changes in the late nineteenth century, such as the guillotine (a device to conclude parliamentary debate on legislation), extended government rights throughout the House and simultaneously marginalised the individual MP (Redlich 1908, vol. 1: 206). While acknowledging the role of the obstructionist Irish Members in accelerating the pace of change, Redlich did not accept that they were the cause of it. Instead, 'the real motive power came from the *alteration in the nature of the British Government itself*' (Redlich 1908, vol. 1: 207, original emphasis). House of Commons procedure, by the start of the twentieth century, had been commandeered by the executive as a political weapon in its own right.

This had consequences for the way the House of Commons functioned. Writing in 1906, for example, Sidney Low remarked that the status of the House of Commons was in decline because of the way that government dominated it, and the way the government's business so often took precedence (Low 1906: 70). Nonetheless, governments still faced difficulties securing their legislation in the early 1900s (Seaward and Silk 2004: 154), a situation that the Balfour government would not long tolerate.

The Balfour reforms

In order to consolidate further the executive's position in the House of Commons, the Conservative government in 1902 pursued a programme of procedural reform, in which the opposition acquiesced, designed to enhance the government's ability to secure its legislation (Redlich 1908, vol. 1: 193). The reforms involved substantial alterations to the organisation of parliamentary time so as to increase those occasions on which government business took precedence, a consequence of which was to restrict further the capabilities of private members (Redlich 1908, vol. 1: 194–5). Time savings were made by alterations and abbreviations at various stages of the legislative process to make the process more expeditious (Redlich 1908, vol. 1: 195–7).

Questions were thereafter to be answered orally by special request only, and the period of notice for questions for oral answer was increased (Borthwick 1979: 478). From the government's perspective, these reforms not only guaranteed it a significant portion of Commons time for its business, but also gave it more certainty about when its business could start. Some changes were also made to the Speakership so as to ensure the House would be in continued operation.

The 1902 reforms marked the beginning of a process of change that lasted throughout the twentieth century, and marked it with considerable enthusiasm also: as Redlich (1908, vol. 1: 197) commented, 'no such thorough or extensive plan for the improvement of the methods of parliamentary work had ever been laid before the House of Commons'. The reforms were geared towards ensuring the expeditious dispatch of government business, and illustrate the increasing success of the executive in shaping the procedural rules of the game for its own benefit, and therefore also of shaping the institutional context of governing.

The 1906 Procedure Committee

Although the 1902 reforms were viewed as successful, the executive nevertheless saw remaining room for improvement in House of Commons legislative efficiency. The Liberal government of 1906 appointed a Procedure Committee to make recommendations to ensure that House procedures were capable of making the demands it wished to place upon them. Procedure Committees have played a considerable role in the last century in changing Commons practices at the behest of government. Walkland (1979: 264) argued that these committees 'were largely supportive in character, developing a system which was as much a reflection of government interest in the Commons legislative procedure as with the rights and opportunities of backbenchers'. Procedure Committees have been extensively used by successive governments as a way to structure the institutional fabric of the House of Commons, and ensure that its norms and values reflect, as much as possible, those of the executive.

The proposals made by the Procedure Committee (HC 89, 1906), and implemented in 1907, involved an alteration to the sitting hours of the House, an extension of the system of standing committees, and an increase in the speed with which divisions were held, all geared towards expediting government business through the House (Redlich 1908, vol. 2: 202). The changes to sitting hours had a streamlining effect by creating one long sitting from two shorter ones (Seaward and Silk 2004: 148), and were conducive to the despatch of government business by shaping Commons hours around the legislative process. Automatic referral of bills to standing committee was pursued as a way to make more efficient use of parliamentary time, and to avoid the more laborious Committee of the Whole House (Redlich 1908, vol.

2: 207, 215–6). The number of standing committees was raised from two to four, with the government ensured a majority on them. Government business also took precedence in all but one standing committee, and chairmen were given powers to curtail committee debate (Seaward and Silk 2004: 158). The committees were organised on an alphabetised basis, rather than according to policy interest, which, arguably, prevented the creation of strong legislative specialisation amongst MPs, even though the Procedure Committee encouraged attention to subject matter when appointing committee members. Changes to the division process also saved some parliamentary time. Although the changes were supported by both front benches, the reform package was eventually forced through the House by means of a guillotine in the face of numerous backbench amendments to exclude certain kinds of bills from automatic referral to standing committee (Walkland 1979: 258).

If the 1902 reforms had been substantial, then the 1906–7 reforms were ground-breaking. Rush (2001: 61) comments that, with their implementation, 'the procedures of the House of Commons had been transformed so that the government effectively controlled the parliamentary agenda and could, through its majority, virtually guarantee the passage of its legislative programme'. Such was the breadth of the 1906–7 changes, that subsequent procedural reforms 'were almost entirely detailed rather than fundamental in nature, tightening the government's grip, improving the productive efficiency of the House of Commons as a legislative machine' (Rush 2001: 61, original emphasis). By the early years of the twentieth century, the path of institutional development at Westminster had enabled the executive to exercise considerable power in changing the institutional context in which it operated. Successive governments had improved significantly their ability to secure their legislation by adapting the rules of the game at Westminster so as to reflect their own preferences, norms and values. Executives had always been powerful, but by 1907 they had mastered the procedures of the increasingly democratised House of Commons and engineered them to reflect its belief that government must be assured of getting its business.

Standing committees cemented

The procedural changes pursued in the early part of the twentieth century soon caused concern for some observers. In 1912, the American scholar A. Lawrence Lowell (1912, vol. 1: 311), commented that the House of Commons had 'solved the question of time by giving most of it to the government to use as it pleases'. Amendments to government legislation carried without the tacit approval of the government had become 'extremely rare', and the standing committee system made it very hard for the House to prevent the government securing its legislation (Lowell 1912, vol. 1: 317–8). Yet despite such concerns, the reform impetus thereafter involved an increased use of the standing committee structure for the purposes of legislative scrutiny. Immediately after the First World War, the standing committee system was reformed once more, primarily to legislate for the promised post-war reconstruction (Walkland 1979: 261). The number of committees increased to six, and they were redesigned to allow them to work faster and with fewer members. Such was the government's desire to dominate the legislative process, that, in 1919, it even attempted (unsuccessfully) to prevent temporarily the introduction of private members' legislation. Thereafter, government did not shrink from acquiring Fridays for its own legislative purposes, which were traditionally reserved for private members' bills (Richards 1979: 302).

Refining expeditious efficiency: 1931–60

Although much had been achieved by the 1902 and 1907 reforms, it nonetheless became clear as the 1920s drew to a close that further efficiency alterations were required. Once more, a Procedure Committee was called into action as the executive continued to adapt the institutional structure through which it worked.

The 1931 Procedure Committee

As economic conditions worsened at the start of the 1930s, criticisms of parliament emerged, largely because its response to those problems was viewed as inadequate. Although much of this criticism was focused on the effectiveness of parliament, the situation still raised questions about its efficiency. The details surrounding the Procedure Committee appointed in 1931 to address the situation are explored more fully in Chapter 5. However, aspects of the Committee's work are relevant in terms of understanding elite views about the need for an efficient House of Commons. In particular, the extensive oral evidence obtained by the Committee from a range of prominent political figures provides a rich insight into perceptions of parliament and its role in the political system.

For example, Ramsay MacDonald, then prime minister of a minority government, appeared before the Committee in his capacity as Leader of the House. In response to a question about whether he thought 'that the main function of the procedure of Parliament should be primarily to get things done as quickly as possible … or should it be really aimed principally at favouring careful deliberation and adequate criticism of the different measures that are brought forward', MacDonald replied that:

> It is really a combination of both … The Standing Orders and Procedure Rules should limit abuses as much as possible but protect the right of the Opposition to be heard, and to give counsel, and to make its position clear to the country;

and, against that, you have to balance up the rights of the government, which are, in a sentence, to get legislation through after due examination. A Parliamentary machine is rather like a living organism, you have to balance up rights and wrongs. (HC 161, 1930–31, Q. 8).

The use of the term 'parliamentary machine' is an accurate reflection of how executives generally view the legislative process. MacDonald pressed home this point when he later argued that 'it is not the function of the Opposition to oppose; it is the function of the Opposition to oppose Second Readings,' and that opposition parties should work to improve bills, not unduly delay them (HC 161, 1930–31, Q. 29). The prime minister also argued that the House should accept the guillotine as a legitimate tool for conducting government business, and as one which was utilised 'for the benefit of Parliament, rather than for the benefit of whichever Party happens to be on the Government Benches' (HC 161, 1930–31, Qs 43 and 7). The Procedure Committee agreed with this view (HC 129, 1931–32), although the guillotine did not feature as a normal part of House procedure in the 1930s (Palmer 1970: 235).

The views of MacDonald, and other witnesses – which characterised parliament as a legislative machine – impacted substantially on the conclusions and recommendations of the Procedure Committee. Yet, there had been a clear divergence in opinion presented to the Committee in the evidence it collected, as its report illustrated:

> Those who considered its primary function to be that of a national forum where great issues were debated, or should be debated, were more concerned with the revival of this function than with the increase of Parliamentary legislative efficiency; while those who considered its function to be that of a legislative machine, or a body charged with the control of expenditure and of Departmental action, were anxious to make far-reaching changes in procedure to improve the performance of these functions by the House (HC 129, 1931–32, para. 7).

Despite these differing viewpoints, the arguments of those who sought further improvements to the speed with which parliament approved government business won out, and many of the Committee's recommendations were focused on enhancing parliament's legislative efficiency (HC 129, 1931–32, paras 10–12).

The post-war Procedure Committee

The Labour government elected in 1945 came to office with an extensive legislative programme, and a Procedure Committee was once more appointed 'to report what alterations, if any, are desirable for the more efficient despatch of business' (HC 9, 1945–46). Not only was the Committee under pressure in terms of time – the government urgently wished to secure its legislation – but it was also under pressure in terms of the increasing volume of business that governments were now placing before parliament (HC 189, 1945–46, para. 4). Continuing to adopt the language of parliament as a legislative machine, the Committee cautioned that '[i]t is therefore a matter for constant vigilance to ensure that the machine is continuously adapted and strengthened to bear the new burdens put upon it' (HC 189, 1945–46, para. 4).

This particular Procedure Committee produced three separate reports between 1945 and 1946 (HC 9, HC 58, HC 189, all 1945–46), which met with broad, if not unanimous, House approval (Morrison 1964: 219). The first report expanded on a scheme devised late in the war by the coalition government, in response to the expected heavy legislative workload once hostilities were concluded (HC 9, 1945–46, para. 4), and focused on an expanded use of standing committees to expedite legislation. It recommended that a greater number of bills be sent to standing committees; that the number of committees be expanded while the number of those serving on them be reduced; that the number of hours of committee work be expanded; and that the committees have time limits placed on their work. Herbert Morrison, then Leader of the House, subsequently observed that, in the immediate post-war era, standing committees had become an integral part of the legislative process, 'instead of mere time-savers', and that the government ideally wanted all legislation, whether controversial or not, referred to them (Morrison 1964: 220–3).

Perhaps the most controversial aspect of the Procedure Committee's proposals was that the guillotine be used in standing committee proceedings (Walkland 1979: 269), a proposal that emanated directly from government and which it viewed as an integral part of the reform package (Morrison 1964: 224). Although clearly convinced that the guillotine was a useful weapon in the procedural armoury against a recalcitrant House of Commons, the government nevertheless wanted to improve the appearance of this tool. Consequently, the government accepted a recommendation that the business committee dealing with issues pertaining to the guillotine be a sub-committee of the relevant standing committee, not a committee of the whole House (Palmer 1970: 236–7). From 1947, whips were also appointed to standing committees in order to reinforce the party view when necessary and ensure the speedy conclusion of legislative scrutiny (Walkland 1979: 272). The inclusion of the whips served to end the standing committee's relative insulation from the partisan atmosphere in the chamber:

> Government backbenchers were made dumb by the presence of whips; ministers and opposition spokespersons would debate a bill with only a second hand knowledge of what it meant; members with specialist knowledge of the subject of the bill were deliberately excluded from participation on the committee. (Seaward and Silk 2004: 159)

Much of the Procedure Committee's attention was devoted to enhancing the expeditious despatch of government business, but it also looked at ways of streamlining the working of the House, although somewhat unsuccessfully. The Committee's second report focused on the potential reform of divisions and questions procedure (HC 58, 1945–46). It explored the possibility of moving to 'mechanical' voting, although the Committee was not persuaded that such a method would be accurate, and parliamentary opinion anyway remained in favour of the traditional division lobbies and the social and political opportunities they afforded backbench MPs. The Committee was also unconvinced by a suggestion to further reduce the number of oral questions Members could table each day, noting it was 'reluctant to restrict a right which has already been severely curtailed' (HC 58, 1945–46, para. 6). Nor did the Committee endorse the government's suggestion that a time limit should be set on speeches (HC 189, 1945–46, para. 59). The Committee's third report examined more detailed matters relating to the mechanics of the legislative process, administration and finance, and private members' business (HC 189, 1945–46). Its recommendations included a reorganisation of supply procedure, a new approach to examining statutory instruments, and the removal of duplication in the examination of budget resolutions and the Finance Bill.

By the end of 1946, then, the executive had succeeded in more fully institutionalising a standing committee system which almost entirely reflected its view of parliament as a legislative machine, and which reinforced the norm of legislative efficiency and the value of procedures which preserved executive strength and capacity for action within the political system.

Reform during the 1950s

Following the changes made in the immediate post-war years, modifications to the House's legislative procedures were thereafter 'relatively minor' (Walkland 1979: 274), and instituted by government directly, rather than through a Procedure Committee. In 1951, the size of standing committees was reduced again, and in 1956 the quorum size was reduced, along with the number required for closure, to enable committees to make decisions faster. Backbench MPs found little time available for private members' legislation, as the regaining of Fridays for this business was still not absolute by the end of the 1950s (Richards 1979: 305).

However, there was a relative absence of any desire to reform further Commons procedure in the interests of greater efficiency in the early 1950s, largely because the executive had already achieved so much (Hanson 1957: 456). It was not until the close of the decade, in 1959, that a Procedure Committee once more came forward with a package of reforms (HC 92, 1958–59). This included minor alterations, such as changes to the order paper and statement of business, changes to the sick-Member pairing mechanism, as well as more substantial suggestions, including extended use of standing committees, and some ideas about the potential for a House business committee. Yet, on many other controversial points, the Procedure Committee remained unconvinced, particularly with respect to a process of formal legislative timetabling, and the suggestion of taking the report stage of bills in standing committee. The Procedure Committee also again rejected proposals to place a time limit on speeches made in debates, and spurned the idea of morning sittings. However, it did finally recommend a further reduction in the number of oral questions that Members could ask each day, and encouraged the Speaker to be harsher with those who abused the use of supplementary questions. While the House broadly endorsed the Committee's recommendations, those relating to standing committees were more controversial, and MPs were especially divided on the merits of their increased use (Wiseman 1960: 240–1).

In terms of the efficiency of the House of Commons, the post-war era was characterised predominantly by consolidation of the earlier reforms instituted in 1931, which had themselves built on what was achieved in 1902 and 1907. By the end of the 1950s, standing committees were fully integrated into the legislative process. Crucially, they were utilised, and justified, as a way not of enhancing the ability of parliament to scrutinise government bills, but of ensuring that those bills were approved by the House of Commons as quickly as possible, and with the minimum level of interference. The executive was highly successful in cultivating a structured institutional context that favoured the pursuit of reforms designed to secure this kind of legislative efficiency, and in shaping norms and values in a way that characterised parliamentary delay of government legislation as inherently against the natural order of things. At the start of the 1960s then, with the standing committee system thus entrenched, attention turned to reforms that might address the need to better streamline the workings of the House of Commons.

Streamlining the work of the Commons: 1961–97

After 1960, successive Procedure Committees came to pay increased attention to that dimension of efficiency that involved streamlining the House of Commons and its working practices. In particular, issues surrounding the use of questions in the House and the structure of Commons sitting hours attracted special attention.

Questions and debates in the House

By the early 1960s, MPs were aware of several problems concerning the operation of Question Time. As the numbers of questions to ministers had increased after 1945, the case for finding the most efficient means of dealing with them became ever more urgent, and the goal was to secure efficient mechanisms for both asking and answering them.

The Procedure Committee examined these issues in 1965, focusing on the low number of questions reached during Question Time and the difficulties MPs had in obtaining prompt oral answers (HC 188, 1964–65). The Committee observed deterioration in the utility of Question Time since 1945, caused largely by an overload of questions tabled for oral answer, and also by over-long supplementaries. Its recommendations were somewhat limited, and merely encouraged a 'brisker approach' to both asking and answering questions, as well as a shorter time limit on the notice required for questions to prevent them becoming stale.

When the Committee returned to the issue again in 1970, it argued that, as far as the efficiency of Question Time was concerned, 'the House can sometimes be its own worse enemy' (HC 198, 1969–70, para. 27). In 1972, a Parliamentary Questions select committee was specially convened to report on the problem (HC 393, 1971–72). It suggested that MPs should be able to stipulate a particular day for a written answer from a minister, to make them more attractive than oral answers (Borthwick 1979: 490), and also recommended the introduction of increased restrictions on the number of questions for oral answer that MPs could table each day. The Procedure Committee nevertheless returned to the subject again in the early 1990s, this time distributing a questionnaire to MPs to gauge their views on how the procedure for questions worked (HC 178, 1990–91). The Committee concluded from the low response rate that there was general satisfaction with how things worked. It nevertheless recommended a further reduction in the period of notice for oral questions, which the government rejected (HC 687, 1992–93).

The Procedure Committee had previously supported the principle of placing a time limit on speeches during debates (HC 92, 1958–59; HC 153, 1966–67; HC 538, 1970–71), and, in 1975, explored the issue in more detail (HC 671, 1974–75). The benefits of a time limit, the Committee explained, were that more MPs could contribute to debates, and that the quality of contributions would improve. However, the downside was that time limits would not take into account the different speech-making styles employed by different MPs, nor the circumstances in which such speeches were made. The Committee once more rejected the idea of time limits, largely on the grounds that they would constrain the ability of MPs to sway the opinions of their colleagues during debates.

However, just a few years later, the Procedure Committee recommended an experimental period of time-limited speeches during second reading debates, to test their merits (HC 588, 1977–78). Subsequently, the Committee concluded that around two or three extra MPs had been called during each individual experimental period than would otherwise have been the case, and argued that the cumulative effect of this increase over a whole session would be substantial (HC 570, 1983–84, para. 4). A further experimental period was pursued, and the Committee recommended that, although frontbench speakers were not subject to the time limit, they should nonetheless try to restrict their contributions to thirty minutes (HC 570, 1983–4, para. 11). The Procedure Committee again endorsed time limits after the second experimental period, arguing that MPs had been broadly happy with the results, although it did also warn against a situation where MPs simply read out speeches during debates (HC 623, 1984–85, paras 3–5). The Committee later recommended that the temporary procedures enabling time limits in debates should be incorporated into Standing Orders (HC 592, 1985–86), to which the House agreed, and also proposed that the Speaker be empowered to impose a ten-minute rule whenever it was deemed appropriate (HC 569, 1990–91).

House of Commons sitting hours

Of all the debates concerning how the procedures and practices of the House can be streamlined, none has provoked more controversy than that over sitting hours. In 1966, the Procedure Committee conducted a substantial enquiry into whether the House could rise earlier at night (HC 153, 1966–67), but discovered that this would be most successful only if instituted in tandem with a move to more voluntary timetabling of bills in order to improve the management of Commons time. After examining a range of different options, the Committee recommended an experiment with morning sittings (the House had heretofore not sat until 2.30pm) along with an extension of Friday sittings to permit more private member opportunities. The experiment with morning sittings was subsequently abandoned, however, because they caused conflict with committee meeting times, government struggled to select suitable business for morning sessions, and late nights in the chamber continued regardless (Seaward and Silk 2004: 149).

The Procedure Committee did not return to the issue again until 1975, when it once more explained that late sittings could only be reduced if the issue was 'considered in relation to the volume and nature of the whole business of the House and the hours and the hours of sitting generally' (HC 491, 1974–75, para. 1). From the Committee's perspective, much of the blame for late sittings rested with the House itself:

> The direct cause of the vast majority of late sittings is the House's acceptance of a Business Motion made each day by the Government to allow business to be proceeded with after Ten O'Clock. In theory, the House can refuse to agree the motion ... but as the Clerk of the House pointed out 'A party wants to get its programme through and so long as it is doing that its supporters will help it to

do that; if it means suspending the rule they will suspend the rule'. (HC 491, 1974–75, para. 9)

The issue remained unresolved until a special select committee on Sittings of the House (the Jopling Committee) was convened in the early 1990s (HC 20, 1991–92). Following lengthy deliberations, the Committee rejected the idea that the problem could be remedied by simply having the House sit earlier in the morning, although it did recommend morning sittings for Wednesdays. Its main proposal, however, was that the House should end its business by 10.00pm on Mondays and Thursdays, and by 2.30pm on Fridays, and that this be complemented by ten non-sitting Fridays each session with the House rising early on the Thursdays to allow MPs to return to their constituencies. The reduced number of sitting hours overall would be facilitated by a comprehensive system of legislative timetabling, by an extension of the ten-minute rule during debates, and by a removal of some business off the floor of the House.

It took two years for the House of Commons to implement any of the Jopling Committee recommendations, with only Wednesday morning sittings and constituency Fridays finding approval. However, the Committee had argued that legislative programming was the key to any attempt to reduce the number of House sitting hours. The idea of a House business committee has always been deeply controversial for frontbench and backbench MPs alike, with the former reluctant to relinquish their control over how legislative business is organised through the usual channels, and with both anxious about exactly what is entailed by a 'House' business committee and who it would contain. Consequently, late nights were not eradicated following the Jopling Committee, and by 1997 the House was sitting as late into the night as ever (Seaward and Silk 2004: 150).

An issue related to the sitting hours debate is that of the potential for a parliamentary calendar, to which Procedure Committees have returned often, albeit without leading to the introduction of any changes (HC 356, 1967–68; HC 588, 1977–78). In 1987, the Procedure Committee made a strong case in favour of moving to a structured parliamentary calendar, on the basis that this would provide predictable sitting times, provide for the planning of workloads, aid business managers in their organisation of the legislative schedule, and promote a more family friendly approach to House of Commons work (HC 157, 1986–87). While some of these issues were picked up by the Jopling Committee, none secured successful adoption prior to 1997.

Expanded use of standing committees

Despite the expansion of the standing committee system after 1945, they remained uncharted territory as far as the Finance Bill was concerned. In 1963, a Procedure Committee examined the case for sending parts of the

Finance Bill to standing committee in order to save time on the floor of the House, but was not persuaded by the evidence. The key point for the Committee was that 'there is a strong body of opinion which believes that even the committal of a part of the Bill would be a breach of constitutional principle, namely that the House as a whole must keep control over the executive in the matter of taxation' (HC 190, 1962–63, para. 3). However, just two years later, the Procedure Committee had experienced an abrupt change of heart on the matter, and published a report that acknowledged the conflict between relieving pressure on House time, while ensuring that the rights of MPs were not infringed (HC 276, 1964–65). The report suggested that separating Finance Bills into their budgetary and administrative elements might be the way forward, with the technical aspects being examined in committee.

The Procedure Committee made further recommendations for the expanded use of standing committees in the legislative process in the 1966–67 session. These included more second reading committees, the use of committees for some report stages and some statutory instruments, and for third readings to be taken without debate (HC 539, 1966–67). Most of these changes were accepted by the House (Walkland 1979: 276). Perhaps the most significant of the changes were those made at second reading stage. Prior to this, second readings were the 'greatest obstacle to the progress of a Bill', sometimes taking a whole day to be completed, and the introduction of second reading committees contributed to a considerable time saving (Boulton 1969: 61). In 1968, the minimum size of standing committees was reduced to sixteen members, which meant that they could consider legislation with only five MPs and the committee chairman present (Walkland 1979: 275), further enhancing the speed with which they despatched government business. The Study of Parliament Group – an esteemed group of parliamentary scholars and clerks – strongly endorsed the merits of reducing further the size of standing committees, advising MPs that this was the only acceptable way of enabling more of them to be created, and therefore the only realistic way of increasing the rate at which bills proceeded through the House (Study of Parliament Group 1969: 214).

Yet, in the midst of this continual refinement of the standing committee system, a central controversy emerged which underlined the particular way that these committees have been engineered inside the House. By 1960, any element of specialisation inside the standing committees had been eradicated, and their permanent membership removed, which thus 'deprived the system of any institutionalised bias which might have existed in favour of continuity and specialisation' (Walkland 1979: 284). The constant turnover of members on the standing committees, and the lack of consistency of subject examined by each committee, worked against the development of a clear legislative knowledge base across the broad range of public policy. This was ultimately detrimental for the Commons as a whole, as Walkland (1979: 285) explains:

> The Commons' talent for the ad hoc cannot be better illustrated than in the present standing committee arrangements. It is evidence that built-in discontinuities militate against committees achieving any corporate sense which can be developed, as has occurred in other legislatures, over a continuous period of common association.

Other observers were similarly concerned about the standing committee system in the late 1970s. Griffith (1977: 104), for example, noted that, although the House decided on standing committee membership based on Committee of Selection recommendations, this meant, in practice, the party whips. Furthermore, the inclusion of certain standing committee members was a foregone conclusion, such as the minister in charge of the bill and the opposition spokesman. Consequently, '[t]he number of places on a standing committee for which a true competition exists may therefore be relatively small' (Griffith 1977: 106). Moreover, willing committee members were hard to come by 'for the large number of unexciting bills which pass through the House of Commons each Session' (Griffith 1977: 106). Opposition members of standing committees were also at an immediate disadvantage because of a lack of access to the kinds of information readily available to ministers and their parliamentary colleagues, leading to a degree of 'superficiality' in legislative scrutiny (Griffith 1977: 108).

A broader look at the legislative process

In response to continuing complaints about the functioning of the legislative process, the Procedure Committee engaged in a broad examination in the early 1970s. The Committee explored many of the most popular concerns – of insufficient parliamentary time and expertise to scrutinise legislation properly – and its report listed many recommendations for minor changes designed to speed up the legislative process still further (HC 538, 1970–71). Some observers remained unsatisfied with the direction that reform had taken, with Drewry (1972) arguing that legislative scrutiny failed to facilitate a differential emphasis on 'technical' and 'controversial' bills. More generally, Drewry (1972: 298–99) argued that the reform direction chosen by the Procedure Committee was itself part of the problem:

> [p]arliamentary reform has become a tactic in political conflict as conceived by actors in the political process: conflict between Parliament and Executive, between front bench and back bench, between Government and Opposition. As soon as one actor is willing to accept radical reform others resist it for fear of upsetting a delicate equilibrium to their own detriment. The narrow approach of the Procedure Committee, while unsatisfying to many outside observers, is fully justified by the hard realities of political life.

The Procedure Committee did not again conduct a broad enquiry into the legislative process until 1985, when it once more explored concerns about the unsatisfactory operation of the standing committee system (HC 49, 1984–85). Its main recommendation involved the creation of a legislative business committee, comprising thirteen MPs appointed by the Committee of Selection, and designed to permit the earlier introduction of timetables on controversial bills that would take over twenty-five hours in committee, and allow the opponents of the bill to be formally engaged in the timetabling process.

However, as noted earlier, the notion of a legislative business committee has never been warmly received either by the government or the opposition front benches, because such a committee would remove the usual channels from the organisation of business and instead place the responsibility with a House committee. The Procedure Committee subsequently explained the reception of this recommendation in these terms:

> The organisation of both front-benches and an unprecedented turnout of Ministers and Parliamentary Private Secretaries on a one-line whip brought about the defeat of the amendment moved by our chairman which would have introduced our proposed new arrangements for timetabling bills for a one year experiment … Those who advanced this objection do not seem to us to have addressed the fact that existing timetabling procedures work to the considerable detriment of back-benchers and minorities. (HC 324, 1985–86, para. 2)

The idea of a business committee was one to which the Procedure Committee returned shortly thereafter, arguing that the time of the House of Commons could only be most efficiently utilised by way of such an institutional innovation (HC 350, 1986–87). However, the government and opposition front benches have been naturally reticent about the idea of a legislative business committee, because it attempts to formalise and place in tentative 'House' control what has long been organised informally through the usual channels. Government business managers are unlikely voluntarily to restrict their room for manoeuvre in such a way, and opposition whips are unlikely to relinquish their own informal role in the management of legislative time. So long as the government and opposition front benches collaborate informally through the usual channels, and so long as they agree on the continued benefits to both sides of doing so, neither is likely to support a recommendation that would remove this power and hand it over to an essentially unknown group of House representatives. The norms of the House of Commons mean that this power resides in the frontbenches, not with the House more generally, and procedural developments have been highly geared towards the preservation of this norm. Strengthening the corporate identity of the House of Commons by way of a legislative business committee is simply antithetical to the norms and values around which successive efficiency reforms have been built.

Conclusion

Reforms to the efficiency of the House of Commons have primarily focused on creating a House that can process government business expeditiously and on ensuring that the House has streamlined procedures that enable MPs to function with the minimum input of resources. As Chapman (1963: 181) noted, '[f]rom a technical point of view, parliamentary procedure is both the aspect of business efficiency in government and also an aid to the ministry in governing; it is an integral part of the art of ruling'. In the past century, governments have allocated more Commons time to government business, through alterations to the parliamentary timetable, and have created procedures that enable the Commons to pass legislation more quickly, through improvements to the standing committee system. Governments have also streamlined the functioning of the House, through many relatively minor alterations that cumulatively result in MPs making the most use of their limited resources, time in particular. Through decades of experimentation and adaptation, sometimes drastic but mostly incremental, governments have modified Commons procedures for their own benefit.

Governments have engineered House procedures to ensure they can secure their business quickly and with the minimum expenditure of energy: their aim has been to ensure that they can govern strongly and effectively. This has been most in evidence when governments have come to power committed to substantial legislative programmes, as demonstrated by the actions of the Liberal government in 1906 and the Labour government in 1945. In such circumstances, governments are convinced of the need to change House procedures because of their electoral victory and the characteristics of their legislative plans. As Chapter 3 demonstrates, this also applies to the New Labour government of 1997, and its approach to reforming the efficiency of the House of Commons.

Also notable is the way that governments have utilised the services of successive Procedure Committees in order to secure the efficiency they seek. The way that governments can use Commons procedures and institutions in order to bring about legislative efficiency and constrain House capacity for intervention nicely illustrates the extent to which the historical development of the Westminster political system has created a particular structural context in which the executive can use its institutional position, and the norms and values which underpin it, to bring about procedural change for its own benefit. As the next chapter demonstrates, this utilisation of House procedure in order to make such procedure ever more efficient has been a key theme since 1997.

The nature of the historical development of the institution of parliament has meant that government can take advantage of the structured institutional context created by its own dominant value system to bring about change that reinforces that dominance. The structured institutional context ensures that elite actors in both the governing party and the main opposition party will share similar outlooks with regards to creating an efficient House of Commons. The governing party will seek efficiency reforms that enable it to secure its legislation quickly and with the minimum expenditure of resources. Simultaneously, the governing party will not wish to take procedural efficiency to extremes, because it acknowledges that it will one day be back in opposition, thanks to the swing of the electoral pendulum. The main opposition party will also give tacit consent to efficiency reforms, because it will expect to benefit from them once back in office. Both front benches will refrain from pressing for changes designed to improve the corporate capabilities of the House of Commons. Their refusal to support the introduction of a legislative business committee is an excellent example of the operation of the structured institutional context at Westminster. Neither party has traditionally supported it because it would impact upon the capabilities of the usual channels and thus restrict the powers of the dominant elite actors, both in government and opposition.

Path dependency, a key component of historical institutional theory, therefore helps us analyse how the executive enhanced its command of House of Commons procedure throughout the twentieth century. The particular conditions of the late nineteenth century which brought about that executive control – the emergence of strong parties, and a desire to reduce the role of the individual Member so as to counter the disruption of the Irish MPs – produced a situation in which the executive was able to change House procedure in order to improve the ability of the government to secure its legislation. Once the Commons had consented to the executive acting in this way, this institutional choice determined the future path dependency of parliament, making it much easier for the governments of the early twentieth century to reform House procedure further still, and ever harder for the Commons to resist. As the dominant actor at Westminster, the terms of the reform agenda were increasingly in the hands of the executive, and institutional change thereafter adopted a particular trajectory that was not easily changed. Consequently, while the twentieth century was replete with examples of continuous procedural change in terms of House efficiency, it was change underpinned by institutional persistence of the norms and values those changes sought to preserve.

Although benefiting from some changes, it is backbenchers from both the government and opposition parties that are most often disadvantaged by reforms designed to improve the efficiency of the House. Backbenchers continue to face the conundrum of their parallel lives as parliamentarians and as party politicians. Despite forming the single biggest group of MPs inside the Commons, party loyalty still inhibits backbench Members from resisting efficiency reforms designed to enhance the ability of government to secure its business. In this respect, an institutionalist perspective predicts that there will be a 'logic of appropriateness' which guides actors' strategies and goals: certainly from the perspective of government backbenchers, that 'logic of appropriateness' regularly guided sufficient numbers of MPs to prioritise the need to deepen executive governing capacity over any desire to develop the abilities of the House of Commons as a 'holistic' institution. As the next chapter demonstrates, this backbench conflict of interest has been a key characteristic of the drive for efficiency reforms since 1997.

4
Efficiency in the House of Commons since 1997

Introduction

The previous chapter illustrated the interest of successive governments in securing efficient procedures in the House of Commons throughout the twentieth century. The Labour government elected in 1997 was committed to an expansive legislative programme after almost twenty years in opposition, and was keen to ensure that the most efficient mechanisms were in place to secure that programme. To achieve this, the government established a Modernisation Committee to implement the necessary changes.

A significant proportion of this Committee's time has been spent on efficiency matters similar to those explored previously by the Procedure Committee. The continued adaptation of Commons procedures therefore exhibits a particularly high degree of path dependency. This path-dependent development is structured by the values and norms of the executive, as the most powerful actor inside the House of Commons, and one that wishes to ensure it can have its business approved with the minimum of parliamentary interference. The name of the new Committee is itself of interest. 'Modernisation' is not necessarily synonymous with 'reform'. While the broader term 'reform' encapsulates a desire to rebalance the relationship between executive and legislature, 'modernisation' refers instead to an updating of procedure. The notion of modernisation has been utilised by the government to update and redesign procedures primarily (although not exclusively) for its own benefit. These changes have included alterations to the legislative process, adjustments to House sitting hours, and the creation of Westminster Hall as a parallel chamber. All these changes were generally described by government as evolutionary and designed to modernise the way the Commons functions. However, these changes, particularly the first two, have been rather more controversial than one might expect from a mere modernisation of procedure.

Two other issues have also provoked argument to varying degrees. First, the Leader of the House of Commons, a government minister, chairs the Modernisation Committee, and this has at times attracted objections from a range of MPs. There are two ways to view this role of the Leader of the House. On the one hand, procedural change of any kind does not always enjoy unanimous government support, and having a cabinet minister shepherd through such reforms at least increases the chances of some change being successfully implemented. On the other hand, a more critical interpretation would argue that, with a cabinet minister in charge of the modernisation project, the executive is even more able to control change inside the Commons and to reinforce its own values and goals. The second issue concerns the large number of Labour MPs who entered parliament for the first time after the 1997 general election. Many of these MPs came to the Commons with new ideas about how the chamber should operate, and this occasionally led to a degree of conflict with more seasoned MPs. Yet at the same time, the 'new intake' of MPs were also keen to ensure that the Labour Party could secure its legislative goals after almost two decades in opposition, and so have often been criticised for accepting changes that strengthen government at the expense of parliament.

The frequently controversial nature of the work undertaken by the Modernisation Committee is demonstrated by a persistent lack of consensus among its members over its recommendations geared towards improving procedural efficiency. Some disagreement is simply an unsurprising result of the partisan nature of the House of Commons. Nevertheless, partisan responses have at times been easier to generate as a result of the nature of the chairmanship of the Modernisation Committee and the frequently skewed impact of the reforms it has pursued.

The Modernisation Committee established

The Labour government's constitutional reform programme included a commitment to establish a select committee for the specific purpose of modernising the House of Commons. The prospects for such a committee were outlined in the Commons just a few weeks after the new government came to office, and the Leader of the House, Ann Taylor, explained that its goal would be to make Commons procedure 'more effective and efficient' (HC Debs, 14 May 1997, col .44). The focus of the committee was also made clear early on, with Taylor noting that its concerns would include improvements to the legislative process, accountability issues, patterns of the MP's working life, and the customs of parliament (HC Debs, 22 May 1997, cols 903–9).

The initial debate on the merits of a Modernisation Committee indicated broad support for such a mechanism, illustrated by Ann Taylor's conclusion that the supportive tone of the debate was 'the best sign that we have had in many years that there is a serious intention to modernise this place' (HC Debs, 22 May 1997, col. 909). Of course, concerns were nevertheless voiced by some MPs regarding the government's reform plans, and in particular about the specific role to be played by the Leader of the House. Conservative MP Sir Patrick Cormack, for example, referred to 'the essential dichotomy' caused by the new dual role of the Leader of the House, who 'in her capacity as a leading Member of the Government, is understandably anxious to get government business through ... but to get business through and to have it properly scrutinised ... is a problem' (HC Debs, 22 May 1997, col. 936). Other Conservative MPs echoed these concerns when the Modernisation Committee was formally established in early June 1997. The Shadow Leader of the House, Alistair Goodlad, argued that 'modernisation may mean changes to the House's procedures in the interests of government', while Robert Jackson (still a Conservative MP at that point) cautioned against equating modernisation with the simple removal of antiquated practices, on the basis that '[d]oing away with such things might become a compensation for a real lack of radicalism' (HC Debs, 4 June 1997, cols 500, 503).

The legislative process

Early concerns about the focus of the Modernisation Committee's work are partially borne out by the way it approached its task of modernising the legislative process. The Committee's work in this area, particularly in the years immediately following its creation, focused predominantly on improving the efficiency of the process, and only latterly began to examine issues relating more to effectiveness. One of the first tasks of the Modernisation Committee was to introduce a structure of legislative programming into the House of Commons, and of all the reforms it has proposed, perhaps none provoked as much criticism of the Committee and its purposes as this.

Traditionally, the legislative business schedule is planned and organised by the government whips and business managers, through informal consultation with their opposition counterparts. The Jopling reforms had led to some voluntary legislative timetabling, whereby the schedule for a piece of legislation was worked out in advance, and clear markers set out formally for the dates at which it would be expected to clear the various parts of the legislative process, thus giving more certainty to both the government and the House of Commons about the timescale for scrutinising and securing business. This limited Jopling timetabling was reasonably successfully, largely due to the uncontroversial nature of the legislation to which it was applied (Donnelly 1997: 253). In addition, in the 1997–98 session, the government secured cross-party agreement on legislative programmes for the Scottish and Welsh devolution bills (Seaward and Silk 2004: 160). Yet the government was clear that it wanted the principle of legislative programming to become a central part of House procedure. Consequently, the first report issued by the Modernisation Committee was entitled *The Legislative Process*, and stipulated that the essential criteria to be met in making any reforms was that the government had to be assured of having its business passed, with Commons approval (HC 190, 1997–98, para. 14). This of course simply reflects the nature of the political process in Britain, which prioritises the need for strong, decisive government. Yet the fact that the first report to be issued by the new Modernisation Committee so clearly stated as much, and stated its task as that of improving legislative efficiency, is revealing. In recommending the adoption of a system of legislative programming, the Modernisation Committee argued the case on the grounds that it would increase the expeditious despatch of government business (paras 57–66). The Committee admitted that the issue was 'emotive and contentious' and that there would always be 'political considerations' involved in the handling of bills (paras 57–8). Yet it also argued that programming could nevertheless be beneficial for all those involved in the legislative process, because it facilitated a third way between the informal usual channels and the rigid guillotine. Crucially, the report pointed to previous work done by the Hansard Society (1993) and to Procedure Committee recommendations for a system of legislative programming predicated on the existence of a House of Commons business committee. Yet the Committee rejected the notion of a business committee on the grounds that it would not enjoy the flexibility of the usual channels, and was too structured for the Commons way of working. The report recommended a trial period of legislative programming, which retained use of the usual channels and enabled the government to set the programme for such bills.

The contentious nature of the legislative programming proposals is illustrated by some of the statements made by MPs on the matter in the Commons. Some Labour MPs found much to be optimistic about. Veteran MP Robert Sheldon supported formal programming on the grounds that it would force both government and opposition to compromise in order to achieve their goals (HC Debs, 13 November 1997, col. 1073). Newly elected Labour MP Phyllis Starkey was supportive because programming allowed scrutiny to be tailored around individual bills, and helped Members by bringing a degree of certainty into the legislative process (col. 1104). Yet, shortly after programming came into operation, senior backbench Labour MP Gwyneth Dunwoody cautioned against the further extension of the system, describing the ability of backbenchers to hold up or advance legislation as 'one of their last remaining powers' and arguing that 'those who talk about timetabling Bills do Backbenchers … a great disservice' (HC Debs, 9 March 1998, col. 16). This is, essentially, the crux of the debate about legislative programming, a debate which is hinged on the perception of MPs about the actual effects of the process. Debates in the first year generally demonstrated cautious support for the principles of programming, largely because MPs perceived it as a way of enabling them to have some structure to their time and discipline to their work (HC Debs, 4 June 1998). As one Labour member of the Modernisation Committee explained in 2002, the reforms had to be viewed as part of a broader legislative overhaul, and argued that the reforms did not 'strengthen the executive in the slightest' (interview, 18 April 2002). This view was endorsed by another Labour member of the Committee in 2002, who argued that programming was a change for the better in the chamber (interview, 13 May 2002). Nonetheless, the flip side of this viewpoint is summed up by MPs such as Dunwoody, who as early as 1998 was arguing that 'the guise of modernisation' was being used easily to restrict backbench capabilities in the House (HC Debs, 9 March 1998, col. 16).

In 2000, the Modernisation Committee returned again to the issue of legislative programming, arguing that such a system had to be characterised by clarity, simplicity and flexibility (HC 589, 1999–2000). The report acknowledged the role played by voluntary informal agreements, but made the case for legislative programming on a much broader, and non-experimental, basis. There were, according to the Committee, benefits for all concerned: the government would know when its legislation would be approved; the opposition would gain a clearer insight into the structure and focus of debate; backbenchers would have more certainty about voting times; and it ultimately would help produce better legislation because government should not need to table so many last-minute amendments (para. 13). The report recommendations paved the way for legislative programming to become more deeply embedded. These included plans for discussions between government and other parties soon after the Queen's Speech to pave the way for the session's legislation, the commissioning of new sessional orders to structure programming motions, and the creation of programming sub-committees for the standing committee stage of the legislative process. The package also included proposals for deferred divisions, whereby votes that would take place after 10.00pm would be held over until the following Wednesday in order to remove the need for MPs to wait around in the House to vote late at night.

The significance of these proposals is most clearly illustrated by the fact that the Modernisation Committee was not unanimous in its approval of the report, and, for the first time, a dissenting report was added by Opposition Members of the Committee. Partisan machinations at work must of course be considered as part of the equation in this instance, with a Labour member of the Committee later describing the dissenting report as appearing 'out of the blue on the last day of proceedings … despite [the Committee] having worked for weeks to reach an agreement' (HC Debs, 7 November 2000, col. 254). This dissenting report, proposed by the senior Conservative MP on the Committee, Sir George Young, linked the opposition's motives to the fact that 'the terms of trade between Parliament and the Executive need to be tilted back towards Parliament' (para. 3). The problem with the legislative programming reforms as outlined by the Modernisation Committee was that, despite what might be said about how they would benefit backbenchers, the fact remained that they would 'make it yet easier for Government to get its legislative programme through the House and, in so doing, lessen rather than encourage proper and adequate scrutiny' (para. 4). A key problem for the authors of the dissenting report was that the Modernisation Committee was pursuing the goal of creating an efficient House at the expense of creating an effective House. Yet, even in terms of the stated desire to create a more efficient House, the dissenting report took issue with the Modernisation Committee's diagnoses of the source of inefficiency. It was not about an inherently inefficient legislative process, nor was it about opposition mischief-making: rather, the main source of inefficiency was the volume and complexity of government legislation, poor legislative drafting, and poor management of the legislative process as a whole. The argument, then, was that legislative programming as proposed by the Modernisation Committee unnecessarily constrained parliamentary scrutiny of bills even although it was not the scrutiny process itself that caused legislative ineffi- ciency. The dissenting report argued that, instead of moving towards a formalisation of the programming structure then in place, there should instead be a more open version of the usual channels. It also rejected the notion of deferred divisions, which, given the way it separated debates from voting, was seen as a way of strengthening the hand of government at the expense of the opposition.

The arguments forwarded in both the official Modernisation Committee report and in the opposition members' dissenting report neatly sums up the two sets of perceptions that have long existed about the problems associated with the legislative process. For government, the problem lies in inefficient procedures that need to be changed in order to ensure more expeditious approval of legislation. For the opposition, the problem lies in the overloading of the legislative machine and of the desire of the executive to use that overloading as a pretext to curtail parliamentary scrutiny mecha- nisms. Indeed, these very arguments were rehearsed in an Opposition Day debate on 13 July 2000, just a week after the Modernisation Committee had published its report on programming and the opposition members of the Committee had made their objections plain. Opposition leader William Hague, for example, argued that the report simply illustrated the failure of the Modernisation Committee to act in the interests of strengthening parliament, and that it had instead become a useful mechanism through which the government could implement procedural change designed to expedite government legislation under the aegis of cross-party approval (HC Debs, 13 July 2000, col. 1091). But when the report itself was debated in the House in November 2000, serious partisan sparks began to fly in the chamber for the first time since the start of the modernisation project. Over two hours were spent initially debating a business motion put forward by the government to limit the length of the debate. Veteran Conservative MP Eric Forth declared, in characteristically inflamed style, that 'the Government, in the guise of the Modernisation Committee – for this purpose the two are identical – have decided to assault the House of Commons' (HC Debs, 7 November 2000, col. 173). Conservative colleague Michael Fallon similarly stated that 'it is particularly deplorable and appalling for debate on a motion that will curtail our rights to be curtailed' (col. 176). Conservative Modernisation Committee member Nicholas Winterton described the business motion as 'the guillotine of guillotines', and argued that the handling of the whole issue of programme motions was 'totally unacceptable' (col. 192). Although Labour members of the Modernisation Committee did not voice any concerns about the business motion, other Labour backbenchers did, with Gwyneth Dunwoody again stating her opposition to the whole notion of programming, and arguing that there had to be full and proper discussion in advance of a division, which was not congruent with a time-limited debate (cols 174–5). She issued a further caution, which highlighted a key problem that has long plagued the reform 'debate', that 'it is always wise for Back Bench members to beware of motions proposed by Front Benchers who argue that the proposals in the motion are for the convenience of Back Benchers' (col. 175). Despite the largely partisan-based opposition to the business motion, it was nonetheless approved on division by 251 votes to 168. All Labour members of the Modernisation Committee supported the motion (except two who did not vote), while all the Conservative and Liberal Democrat members voted against, demonstrating the clear partisan divide precipitated by the issue of programming and its handling in the House.

Once underway, the debate on legislative programming proper was similarly conducted along partisan lines. Throughout, Labour MPs generally endorsed the generic benefits of programming, as previously outlined by the Modernisation Committee, while Conservative MPs echoed the criticisms and concerns of the dissenting report. Opposition MPs also blamed the unsatisfactory construction of the Modernisation Committee for the unacceptable nature of the proposals it had made. One Conservative member of the Committee, John Bercow, asked:

> Is the meagre fare proposed by the Modernisation Committee any surprise, given that the Committee is chaired by a member of the Cabinet, and contains no fewer than three parliamentary private secretaries to Ministers, who are, of course, members of the Government payroll vote? The fingerprints of the Government Whips Office are all over the Committee. (HC Debs, 7 November 2000, col. 228)

Sir George Young, both a former member of the Committee and a former Shadow Leader of the House, pinpointed the central problem surrounding the reform issue, stating that 'two debates are taking place this afternoon – one about modernisation and one about strengthening', and arguing that he viewed these 'as two circles which overlap in part' (col. 255). The legislative programming recommendations, according to Young, were about modernisation, but of a kind that weaken parliament, because 'the Opposition do not have many weapons, and the report invites us to put some of them beyond use, while the Government sit on their substantial arsenal' (col. 255). Yet, despite such concerns, the government motion to introduce programming as outlined by the Modernisation Committee report was supported on division by 296 votes to 137. Unlike during the preceding business motion, the Liberal Democrat members of the Modernisation Committee voted with their Labour colleagues, with the Conservative members voting against. The debate was later described by one MP as emphatically not about accountability, but more 'like moving deck chairs on the deck of an oil tanker and suggesting that that would somehow make it change course' (HC Debs, 9 November 2000, col. 502).

If the Modernisation Committee's focus until that point had been almost exclusively on the question of enhancing legislative efficiency, then the Committee thereafter fell into something of a fallow period. In the 2000–1 session, the Committee published just one report, which reviewed the experimental programming that had been undertaken, and was a response to continued problems with its operation (HC 382, 2000–1). Cross-party agreement had not been reached on the sessional orders, and every programme motion had consequently faced opposition. What had started life in the House of Commons in 1997 as procedural change that attracted a degree of cautious all-party support, had, by 2001, become a significant partisan wedge in the modernisation project. The 2001 Modernisation Committee report therefore suggested a range of further alterations to how programming should work in practice. Yet, this report also attracted another dissenting report from the Conservatives on the Committee, who argued that programming had impeded the proper consideration of bills, and had managed to provoke principled opposition, when it should have alleviated it. The dissenting report contested the Modernisation Committee's claim that programming had improved the 'terms of the trade' for everyone:

> It is clearly to the disadvantage of the Official Opposition, to the expressed disadvantage of backbenchers and minorities and to the balance between the majority and the minority within the House. It has strengthened the Government's control over procedures with no discernible concession to the Opposition. It is true that the Government will get greater certainty for its legislative timetable. The proposition that Opposition parties and backbenchers will get greater

opportunities to debate and vote on the issues of most concern to them simply has not been borne our by experience in this Session of the experiment. (HC 382, 2000–1, Appendix)

The authors of the dissenting report therefore questioned one of the basic premises forwarded in defence of legislative programming – that it would enable the opposition to decide on which parts of a bill it wished to focus its scrutiny, remove the temptation to waste time by debating each clause at length, and therefore contribute to a far more effective legislative process, as well as a far more efficient one. In addition, the dissenting report authors also questioned the way that the Modernisation Committee had approached the task before it:

in seeking to amend the procedures of the Programming of Bills, the Modernisation Committee has not taken evidence from Members of Parliament, the Clerk of the House, nor apparently consulted with the Speaker ... Neither has there been any structured analysis of the obvious defects in the proceedings set out in the Sessional Orders made by the House on 7 November 2000. (HC 382, 2000-01, Appendix)

Much of the controversy over legislative programme took place while Margaret Beckett was Leader of the House and in the chair of the Modernisation Committee, an individual who was viewed as largely disinterested in broader issues regarding Commons reform, and as focused predominantly on utilising the Committee as a means to enhance legislative efficiency. Yet, although in operation for just a few years, the legacy of legislative programming very quickly left its (largely partisan) mark on the House, and when Robin Cook took over from Beckett in 2001, attention turned towards rectifying some of the worst aspects of programming. A subsequent report from the Modernisation Committee expressed concern that, 'since its introduction, programming has moved from a procedure for which there was broad agreement, to a process secured on a majority vote' (HC 440, 2001–2, para. 47). It reiterated arguments made in previous reports, that 'the strategic objective must be to find a consensual way of securing agreement to the timetabling of Bills' and that finding such consensus 'depends on all sides recognising that they each have more to gain from agreement than by confrontation' (para. 48). Crucially, the report counselled that:

[a]ll sides should be willing to abandon entrenched positions. Government should accept that better scrutiny can produce better legislation. Opposition should not mistake obstructionism for effective scrutiny. These though are matters of political culture. They cannot be resolved by amending the rules of procedure. (para. 48)

As part of a balanced agreement whereby both government and opposition gave ground as a way to secure programmes, the recommendations to improve the way the process worked subsequently found approval in the House as part of a broader reform package in October 2002. Indeed, Robin Cook viewed the mechanism of using a substantial package of reforms that reached across a range of efficiency and effectiveness issues as the only way to secure change in any of these areas, and to prevent the House descending into a partisan battle over possibly quite minor procedural points. From this perspective, the aim of a substantial package such as that produced in 2002 (and examined fully in Chapter 6), was that it would convince the House to accept some changes it might not like because to reject them would also mean rejecting other changes which it did like.

Nonetheless, the Modernisation Committee did return once more to the thorny question of programming, to recommend that the sessional orders which enabled timetabling be renewed. It again attempted to dampen the on-going partisan controversy by demonstrating that programming was 'not a new idea' and had, since 1887, 'been used regularly to impose a timetable on proceedings on public bills' (HC 1222, 2002–3, para. 1). Moreover, 'the suggestion that more routine use might be made of some kind of timetabling procedure has been advanced from time to time for nearly two decades' (para. 1). The report emphasised not only that 'it is important for all sides to recognise that programming is here to stay', but that programming 'is not simply a tool of Government', but rather 'a set of procedures of the House and, as such, Members in all parts of the House bear responsibility for its efficient operation' (para. 28). The report included recommendations for ensuring that sub-committees have enough time to consider government amendments, and that the time allocation provided by the bill timetable be extended if required. Once more, a dissenting report was attached, which disputed that there had in fact been a system of legislative programming in operation, and argued instead that what had actually been taking place was the guillotining of every bill and the exclusion of the opposition parties from programming discussions. However, this dissenting report did not secure support from all the Conservative Committee members, with only two voting in favour.

Clearly, then, moves towards structured legislative programming provoked partisan objections from MPs both inside the Modernisation Committee and in the House of Commons at large. Even those Conservative members of the Committee who are broadly supportive of the modernisa-tion project have nonetheless criticised the programming project and, in particular, the perceived role of the new 1997 Labour intake in securing its introduction. One senior Conservative MP explained his view that the new MPs 'do not appreciate the role of opposition in democracy', and that they were consequently content to support programming, which this MP believed to be 'a euphemism for guillotining' which served 'to limit the ability of the opposition … to delay legislation, and, in some cases, to amend legislation' (interview, 23 May 2002).

The controversy surrounding legislative programming was compounded by the decision of the Procedure Committee in the 2003–4 session to conduct an investigation into its operation. Such issues concerning the legislative process had, prior to 1997, been the preserve of the Procedure Committee, with the Committee taking a step back from their exploration so long as their chairperson was afforded a seat on the Modernisation Committee. Yet, with the deep partisan cleavages opened up by the operation of legislative programming as instituted by the Modernisation Committee, the Procedure Committee eventually judged the time as ripe for it to return to this familiar territory on its own terms. It is also notable that the Procedure Committee, at the time of that investigation, was chaired by Conservative MP Nicholas Winterton, who was a long-term critic of the role of the Leader of the House in the chair of the Modernisation Committee. A crucial point for the Procedure Committee was that legislative programming had never actually operated as originally intended when introduced in 1997, illustrated 'by the fact that most programme orders have been the subject of divisions … and by frequent complaints that many groups of amendments and new clauses and schedules were going undebated' (HC 325, 2003–4, para. 8). The Procedure Committee set itself the task that had ostensibly been that of the Modernisation Committee all along: to find a point of consensus between different views of the legislative process, on the attendant roles of government and opposition therein, and to devise a system of legislative programme that could successfully operate at the point of that consensus. Of course these differing views on the legislative process are almost completely diametrically opposed, which is why the issue has been so contentious, and were nicely summarised during the Procedure Committee's evidence sessions held during the enquiry. According to the Conservative 'traditionalist' Eric Forth:

> everything in this rests on the assumptions that one makes about the relative roles of government and opposition in the legislative process and particularly in standing committees. If one assumes, as I do, that in our system of parliamentary government where the government has, by definition, a majority and where it is the government's legislative programme that is being scrutinised by parliament, I believe it is of the utmost importance for the effectiveness of that process that it is the opposition which essentially has the dominant hand in determining how much time will be spent in committee. (HC 325, 2003–4, Q. 87)

Labour MP Barbara Follett, on the other hand, who had first entered parliament in 1997, pointed to her early experience sitting on bills where scrutiny apparently seemed to be at risk of going on indefinitely, and which had convinced her (and, she maintained, the government) that programming was

the ideal mechanism to prevent legislative scrutiny being used as an excuse
for irrelevant standing committee debates and filibustering by the opposition
parties (Q. 88). The Procedure Committee's many detailed recommendations
can, in part, be viewed as at least an attempt to reconcile these clashing
perceptions of the legislative process, and to iron out some of the more
uneven aspects of the operation of programming. In its response, however,
the government carefully described the Procedure Committee's work as one
that 'usefully supplements' the work of the Modernisation Committee, and
accepted only some of the recommendations made, incorporating them into
a motion to turn the sessional orders into permanent Standing Orders of the
House (HC 1169, 2003–4). Legislative programming procedures were incorporated into House Standing Orders on 26 October 2004, following a
division which largely rehearsed the same arguments for and against the
reforms, on a division of 261–173, with the House split along party lines,
albeit with some senior Labour backbenchers, such as Gwyneth Dunwoody
and Frank Field, entering the opposition lobby.

The final inclusion of legislative programming procedures into House of
Commons Standing Orders marks yet another government success in
adapting parliamentary mechanisms for its own ends. It fully formalised what
governments had anyway been doing for quite some time – constraining the
time opportunities available to the House of Commons for legislative
scrutiny, and severely disabling one of the weapons that has been traditionally viewed as the most useful in the parliamentary armoury, that is, the
ability to delay government legislation.

Yet, while much parliamentary attention was placed on the impact of
legislative programming, it arguably masked other kinds of efficiency
changes pursued by the Modernisation Committee. For example, the
Committee proposed changes to the explanatory material for bills to enable
Members to engage more quickly with their content and substance (HC 389,
1997–98). Crucially, also, it explored the case for the carry-over of bills from
one session to another (HC 543, 1997–98). The aim of this reform was to
allow legislation to be more evenly spread over the parliamentary calendar,
and to avoid the traditional glut of bills which always happened at the end of
the session, when government was anxious to get its remaining business
through the final stages of the legislative process. The principle of carry-over
received a reasonable level of support when it was first discussed in the
House (HC Debs, 4 June 1998), which agreed to experiment with an ad hoc
system of carry-over. Yet, by 2002, there had only been one bill subjected
successfully to the procedure, and a subsequent report from the
Modernisation Committee argued that carry-over was essential in order to
solve the problem of limited parliamentary time for legislative scrutiny, as
well as to tackle some of the most obvious difficulties with the way that
programming worked (HC 1168, 2001–2, paras 35, 38). The Committee,

then under the stewardship of Robin Cook, recommended that House Standing Orders should be amended to permit carry-over for another experimental period. Crucially, the Committee argued that carry-over should be viewed as a tool 'not to increase the volume of legislation but to provide more time in which to scrutinise the existing volume', and argued that it was therefore probably more beneficial to parliament than to government (para. 41). The House agreed to a temporary Standing Order to enable government bills to be carried over in October 2002, and a further three bills were then subjected to the procedure. Taking these examples to be evidence of its success, the Leader of the House, Peter Hain, tabled a motion in October 2004 to make the carry-over procedure a permanent part of House Standing Orders. The key point about the initial proposal from the Modernisation Committee to enable carry-over was that the ad hoc procedure should be facilitated only by cross-party agreement. During the debate to incorporate the mechanism permanently into Standing Orders, the opposition parties reiterated this need for the government to seek out cross-party agreement in advance for carry-over, a commitment that the Leader of the House was largely unwilling to give, on the grounds that such a process should not be blocked because of an absence of consensus (HC Debs, 26 October 2004, col. 1317). Despite complaints about both the principle and the potential practice of carry-over from opposition parties and from various backbenchers, the new Standing Order was approved by the House of Commons. By the end of 2007, five bills had been subject to the carry-over procedure. Crucially, too, the existence of the mechanism as a permanent part of House procedure had already enabled the government, through the Modernisation Committee, to attach new norms to it. In another wide-ranging report on the legislative process in 2006, the Committee recommended that when a bill is introduced late in the session as a result of being subject to pre-legislative scrutiny, there should be an *assumption* that it will be carried over to the next session as permitted in the Standing Orders, and that there would be an expectation of cross-party support being forthcoming (HC 1097, 2005–6, para. 29).

The formalisation of the carry-over procedure is a significant institutional innovation, perhaps not as contentious as legislative programming, but no less important in the broader scheme of things. Carry-over has long been viewed as a common-sense mechanism designed to alleviate the legislative burden that falls on parliament at particular times of the year, and partially to dismantle the structural edifice that is built (inappropriately for some) around sessions. Government benefits from carry-over because legislation is less likely to fall because of sessional cut-offs. Parliament benefits because it alleviates the legislative bunching that can occur at particular points in the session, and therefore contributes to a more streamlined House. Depending on one's perspective, it is also possible to argue that carry-over in fact contributes to a more effective House: if MPs are no longer having to race through any remaining legislative stages so that government bills are approved before a session ends, then it is conceivable that the procedure also facilitates not just more efficient scrutiny, but also more effective scrutiny, although this is certainly by no means guaranteed. In this respect, then, efficiency and effectiveness are demonstrably not mutually exclusive.

Westminster Hall

The creation of sittings in Westminster Hall did not produce controversy commensurate with that which accompanied the legislative programming proposals. What is of particular interest about this reform is that the Modernisation Committee promoted it as a significant step forward in securing an effective House of Commons. However, given the criteria and definitions laid down here with regards to how we can define the terms 'efficiency' and 'effectiveness', given the structured institutional context in which these reforms take place, and the norms and values that structure parliamentary life, the Westminster Hall innovation must instead be defined as a reform that is essentially about enhancing the efficiency of the House.

The key to understanding why this reform is mainly efficiency-driven lies in the first Modernisation Committee report to suggest it as a possibility. That report was on the topic of changing the parliamentary calendar (HC 60, 1998–99), and the Committee raised the idea of creating a parallel chamber to provide a forum for those issues that failed to find time on the floor of the main chamber. From the beginning, then, the whole notion of a parallel chamber was predicated on the issue of time constraints and the availability of House resources. This emphasis can also be found in the subsequent Committee report that recommended the creation of Westminster Hall sittings (HC 194, 1998–99). The report again pointed to the time constraints that prevented the House from 'effectively carrying out its fundamental duties of legislating, debating the major issues and holding the Executive to account' (para. 3). Crucially, the report argued that Westminster Hall would 'offer fresh opportunities to back-bench Members and enable the House to hold the Government to account on a wider range of issues' (para. 23). The new parallel chamber would be institutionally distinct from the main chamber, in that it would not be allowed to hold divisions, and so could only approve measures unanimously, meaning that only non-controversial business could proceed there.

From the perspective of the Modernisation Committee, Westminster Hall was conceived as a forum for three particular purposes (HC 194, 1998–99, paras 23–33). First, it would provide additional time for private Members' business, such as adjournment debates. Second, it would enhance the available opportunities for select committees by finding more time to discuss their work and reports. Finally, it would serve as an opportunity for business that failed to find House time, such as green paper debates and English regional concerns. It was, therefore, designed in response to complaints about the absence of time for backbench MPs in the main chamber, and as a mechanism that would better enable backbenchers to participate in the task of holding government to account. And this was the way that the parallel chamber was commended to the House of Commons, when it was debated in May 1999. Leader of the House, Margaret Beckett, even went as far as stating that the recommendation for Westminster Hall had not originated with government, but had emerged solely from the work of the Modernisation Committee itself (HC Debs, 24 May 1999, col. 82). A Conservative proponent of the Westminster Hall idea, Sir George Young, emphasised that the aim of the experiment was 'to give the House a greater ability to hold the Executive to account, rather than to enable the Executive to push through more inadequately considered legislation' (col. 87). Similarly, Liberal Democrat Chief Whip, Andrew Stunnell, noted that the innovation would assist Commons backbenchers in performing their scrutiny functions, with which they struggled because of time constraints (cols 100–3). Many other MPs also noted the benefits that would accrue for the dissemination and debate of select committee scrutiny work.

If these, then, were the aims of Westminster Hall, then why is it being described here as an efficiency reform, rather than effectiveness? According to the definition provided earlier, effectiveness reforms are those that are geared towards rebalancing executive-legislative relations in a way that benefits parliament in its task of holding the government to account. The stated aim of Westminster Hall was to provide more time for backbenchers for the express purpose of holding government to account: to debate constituency issues that had no chance of being discussed on the floor of the House, to discuss select committee reports, and to explore government green papers in detail. However, the crucial point is that the parallel chamber was designed as a forum to 'mop up' those issues that time did not permit exploration of in the main chamber, and this aspect of its institutional design immediately means that any executive scrutiny taking place there will be of a qualitatively different kind to that in the main chamber or in the standing or select committees. Westminster Hall was not constructed with a specific scrutiny function in mind – as were, for example, the select committees – and therefore as a mechanism aimed at addressing a particular imbalance in executive-legislative relations. It was, instead, constructed with an eye towards moving non-contentious legislation away from the main chamber, and of creating time elsewhere for backbenchers, time that is not available in the main chamber because of government dominance of resources there. Yet, recreating that time somewhere else for backbench purposes does not in and of itself help in rebalancing executive-legislative relations. As one Conservative MP remarked during the debate on the proposals, it was questionable whether 'Government would introduce and support these proposals if they thought that they would result in the Government having to be more accountable to Parliament' (HC Debs, 24 May 1999, col. 111). Indeed, the very fact that the government not only acquiesced in this reform, but actually also supported it, strongly supports the argument that Westminster Hall has not really contributed to enhanced parliamentary effectiveness, but has instead enhanced efficiency by moving yet more business out of the main chamber. Furthermore, the existence of Westminster Hall arguably makes it harder for backbenchers to claim more time in the Commons chamber in future: it was set up as a forum for backbenchers, and if that premise frames its future development, it may, over time, mean that any additional call for backbench opportunity may be answered by way of the parallel chamber.

Yet, any such path dependency of the institutional development of Westminster Hall may also, over time, actually help turn what must now be considered an efficiency reform into an effectiveness reform. The development of standing and select committees have, over time, contributed to a general rethink of how the main chamber of the House of Commons should be perceived, and to an acceptance that a great deal of useful scrutiny work can take place in forums other than the main chamber. In this respect, shifting work out of the main chamber and into other, specifically designed institutional platforms may eventually help define Westminster Hall as one of the important locations where executive scrutiny takes place, even if it is not clear that it is perceived this way at present. That is not a rethink that has encompassed all parts of the House, nor is it an accurate reflection of the current nature of the parallel chamber. The Shadow Leader of the House, Angela Browning, commented on the shifting of scrutiny debates away from the main chamber in a debate on Westminster Hall shortly after its creation:

> Such debates deserve full debate and scrutiny on the Floor of the House, with the relevant Secretary of State answering for himself or herself from the Dispatch Box. The practice, under the guise of more is better, of shuffling some of the more controversial Select Committee reports into Westminster Hall – where, by general acknowledgement, the nature of the debate is non-controversial – does not allow the House to call a Secretary of State to the Dispatch Box to answer Select Committees ... (HC Debs, 20 November 2000, col. 32)

Westminster Hall was designed as a non-contentious forum, where the partisan sting of debate could be removed from scrutiny. Yet, scrutiny is a contentious and controversial activity, as it should be, and so long as the parallel chamber is viewed as non-controversial, the nature of the work undertaken there will also be considered non-controversial and therefore, for much of the time, unimportant. Increasing the volume of backbench debates on select committee reports and government proposals in itself means little if it is not linked in a concrete way to specific outcomes with consequences for government. Furthermore, although Westminster Hall may, given time, develop institutionally and gain in significance and importance, it could just as equally go the other way: the parallel chamber could serve as a way to increase time on the floor of the House for government by creating an institutional precedent for diluting what takes place at Westminster Hall by continually adding to its varied workload, and thereby increasing the efficiency of the main chamber in terms of government business. From the most pessimistic viewpoint, if the aim of the government is continually to enhance Commons efficiency, then Westminster Hall serves as little more than a mechanism to remove tedious backbench scrutiny matters from the main chamber.

The parliamentary calendar and sitting hours

A perennial theme in most discussions about the possibility of 'modernising' the House of Commons concerns the working hours of the chamber, and one of the first things that MPs called upon the Modernisation Committee to examine was the erratic nature of the parliamentary calendar and the pattern of Commons sitting hours. This became a focus for the Committee's work in its second year of existence, and its report on the parliamentary calendar afforded a particularly good insight into how the Committee conceptualised reform:

> The purpose of reform is to make Parliament more effective. This means allowing Members to make the best use of their time, and to balance their various commitments in the House and its Committees with the increasing workload demands in their constituencies. (HC 60, 1998–99, para. 1)

As far as effectiveness and efficiency have been defined here, however, reforms in the area of the parliamentary calendar are far more concerned with enhanced efficiency than enhanced effectiveness: reforming the calendar or sitting hours is rooted in a desire to make the best use of the available parliamentary resources – in this case, time. The efficiency-based nature of this type of reform is further underlined by the fact that the Modernisation Committee's proposals for change were identical to those originally suggested to it by the government. Those recommendations largely pertained to the way the House operated on Thursdays, and involved the House meeting for Questions at 11.30am, with the moment of interruption coming at 7.00pm, and with standing committees meeting between 9.00am and 11.30am and 4.30pm and 7.00pm. The Modernisation Committee proposed that if the House did not like these suggestions, it would then put forward its own alternative strategy, which was different only in as much as Questions would be taken at 2.30pm. The report also recommended the introduction of a non-sitting week in February, to allow MPs to spend time in their constituencies. In the interests of flexibility, it further recommended that standing committees should be able to meet any time the House is sitting, except during Question Time, and that a period in September should be set aside as a designated 'Committee Week'.

The nature of the Committee proposals, and their origins as government recommendations, provoked much controversy when they were debated in the House in December 1998. There was confusion regarding whether or not the recommendations had been unanimously approved by the Modernisation Committee, as well as some discord over the opposition parties' decision apparently to support the government recommendations in Committee but vote against them in the House (HC Debs, 16 December 1998, cols 986, 933). Conservative MP Nicholas Winterton, a member of both the Modernisation Committee and the Procedure Committee, remarked on the particular role of the government in producing the sitting hours recommendations in these terms:

> Is not one of the problems facing the House the fact that this is a House of Commons matter, yet we are considering Government proposals? ... I am not sure that I believe that the Committee should be chaired by a member of the Government and Cabinet. That is the problem. We are debating Government proposals which the Government want to get through when it should be entirely a House of Commons matter. (HC Debs, 16 December 1998, cols 1000–1)

As with aspects of the legislative programming reform agenda, the origins of the recommendations made by the Modernisation Committee with respect to parliamentary sitting hours again provoked consternation about their intended impact. As Sir George Young commented during the debate, 'any Select Committee, and particularly the Modernisation Committee, will want to develop its own agenda and not just accept the Government's ... the House of Commons should control the Executive, not the other way around, particularly on this sort of issue' (col. 1001).

Indeed, the governmental origins of the recommendations served as an excellent partisan wedge during the entire debate, and greatly aided MPs in their task of flagellating each other with the entire modernisation project. One Labour member of the Committee, Clive Solely, for example, argued that Conservatives were undermining the basis of modernisation by attaching unnecessary dissenting reports to the Committee's work, and warned that since 'the majority of the House favours reform' the opposition should 'prove that it is prepared to work towards consensus' (col. 1005). Furthermore, the debate was characterised by (not untypical) confusion about the wording of the motion that the House would vote on, and the extent to which it was even being given an opportunity to express a view on the alternative scenario outlined by the Modernisation Committee. The issues under consideration in this instance looked, to the untrained eye, to be relatively simple ones regarding the nature of the parliamentary working week. However, the fact that the proposals were government-driven added an additional element of controversy to the proceedings, and sparked criticisms about the role that the Modernisation Committee was actually playing in the modernisation project.

Nonetheless, the House approved the government-sponsored changes to the Thursday sitting hours, and in July 1999, the Modernisation Committee recommended that the experiment be continued for another parliamentary session (HC 719, 1998–99). The fact that the changes proceeded only on an experimental basis underlines the divisions within the Modernisation Committee regarding their merits, and the absence of support sufficient enough to allow the new sitting hours to be solidified in Standing Orders, further illustrated by the tenor of the debate that approved the continued experiment (HC Debs, 25 October 1999).

The Modernisation Committee again recommended the continuation of the new-style Thursday sittings in a report of November 2000 (HC 954, 1999–2000). When the report was debated by the House, concerns were once more voiced about the impact that the new arrangements had on the work of the chamber. Gwyneth Dunwoody complained that the changes meant that MPs had lost the right to vote on important matters on Fridays (HC Debs, 20 November 2000, cols 30–1). Conservative MP John Bercow raised concerns that, when the new sitting hours arrangements were combined with the system of deferred divisions, the result would be that votes from Thursdays would lay over until the following Wednesday, and that 'a dramatic and disastrous reduction in Thursday attendance is obvious' (col. 31). Yet, this simply highlights the confusion caused by various Modernisation Committee changes brought into operation, because, as the Leader of the House pointed out during the debate, deferred divisions did not affect Thursdays, because deferment only happened after 10.00pm, but the House rose at 7.00pm on Thursdays (col. 31). At any rate, the House approved the continued operation of the Thursday sitting hours for a further session by 275 votes to 22.

Yet, it was clear that there was still disquiet about how the new sitting hours arrangements were working in practice, and when Robin Cook took over as Leader of the House, the Modernisation Committee pledged to re-examine the impact of the Thursday changes (HC 440, 2001–2). The Committee's subsequent report noted concerns about the relatively late hour at which the House began business in the chamber, arguing that this caused it to simply respond to the political agenda, rather than set it (HC 1168, 2001-02). The report recommended that the House sit and rise earlier from Tuesday to Thursday. It also proposed that constituency work should take precedence on Fridays, stating that 'if we are to address the growing gap between the electorate and politicians ... there is a solid case for arguing that more time should be provided within the Commons calendar for MPs to be among their constituents' (para. 73). The Committee also recommended that the Commons calendar should be announced a year in advance, that there should be an additional constituency week in the first half of the year, and that the summer recess should be shorter.

Yet, these recommendations proved to be even more controversial than any others on the sitting hours question previously proposed by the Modernisation Committee. In particular, the opposition criticised the proposals on the basis that they emanated from the government. Shadow Leader of the House, Eric Forth, cast doubt on 'whether what the Government – thinly cloaked as the Modernisation Committee on this occasion – propose will make the House of Commons more effective in scrutinising the Government and holding them to account' (HC Debs, 29 October 2002, col. 706). Liberal Democrat member of the Committee, Paul Tyler, objected to this characterisation, arguing that:

> The media and Members of the House seem to treat the proposals as though they are Government proposals. They are the proposals of a Select Committee, just as the proposals of the Procedure Committee … are from an all-party Committee. It is important to recognise that. (cols 717–8)

Yet Eric Forth went on to raise the key feature of the Modernisation Committee that has characterised its existence ever since the beginning – that 'unusually and wrongly … it is chaired by a Member of the Government and, indeed a Cabinet Minister' and that this made it quite different to any other House committee (col. 718). The ever-present fact that the Modernisation Committee was chaired by a government minister framed the concerns of other MPs about the likely impact of the proposed changes, and the debate contained many different suggestions about how the new sitting hours would interfere with the ability of the House to scrutinise the government, rather than improve it. The highly contentious nature of the proposed changes, and the concern from across the House about how they would operate in practice, is reflected in the narrow defeat of Labour MP Chris Mullin's amendment to prevent the changes applying to Wednesdays, which was overcome by just 288 votes to 265. Furthermore, while the main question on sitting hours was approved by 311 votes to 234, the recommendation for earlier sitting hours on Tuesdays was carried by just 274 votes to 267. In January 2003, therefore, the House began to sit from 2.30pm to 10.00pm on Mondays, 11.30am to 7.00pm on Tuesdays and Wednesdays, 11.30am to 6.00pm on Thursdays and 9.30am to 2.30pm on Fridays.

The sitting hours issue has been a significant wedge issue in the modernisation project. The Modernisation Committee has consistently reiterated that such plans are formulated for the benefit of parliament, and successive Leaders of the House have stressed that the primary aim has not been only to make parliament more 'family friendly', while still accepting that improved hours of work are undoubtedly a desirable outcome. Nonetheless, many of those involved in the modernisation project have pointed specifically to the need to improve hours for the benefit of MPs. For example, one Modernisation Committee member cited her frustration at the all-night sittings and working patterns as the central reason why she sought membership (interview, 16 April 2002). A Liberal Democrat member of a backbench All-Party Group for Parliamentary Reform commented on the frustration amongst the new intake of MPs after 1997 'about the whole way in which this building operates' and the impact it had on those with families (inter-view, 14 May 2002). For those with such views, there is a sense that it was the new intake of MPs who forced this matter onto the agenda in the first place.

Yet, the changes nevertheless provoked considerable debate and controversy, and the existence of the new intake of MPs helped to fuel this. One Conservative MP on the All-Party Group for Parliamentary Reform, for example, described an 'unholy alliance' between the government and the new MPs elected in 1997, which had worked to force unwanted changes on the rest of the House (interview, 14 May 2002). This MP was not opposed to improved hours of work for MPs, but was less sure as to whether the various reforms had actually achieved any improvement:

> I think there has been an unfortunate confusion between the very clear fact that our hours and our procedures are not in the current parliament family friendly – I think there's been a confusion between a reasonable desire to try to change that, and some of the steps which have been taken … which actually don't necessarily make parliament that much more family friendly, do make the hours shorter, and which certainly constrains the ability of parliament to do its job. (Interview, 14 May 2002)

Indeed, such was the continued controversy over the operation of the new sitting hours that the Procedure Committee conducted an inquiry into the matter. Since the creation of the Modernisation Committee, the Procedure Committee had stayed out of the sitting hours debate. The Procedure Committee's survey of MPs demonstrated what was by then obvious to anyone – that no one option on reforming House sitting hours could command a clear majority amongst MPs, although there was some sentiment for a reversion to the previous Tuesday sitting hours (HC 491, 2003–4). The main concern with the new way of working was the impact it had on standing committees, which traditionally met in the mornings. The Modernisation Committee therefore returned yet again to the sitting hours issue, publishing a report in January 2005 that largely endorsed the new system of sitting hours, although it did recommend the need to restore Thursday to a full parliamentary day, and therefore recommended the House sit one hour earlier on Thursdays at 10.30am.

When the House debated the Modernisation Committee proposals in January 2005, the deep divisions about the impact of the new hours instituted in 2003 came to the fore. In particular, opposition MPs complained that the new hours had reduced the time available for scrutiny of the government, while some Labour and Liberal Democrat MPs tried to argue the case for thinking more holistically about the work of the House of Commons in terms of its committees and Westminster Hall, rather than focus only on what happened in the chamber. Yet, the House ultimately decided that, while it could accept much of what the Modernisation Committee proposed, it could not accept the House continuing to sit at 11.30am on Tuesdays, and supported an amendment tabled by Labour MP George Howarth to that effect by 292 votes to 225. Indeed, with the amendment incorporated into the government motion, the House supported the adjusted sitting hours by 375 votes to 14. From the start of the 2005 parliament, the new sitting hours of the House were 2.30pm to 10.00pm on Mondays and Tuesdays, 11.30am to 7.00pm on Wednesdays, 10.30am to 6.00pm on Thursdays and 9.30am to 2.30pm on Fridays.

Depending on their nature, changes to House sitting hours can be of benefit to both government and parliament. Such changes are always about creating an efficient chamber – a chamber that is best disposed to make the most out of the limited time it has available to it. Whether such enhanced efficiency does then lead to enhanced effectiveness has been the rub throughout the controversy provoked by these reforms since 1997. Depending on the persuasion and outlook of any given MP, sitting hours changes either help MPs to find more time for their constituency and committee work, or they hamper MPs in their ability to hold government to account. Even those changes implemented by parliamentary-minded Robin Cook – ostensibly for the purpose of making the MP's working life more manageable – caused tremendous debate because of the varying ways they were interpreted. Indeed, several Conservative and Liberal Democrat MPs commented in interviews that one of the main motivations behind reforming sitting hours was to ensure marginal Labour MPs could find more time in their constituencies shoring up their votes (interviews, April/May 2002; June 2007). In other words, the notion that organising the House of Commons working week should really be a value-free exercise is a misguided one – it is at heart about values and about the norms that structure the way in which MPs approach their various parliamentary tasks.

Proceedings in the chamber

The Modernisation Committee also examined a range of other procedural issues pertaining to the way the Commons goes about its work, not all of which need detain us here. For example, in 2002, the Committee proposed that ministerial statements should come earlier in the day, to allow for better media coverage of parliament, and that the House employ shorter debates when prudent (HC 1168, 2001–2). It also recommended that backbench contributions to debates should be limited to ten minutes, a proposal which once more provoked debate in the House about whether modernisation was meant to benefit government or parliament (HC Debs, 29 October 2002). In that instance, however, then Leader of the House, Robin Cook, had rolled a number of modernisation proposals into one package, forcing the House to accept all changes, or risk securing none at all: indeed, it was this package which also brought about the unpopular changes to sitting hours discussed in the previous section. Formalising the time limits in 2002 simply made concrete something the House had previously experimented with: in this instance, however, the main point of contention was that frontbench speeches were not also formally time-limited.

However, there are a range of things with which the Modernisation Committee has not concerned itself. Issues pertaining to parliamentary questions remained the preserve of the Procedure Committee after 1997, which reported on the matter in 2002 (HC 622, 2001–2) following a range of concerns raised by the Public Administration Committee in the course of its work on ministerial responsibility (HC 820, 1997–98; HC 821, 1998–99; HC 61, 2000–1; HC 1086, 2001–2). The Procedure Committee's recommendations aimed to improve the overall utility of question time and tilt the terms of trade back towards backbenchers from a procedural perspective. The government did accept some of the Committee's recommendations in this vein, although it naturally rejected the claim that ministers gave too many 'evasive and unhelpful replies' (Cm 5628, 2002, para. 19).

The Modernisation Committee and efficiency in the Commons

In the 1998–99 session, the Modernisation Committee noted its programme of work had 'produced a mixed response in the House', noting that while some MPs believed the process of reform had 'gone far enough', others maintained that it had been 'merely tinkering at the edges of the far more radical reforms needed' (HC 865, 1998–99, para. 12). Yet it was not just MPs who had concerns about the focus of the modernisation project. Outside organisations had similar concerns, with Charter 88 describing the implemented reforms as 'typified by minor amendments to existing practice and little, if any, firm commitment to reform' (Charter 88, 1998).

One particular question posed by Shadow Leader of the House, Eric Forth, in 1999, nicely pinpoints the contradictions of the modernisation project and the Committee charged with delivering it:

> Given the President of the Councils' role as representative of the House of
> Commons within government, will she give an absolute guarantee that,
> whatever changes are proposed for consideration by the House under the rather
> dubious rubric of modernisation, the one thing that will not happen is a
> reduction of the time available to the House to scrutinise and hold to account
> the Government? (HC Debs, 1 March 1999, col. 738)

This comment, which is hardly unique in Hansard, illuminates two different
points regarding the progress of efficiency reforms in the House. First,
Forth's point is obviously partisan, and partisanship has been a significant
wedge in the modernisation project, and one which has facilitated competing
interpretations of the aims and outcomes of the reforms instituted. Second,
Forth's comment highlights that efficiency reforms can be, and have been,
used as mechanisms to prevent systematic executive scrutiny, because the
government perceives improvements in Commons efficiency as opportunities to accelerate the progression of its own business. In this respect, then, the
chairmanship of the Modernisation Committee has been extremely problematic. The Committee chairman is also the same government minister in
charge of securing the government's business, and therefore has an interest
in using modernisation in order to ease government business through the
House, rather than in creating conditions to impede it. One Conservative MP
on the Modernisation Committee commented on the chairmanship in these
terms:

> I'm not sure that a select committee of the House, which is looking at how we
> use our time, how we are effective in respect of the electorate at large and the
> public, how we deal with ... the parliamentary calendar, I have some doubts as
> to whether control of that committee, or the chairmanship of the committee,
> should actually be in the hands of a cabinet minister. Because, to an extent ... it
> would clearly be understood that if that committee produces a report, it has the
> blessing of the government, and the blessing of the government may not be in
> the interests of the House of Commons, because any government is keen to have
> a system whereby it can get its business as quickly and as easily as possible.
> (Interview, 23 May 2002)

One Labour member of the Modernisation Committee, by contrast, had a
more resigned attitude on the matter, stating that, 'I think it is an under-
standable practical compromise at the moment on the basis that it re-empha-
sises just how strong the executive has become in its domination of
parliament, because we can't even make reforms unless we can negotiate
some approval by the executive to give up things to us' (interview, 13 May
2002).

The relationship between efficiency and effectiveness is not zero-sum.
Some reforms in the interests of securing efficiency in the Commons,
however they might be promoted, may also impact upon its effectiveness. A

good example is the carry-over of public bills. This is of benefit to the government, which avoids losing its legislation. It is also of benefit to the House of Commons, which avoids a glut of work at various points in the session. Such an observation does not, however, alter the basic reasons why government engages in parliamentary reform. The ultimate reason is to create the most efficient procedures for passing government legislation through the House. Prior to 1997, the government utilised the Procedure Committee towards this end, and since 1997, it has utilised the Modernisation Committee instead, the latter arguably proving more pliant than the former because of the ministerial presence within it.

Such a statement may seem to sympathise with the views of some members of the Conservative Party on this theme, but it is not intended as a value judgement. Instead, it is an assessment of the sensibilities of the dominant elite that operate inside the House of Commons. The emphasis on legislative efficiency is simply a result of the historical development of the House, and the structured institutional context of norms and values within which MPs operate. In this perspective, modernisation is predominantly about creating a set of conditions inside the House of Commons that augment its efficiency in delivering the government's legislative programme. Labour MP Tony Wright emphasised as much when he noted that 'we are engaging in some modernisation of the House, but the question is whether we are engaging in parliamentary reform' (HC Debs, 9 November 2000, col. 510). The initially ad hoc way in which the Committee approached its task was also called into question, with Wright commenting that, when it was first established, 'the Modernisation Committee did not take a view in the round on what parliamentary reform required', with the result that '[w]e do not know to what purpose and in what direction we are modernising, and we are suffering greatly as a result' (col. 510). For Conservative MPs, however, the purpose of modernisation was always clear, summed up by Sir Peter Emery's argument that the government's 'purpose in modernisation is to strengthen the Executive and override a major suggestion of allowing Parliament to have a greater impact on the Executive' (col. 513).

This executive preference for altering House procedures in order to ensure its business can be secured quickly forms part of a consistent pattern of behaviour, as the previous chapter demonstrated. Consequently, modernisation is not a synonym for parliamentary reform. Indeed, '[t]he government's approach to legislative modernisation always owed more to its desire to secure the passage of its business than to a desire to improve the effectiveness of parliamentary scrutiny' (Cowley and Stuart 2001: 238). The institutional norms and values in operation at Westminster mean that executives focus on ways to secure ever greater legislative efficiency, and the nature of institutional development means that the logic of such reform necessarily closes down some reform alternatives while loading the dice in favour of others: for example, once the principle of standing committees or legislative programming, controlled by the government, have been introduced, it becomes easier, not harder, to adapt and refine them further.

Historical institutionalism emphasises that institutional change does not take place on a blank slate, and that previous institutional choices impact significantly on future ones. Consequently, it is in analysing efficiency reforms at Westminster that historical institutional theory has most explanatory validity. The Westminster institutional context is structured by certain key norms and values, and those which are of most relevance in the context of efficiency reforms are parliamentary sovereignty and strong party government. As the dominant actor at Westminster, the government seeks not just to preserve but also to deepen these norms, because by so doing it expands its capacity for action. According to historical institutional theory, the structured institutional context favours some strategies for change over others, and governments thus favour strategies that enhance legislative efficiency. Therefore, the key changes secured early in the twentieth century – which constrained parliamentary input into the legislative process and instituted procedures and mechanisms that enhanced legislative efficiency – not only built on the re-emergence of a strong and ascendant executive by the close of the nineteenth century, but also consolidated a new path for institutional development from which parliament has not significantly deviated. The previous weight of institutional choices has consequences for future choices, and once the logic of those embryonic procedures for legislative efficiency was accepted, that logic could not thereafter be disputed. Consequently, the institutional products of that logic, which all sought to further government dominance of the legislative process, became the foundation for all future developments. In this respect, historical institutionalism helps us to understand why the House of Commons accepted the introduction and continued use of legislative programming procedures after 1997, despite the controversy which accompanied them: such procedures were a simple extension of government control of House legislative procedures, control which had long ago been asserted. The various efficiency reforms pursued by the Modernisation Committee – legislative programming, changes to sitting hours, and so on – are therefore not actually about institutional change, but are instead entirely about institutional continuity. A historical institutionalist approach compels us to look beyond individual episodes and instances of change, and to place them in a much broader historical frame of reference, and by so doing, to see the longer-term processes of continuity that underpin individual reforms. The framework helps us to analyse that continuity through the language of path dependency: once the executive successfully took control of House procedure, institutional development thereafter proceeded along a path whereby the executive used that control to meet its own particular needs. In this respect, path dependency is not simply the convenient descriptive device alleged by critics: it is rather a tool which has empirical explanatory capacity.

Nonetheless, as Chapter 6 demonstrates, the Modernisation Committee did gradually move away from these efficiency-based reform packages. In part, this was because some of these efficiency issues had been largely settled as far as MPs were concerned. As one Labour member of the Modernisation Committee remarked, 'the things it [the Committee] was dealing previously with were things like sitting hours, the parliamentary week and the parliamentary year, and so on, and I think most people now think that parliamentary hours are now pretty much a done deal' (interview, 19 June 2007). In time, the Modernisation Committee came to think more about broader House of Commons issues, and more about the question of effectiveness. Of course, debates about how to improve the effectiveness of the Commons are not new, and have a long pedigree, as the next chapter demonstrates.

5
Effectiveness in the House of Commons 1900–97

Introduction

The institutional make-up of Westminster is characterised by the norm of strong government, and consequently places much value on ensuring that government can secure its business. Successive governments have been able to use their dominant position inside the House of Commons to exploit those norms and values in order to reform parliamentary procedure and ensure that legislation is approved expeditiously and that the chamber functions in a streamlined way. Governments have also used their institutional dominance with respect to effectiveness reforms, although for quite different purposes. Following the logic utilised previously in discussing the structured institutional context in existence at Westminster, effectiveness reforms are defined as those which seek to rebalance executive-legislative relations. Such reforms challenge the norms and values that comprise the structured institutional context in which the Commons exists, and, as the dominant actor within the Commons, the executive in turn uses these same norms and values in order to resist such change. The historical development of Westminster – which has been predicated on executive sovereignty, ministerial responsibility and strong party government – has made it remarkably difficult to realign executive-legislative relations in a meaningful way. Government enjoys pre-eminence inside parliament and the norms and values that maintain that pre-eminence are embedded in the very fabric of the structured institutional context that parliamentary reformers seek to overhaul. From a historical institutionalist perspective, the structured institutional context at Westminster has meant that strategies for change in favour of rebalancing executive-legislative relations have not been favoured, impinging as they necessarily would on executive sovereignty, ministerial responsibility and strong party government. Consequently, the path of institutional development has been one where such reforms are not easily accommodated.

This chapter examines some of those reforms in the years prior to 1997, suggested for and implemented in the House of Commons, which have been geared towards enhancing its effectiveness. While effectiveness reforms in the early part of the century tended to suggest particularly radical solutions to the 'problem of parliament', such as electoral reform and devolution, that tendency was largely replaced in the post-war era by a desire to enhance effectiveness by promoting internal reform of the House of Commons itself.

Effectiveness in the House of Commons

The historical evolution of the Westminster parliament, and the norms and values that have evolved alongside it, have forged path-dependent development that has reinforced the centrality of government within the political system. The practical operation of parliamentary sovereignty, the impact of ministerial responsibility, and the values fostered by the operation of party government, all structure parliament's institutional existence and effectively delimit its capabilities and spheres of action. Parliamentary sovereignty, while theoretically referring to the legislative authority of parliament, in practice means executive sovereignty, as a result of the government's ability to command majority support inside the Commons. Ministerial responsibility is supposed to ensure that government remains responsible to parliament, and in theory acts as a mechanism to facilitate both strong and accountable government, yet it has instead been inverted to prevent effective accountability and to strengthen further the capability of government. The practical operation of party government at Westminster, characterised by a government-opposition mentality, and underpinned by strong party discipline and loyalty, has consolidated the development of a dominant value system within the Commons predicated on the need to ensure that government secures its business.

This structured institutional context not only provides the environment within which parliament operates, it also provides the environment within which reform of parliament takes place. How one views parliament, and its relationship with government, will inform the formulation of reform proposals. Those interested in securing an efficient parliament will, as the previous chapters demonstrated, be drawn towards those reforms aimed at expediting the legislative process, streamlining sitting hours in the House, and generally ensuring that scarce parliamentary resources are used for maximum effect. Those interested in securing an effective parliament will instead be interested in reforms that seek to alter the structured institutional context within which the Commons operates, and thus seek to alter the dominant value system inside the Commons. However, it is worthwhile stressing again that the relationship between efficiency and effectiveness is not zero-sum. Efficiency reforms, depending on their formulation, may contribute to a more effective parliament, and vice-versa. On the whole, however, efficiency reforms are often criticised more for inhibiting the effective operation of the Commons than they are praised for enhancing it. Similarly, some effectiveness reforms will likewise attract criticism on the grounds that they inhibit the efficient operation of the Commons.

So, what kind of impact would various sorts of effectiveness reforms have on Westminster? As far as parliamentary/executive sovereignty is concerned, effectiveness reforms might restrict the legislative capabilities of the executive and its ability to secure legislation with relative ease, and at least enhance the rigour of the legislative scrutiny that takes place. In terms of ministerial responsibility, effectiveness reforms might entail the construction and implementation of alternative scrutiny systems to make parliamentary oversight of government departments more demanding. In terms of party government, effectiveness reforms might aim to reduce the impact of the whips' offices in the daily lives of MPs, create alternative career paths to that of government, and enhance the parliamentarian instincts of MPs in relation to their party instincts.

Tony Wright made clear this distinction between efficiency and effectiveness in these terms:

> When we talk about modernising Parliament, I get rather uneasy, as modernisation can mean two different things. It can mean allowing the Executive to have an easier life and to get their business through in a more straightforward way, as well as tidying up some of the untidy bits of how this House operates, including things that I like, such as ensuring that we get home earlier at night. Those are important matters, but let us not believe for a second that they go to the heart of the constitutional issue, which is that there has been a drift of power away from Parliament and towards the Executive as party discipline has tightened in the past century or so. We have to decide either that this is how politics now is ... or that that shift has to be reversed. (HC Debs, 14 May 2002, cols 685–6).

A radical approach to securing effectiveness: 1900–30

Effectiveness reforms, therefore, aim to restructure and rebalance executive-legislative relations at Westminster. Several scholars at the start of the twentieth century discussed the specifics of the relationship between government and Commons, and their work helps to frame the nature and content of the debate regarding the prospects for an effective chamber.

Theorising the House and its relationship with government

In 1904, Sidney Low summed up the position of the House of Commons as a result of its historical development as follows:

Its supremacy is qualified by the growth of rival jurisdictions. Its own servants have become, for some purposes, its masters ... The Cabinet is more powerful, and has drawn to itself many attributes which the Commons are still imagined to possess. The Electorate, more conscious of its own existence under an extended franchise, wields a direct instead of a delegated authority. And causes, internal to the House itself, have deprived it of some of its functions, and limited the exercise of others. (Low 1906: 58–9)

For Low (1906: 76–7), 'a member's views as to the growing encroachments of the Government on the right of discussion are apt to be coloured by his own relations to it'. The executive had come to control the Commons, rather than the other way around. Despite the theory that a failure by ministers to justify their actions to the House would result in them being turned out of office, the Cabinet in practice 'is scarcely ever turned out of office by Parliament *whatever it does*' (Low 1906: 81, original emphasis). Low concluded that 'the weakness of the private member, and of the House generally, and the growing strength of the Cabinet, are not due in the main to the Rules of Procedure' and that 'their amendment would not affect the deeper causes, which have altered the balance between the Legislature and the Executive' (1906: 83–7). Part of the problem with the Commons lay in 'the multiplicity of its nominal duties, the variety of its functions [and] the mountainous mass of its interests' (Low 1906: 88). So many were its functions, in fact, that it was failing in its duty to fulfil any of them satisfactorily.

In his 1912 study of the 'English' political system, American scholar A. Lawrence Lowell also examined executive dominance of the House of Commons. The situation was one in which the cabinet 'initiates everything, frames its own policy, submits that policy to a searching criticism in the House, and adopts such suggestions as it deems best' (Lowell 1912, vol. 1: 327). The House operated in the context of a two-party system, and could only accept government proposals or reject them (Lowell 1912, vol. 1: 355). Consequently, 'the programme of the ministers must be accepted or rejected as a whole, and hence the power of initiative, both legislative and executive, must rest entirely with them', even if that caused a decline in the ability of the Commons 'in passing any effective vote, except a vote of censure' (Lowell 1912, vol. 1: 355). The main power of parliament, then, was as 'the great inquest of the nation' (Lowell 1912, vol. 1: 355), and as a forum where the issues of the day were aired and debated. Indeed, Lowell was remarkably upbeat in terms of how he perceived the role of the House of Commons:

If the parliamentary system has made the cabinet of the day autocratic, it is an autocracy exerted with the utmost publicity, under a constant fire of criticism; and tempered by the force of public opinion, the risk of a vote of want of confidence, and the prospects of the next election. (Lowell 1912, vol. 1: 355)

For those with experience inside the House of Commons, things did not seem so rosy. Labour MP F.W. Jowett, for example, was a vociferous critic of the impact of party on parliamentary government, and his 'Jowett Plan', surprisingly approved by the Labour conference in 1914, advocated a system where MPs would be freed from the yoke of party and enabled to vote on matters according to their merits, rather than according to party dictat (Hanson 1957: 460). Jowett even went as far as arguing that government departments should be partly run by all-party committees of MPs, and that government ministers should be charged with enacting the collective will of the committee. Naturally, the extremity of this plan, and its intentional crippling of the norm of strong government, was not widely endorsed, but it is nevertheless a good example of the action some observers believe to be required in order to dampen the impact of party at Westminster.

The case for devolution

Following the First World War, fresh calls emerged for systematic reform of parliament, and the Commons in particular. The wartime government had accumulated a new range of duties for itself, which were not relinquished by the executive at the conclusion of hostilities, and, consequently, the relative weakness of the Commons in comparison with government seemed even more marked. As Butt (1969: 97) notes, '[t]here was a clear connection between the new duties being performed by the central government on behalf of the community and the feeling that the House of Commons was no longer able to exercise adequate influence over the Executive'. The House seemed to be engulfed by the new organisational imperatives of the parties, which were then reacting to franchise expansion, resulting in the emergence in the 1920s of parliamentary-based party committees on a range of subjects (Butt 1969: 100). Of particular concern was the evidence that the individual MP seemed paralysed in the face of the immense workload now facing the Commons as a result of the freshly assumed responsibilities of government (Butt 1969: 106).

In light of these concerns, suggestions emerged that there was an urgent need for parliamentary devolution. Sidney Low had already made such a case in 1906. Devolution was justified as a way to separate 'imperial' functions from 'local' ones, and therefore to make a clearer distinction 'between great and small, between subjects merely local and transient, and those of imperial and enduring importance' (Low 1906: 290–1). Such a process would result in 'national councils' that would be an extension of the existing levels of subordinate government, except along a federal model, with sovereignty remaining at Westminster. Devolution of this sort would mean that '[t]he House of Commons will gain in dignity, as well as efficiency' because it could discuss major issues free from the pressures of attending to minor legislation (Low 1906: 294–5).

If Low had found the case for devolution compelling well in advance of the First World War, then it was arguably even more so in the years immediately following the conclusion of hostilities. In June 1919, the House of Commons passed a motion favouring the creation of subordinate bodies within the UK, and established a Speaker's Conference to examine the matter in detail, which debated the merits of having an imperial parliament for the 'great issues of the day' and subordinate bodies for more domestic matters (Butt 1969: 109). The Conference on Devolution, which met under Mr Speaker Lowther and comprised thirty-two MPs hand-picked by the prime minister, reported in April 1920. While the Conference was successful in deciding which powers should be devolved, it was less sure about how to write the constitutions of the various devolved bodies proposed (Butt 1969: 109–10). The failure to reach clear conclusions meant that, by 1920, in Westminster at least, 'the issue was running into the political sands' (Lenman 1992: 67).

Regional devolution did, however, continue to attract interest away from Westminster. The Scottish Council of the Labour Party became increasingly committed to regional devolution, and passed resolutions supporting Scottish home rule at every conference between 1915 and 1923. Collaboration between the regional and central elements of the party even resulted in the framing of a Scottish Home Rule Bill, which was unsuccessfully presented to parliament in 1924 (Lenman 1992: 67). However, devolution was supported on these occasions, not as a way to improve the effectiveness of parliament, but in order to initiate home rule as a principle in itself (Hansard Society 1967: 37). Even Ramsay Muir's (1930) advocacy of regional devolution had more to do with preventing the over-centralisation of government than it had with securing an effective parliament (Hansard Society 1967:37).

Nevertheless, broader interest in devolution as a method of improving the effectiveness of the House of Commons was present throughout the 1920s. While the Speaker's Conference had been primarily interested in regional devolution, the concept of functional devolution was soon being championed. Ramsay Macdonald, for example, argued that while 'defending the Parliamentary method and Parliament, one must be careful not to be committed to defend Parliament in its existing form' (Macdonald 1920: vi). Macdonald insisted that parliamentary methods had to be 'embodied in an efficient organisation' in order to resist revolution, and reasoned that 'reform is not to be found in new electoral systems [or] in committee government', but in ensuring that parliament be adapted to 'modern social conditions' (Macdonald 1920: vii–iii). He advocated two 'aspects of democracy', one political and the other industrial, but argued for the creation of 'a community within the community, as against a function within the community', with the ultimate aim being to strengthen the links between the individual and parliament (Macdonald 1920: 70). For Macdonald, therefore, devolution could improve the effectiveness of parliament by bringing it closer to the people (Macdonald 1920: 72–3). In this instance, parliamentary effectiveness was understood in particularly broad terms, and not confined simply to issues of procedural efficacy.

Somewhat more specific were Sidney and Beatrice Webb's plans for parliamentary devolution outlined in 1920. They identified the problem as 'not too much democracy but too little, not too many thoroughly democratic institutions but too few' (Webb 1975: 89). They advocated the creation of a political parliament and a separate social parliament, because:

> The whole body of citizens … must have two channels – one through which they can express their will in the group of issues involved in the protection of the community and the individual against aggression, including the maintenance of personal liberty; and the other through which they can exercise their creative impulse towards such a use of the national resources as will provide for themselves a finer and fuller civilisation. (Webb 1975: 93)

The plan involved splitting the House of Commons, and its powers and functions, into two national assemblies, each with its own competencies. As the Webbs saw it, an effective division of labour was the best way to maximise parliamentary effectiveness, and ensure that the executive could be held to account.

Winston Churchill was also concerned with the status of the House of Commons during the 1920s and early 1930s. He had been advocating 'home rule all round' since the early 1900s, mainly as a cure for the Irish problem (Theakston 2004: 66–7). Churchill naturally held parliament in high regard, and perceived devolution as a means to enhance the status of Westminster. In a speech at the Guildhall in November 1923, he remarked:

> The House of Commons, if I am rightly informed … is dead. Whether it has committed suicide or whether it has been put away I cannot tell. Whether it is a voluntary or a compulsory act no one can know, but at any rate the appearances have been well maintained, and the representative assembly, the House of Commons, is marching silently and docilely to execution blindfold. (James 1974, vol. 4: 3394)

Churchill was well aware of the 'great reaction against parliamentary institutions' then occurring across Europe, and regretted that parliaments were no longer the arenas in which 'the real important issues of national life have to be decided' (James 1974, vol. 4: 3395). The need to defend parliamentary institutions grew more urgent for Churchill in the 1920s as the economic depression worsened in the UK. The period 1929–31 has been described as the 'high tide of criticism of the existing parliamentary system', and the point at which serious questions were asked of the problem-solving capabilities of the UK's political institutions (Butt 1969: 118). This sentiment is illustrated by Churchill's Romanes lecture at Oxford University in June 1930, described as 'a strong defence of parliamentary democracy' (Gilbert 1976: 361), in which Churchill argued that parliament was 'precious … beyond compare' (James 1974, vol. 5: 4853). Nonetheless, Churchill maintained that parliament was poorly structured to deal with the economic questions of the day. He explained that:

> It must be observed that economic problems, unlike political issues, cannot be solved by any expression, however vehement, of the national will, but only by taking the right action … What is wanted is a remedy. Every one knows what the people wish. They wish for more prosperity. How to get it? That is the grim question, and neither the electors nor their representatives are competent to answer it. (James 1974, vol. 5: 4854)

For Churchill, electoral imperatives prevented political parties from tackling serious economic issues, and party leaders were reluctant to engage in serious discussion about how to solve them. What was required, therefore, was a 'non-political body, free altogether from party exigencies, and composed of persons possessing special qualifications in economic matters' (James 1974, vol. 5: 4854). Churchill advocated the creation of a subordinate economic parliament, which would make recommendations to parliament about solutions to economic problems, and do so free from the influence of public opinion. He accepted this would be 'an innovation', but believed that the constitution was flexible enough to accommodate it (James 1974, vol. 5: 4854).

While individuals such as Sidney and Beatrice Webb and Winston Churchill perceived devolution as a way of enhancing the effective operation of the House of Commons, few others cast it in these terms. Thereafter, when the question of devolution arose, it largely concerned the merits of home rule as a goal in itself, rather than as a contribution to the effectiveness of the Commons. While the issue therefore did not disappear from the political agenda, the nature of the arguments for devolution during the remainder of the century means that it does not form any significant part of our discussion hereafter.

The case for electoral reform

Devolution was not the only radical solution suggested to cure the defects of parliament. Some commentators believed that parliamentary ineffectiveness was primarily caused by the way in which party, by means of the electoral system, had come to dominate the organisational structures inside the Commons. This created conflict for MPs between their party and parliamentary roles, with ramifications for the relationship between the House and the government. For such observers, the solution was to alter the institutional structures inside the Commons, in contrast to the devolutionists who argued instead for the 'farming out' of either powers or functions. Electoral reform therefore appealed to those who favoured structural institutional change at Westminster, and many of its advocates were convinced that it would bring about an improved quality of representation. However, many also favoured reform because it would restructure executive-legislative relations, enhance the status of the individual MP inside the Commons, and facilitate improved Commons effectiveness. Indeed, the arguments made for electoral reform sat comfortably with those for devolution, 'all of which were treated with a seriousness that reflected not only immediate political crises but also an underlying dissatisfaction with the system of representative democracy as it had evolved in Britain since the late nineteenth century' (Pugh 1978: 5).

Following a campaign by the Proportional Representation Society, the government announced in 1908 that there would be a Royal Commission on Systems of Election, whose terms of reference were to examine the options for securing 'a fully representative character for popularly elected legislative bodies' (Hart 1992: 155). Yet, several of the witnesses who gave evidence to the Commission 'based the case for [electoral reform] not so much or indeed at all on the frequent misrepresentation of parties in the House of Commons, but on what they saw as other defects in the existing political system', which included the reduced independence of MPs, a problem that could only be solved by weakening the hand of the parties inside the Commons (Hart 1992: 156). In this respect, electoral reform was viewed as a way to improve parliamentary effectiveness by adding value to the roles played by individual MPs. At any rate, the Royal Commission did not support a proportional system in its recommendations, although it did suggest the use of the alternative vote in seats with more than two candidates.

Yet the idea of reforming the Commons by reforming the electoral system persisted, on the grounds that electoral reform would loosen the grip of party over MPs, increase parliamentary control of the executive, and address disillusionment with the political system (Hart 1992: 177). For example, J.H. Humphreys, in his 1911 book, *Proportional Representation*, argued mainly for reform in order to secure fair representation, but nonetheless stated that such change would strengthen the House of Commons because a more proportional House would be 'more competent to discharge its true functions', and thus enable it to 'resume its proper function of controlling legislation' (Humphreys 1911: 226–7). Furthermore, in 1916, the government established a Speaker's Conference to examine issues concerning the franchise, seat redistribution and the electoral register, and its remit soon came to cover electoral reform. The Conference went on to recommend the adoption of proportional representation in some constituencies (Hart 1992: 178–82), which has been described as 'astonishing', not least because the Royal Commission of just a few years previous had refused to countenance such a move (Butler 1963: 7). During the course of the Conference, arguments were heard about how the adoption of a PR system would reduce the power of party and the executive, and strengthen the capabilities and effectiveness of the House of Commons, which naturally served to consolidate opposition to PR from those groups who would be adversely affected (Hart 1992: 191–2). Ultimately, however, the government legislation that resulted in the Representation of the People Act 1918 did not contain any elements of proportional representation.

Regardless of arguments about how electoral reform would help restructure the relationship between executive and legislature, and how it might enhance the perceived effectiveness of parliament, the parties resisted such reform for reasons of self-interest. The October 1924 general election was disproportionately favourable towards the Conservatives, who 'had therefore little incentive to change the system', and the Labour Party passed a resolution in 1926 against PR on the grounds that such a mechanism would not help them gain office (Hart 1992: 225). The Labour Party not only sought socialism by parliamentary means, but was also acutely aware that it stood to gain from the electoral vacuum caused by the decline of the Liberal Party (Butler 1963: 47). The Liberals themselves came to support PR just as their electoral fortunes under first-past-the-post rules were beginning to wane (Hart 1992: 225–6). Another Speaker's Conference on the electoral system, in 1929, failed to make any firm conclusions because of the irreconcilable views of the three main parties (Hart 1992: 232–9), and operated in the context of little widespread demand for electoral reform either inside or outside parliament (Butler 1963: 14).

Thereafter, while electoral reform, like devolution, never disappeared from the political agenda, it was not debated primarily in terms of how it might contribute to a realignment of executive-legislative relations. Subsequent discussions of electoral reform often concerned issues to do with constituency boundaries and how their manipulation might contribute towards securing clear government majorities (Catterall 2000: 171). Proportional representation generally attracted few advocates (Hart 1992: 264) and when it has been discussed recently, it has been largely from the perspective of securing a fair electoral system, with any changes to executive-legislative relations being cast as a welcome by-product of reform, rather than a primary motivation for it. This kind of reform, therefore, hereafter falls somewhat under the radar of our discussion.

Emerging support for Commons committees: 1931–60

Although calls for increased Commons effectiveness by means of electoral reform and devolution were successfully resisted by the dominant actors who would have been detrimentally affected by them, the central problems that had generated those calls became increasingly more desperate as economic conditions worsened in the 1930s. Serious economic problems persisted throughout the 1920s, caused largely by the necessary adjustments to peacetime, and demonstrated by the decline in Britain's export market, in difficulties following the return to the Gold Standard in 1925, and by endemic unemployment (May 1995: 373; More 1997: 216). Britain's staple industries, such as coal, endured extreme difficulties, and the nation struggled under the weight of national debt accumulated during the war (Robbins 1994: 142; Thorpe 1992: 61). Consequently, when the Wall Street crash occurred in late 1929, the economic outlook was bleak to say the least (Douglas 1986: 11). By 1931, with a crippling balance of trade and deepening unemployment, Britain had succumbed to serious economic depression.

Crucially, the apparent inability of the House of Commons to solve the economic problems of the day seemed to provide incontrovertible evidence that the effectiveness of the institution needed to be enhanced. Much of Churchill's advocacy of an economic parliament after 1929 stemmed from the existence of acute and prolonged economic problems, and his observation that existing institutions were incapable of solving them. The *Political Quarterly* journal featured regular contributions from those who were concerned about the state of the nation at the start of the 1930s, ranging from specific economic worries to broader concerns about a future European war, all of which fed into general criticism about the effectiveness of parliament in dealing with these issues (Samuel 1931; Strachey and Joad 1931).

So extensive was the concern regarding the ineffectiveness of the Commons that a Procedure Committee was established and charged with examining the problem in detail. Of course, different actors define 'effectiveness' in different ways. Chapter 3 demonstrated the thinking of the prime minister, Ramsay Macdonald, that effectiveness essentially equated with efficiency. His evidence to the Procedure Committee indicated his belief that the Commons interfered too much with the ability of the government to govern, and that it should have its abilities curtailed. This no doubt reflected his position at the head of a minority government facing grave economic problems that seemed almost insoluble, and his frustration that he could not get the government's most radical legislation through parliament (Thorpe 1992: 23). However, a good deal of the evidence provided to the Procedure Committee affords an interesting insight into how effectiveness was defined by other political actors at the time, and how they perceived the need to enhance the position of the House of Commons. One particular discussion that framed the Procedure Committee's enquiry was that regarding the merits of a comprehensive Commons committee system. Just as there had been an attempt in 1931 to pull Britain from depression by means of a new approach to government – the National Government – so too was there a growing assumption that substantial institutional reform of parliament was one way to tackle the enveloping crisis.

The case for committees

The idea of investigative Commons committees was not new when the Procedure Committee came to discuss them in 1931, and select committees had been used with varying frequency for a considerable length of time (Johnson 1979: 426–9). In 1902, a select committee had examined the merits of using committees to examine government policy and public expenditure (Norton 1981: 163), and in 1912 the House had established the Estimates Committee (Hanson 1970: 44). Sidney Low had, as a complement to his devolution plans, advocated the use of a committee system, and particularly a Foreign Affairs Committee, which would be a joint committee between both Houses that would seek 'to advise, to discuss, to investigate, and generally to act as the eyes and ears of Parliament' (Low 1906: 302). The Committee would have the power to call for papers, and to request the attendance of ministers to provide explanations, although government would not be bound by any decisions or views taken. The sanction for Low was that 'when ministers differed from the Committee, they would do so under a grave sense of responsibility; for they would have the full knowledge that this weighty little council, composed of the most competent and influential private members of both chambers, was against them' (Low 1906: 302–3). Low hoped that the new committee would not only augment the scrutiny capabilities of the Commons, but would also serve to enhance the standing of the chamber in the eyes of the public.

From the early 1930s, however, parliamentary observers sought to examine how the House of Commons might more effectively function as a holistic institution in its own right, in order that it might not only be better placed to address the serious economic problems then facing the nation, but that it might also find for itself a very clear role as an institution distinct from that of government. As the evidence given to the 1931 Procedure Committee demonstrated, many commentators were becoming increasingly convinced that a well-structured committee system might be the way forward in strengthening the effectiveness of the House of Commons. On the whole, the evidence heard suggested that the House was seemingly in decline, that it was unable to function properly, and that the public was less interested in its work than ever before. Elder statesmen David Lloyd George, for example, told the Committee that '[t]here is a growing feeling that Parliament is not coping with its task and not altogether discharging the trust which the nation has reposed it in' (HC 161, 1930–31, Q. 351). In pointing to the low turnout during Commons debates on the economic problems of the time, he remarked that:

> If I am asked what was responsible for this slackness, I come straight to the question of procedure. It was not because there was a lack of interest on the part of Members in this vital question, but because they felt these discussions would lead nowhere. You could not carry things any further by these mere broad discussions. The House of Commons has no machinery ... for pursuing the subject in the practical details and for investigating these questions closely. (HC 161, 1930–31, Q. 355)

Labour MP F.W. Jowett concurred with this viewpoint, explaining in a memorandum to the Committee that:

> There can be no doubt that the authority and prestige of the House of Commons have been in decline in recent years. The cause of this decline must primarily be traced to its unsuitable machinery of procedure, which renders the activities of opposition parties and private Members largely ineffective except for the purpose of obstruction. (HC 161, Q. 1669)

David Lloyd George based his reform proposals on a similar analysis which argued that:

> The control of the Executive by the House of Commons is confined to rather perfunctory discussions which do not excite any real interest, apart from an element of censure, which is conducive to excitement, but does not achieve the real purpose of establishing control over the Executive. (HC 161, Q. 353)

Both Lloyd George and Jowett advocated the introduction of comprehensive committee systems into the House of Commons as a means of improving its effectiveness in dealing with national problems and in holding the government accountable. Their plans differed in detail, but were aimed broadly at encouraging specialisation amongst MPs as individuals, so that this specialisation could then be brought to bear at the collective level when the House discussed broad policy issues. Indeed, Jowett recommended abandoning the Committee of the Whole House entirely, a proposal that was endorsed by Ramsay Muir, who also argued the case for the use of small committees to consider all bills before the House, and advocated the creation of a committee system to scrutinise government departments (HC 161, Q. 2642). Yet, even with such reforms in place, Muir remained sceptical about their likely impact on the problems that faced the House of Commons:

> The roots of the evil are far deeper. They lie in the forms which our system of government has insensibly taken during the last two generations, and which have almost reduced Parliament to insignificance; in the all but irresponsible autocracy of the Cabinet, behind which bureaucracy has become alarmingly powerful; in the rigidity of party organisation and the formidable power of party caucuses; and in the transformation of every General Election from what it theoretically is – the choice of individual members capable of playing an effective part in the government of this country – into a sort of plebiscite to

determine which of the rival party caucuses shall wield dictatorship. (HC 161, Q. 2642)

For Muir, these developments meant that mere procedural changes in the Commons – even those with significant structural implications for account-ability mechanisms – were not in themselves enough to enhance the power and effectiveness of parliament. Yet this sort of analysis ultimately had a limited impact on the Procedure Committee's conclusions. It was rather more persuaded by the advice provided to it by Winston Churchill:

> On this question of procedure of the House of Commons, it depends on what you want the House of Commons to do, whether you want to make it a highly efficient machine for passing all kinds of Bills into law? Is that the principle emphasis that you wish to give its functions or do you wish to make it a grand forum for national debate? Of course, it partakes of both functions; but in reviewing its procedure, to which of these two do you wish to assign your chief care? (HC 161, Q. 1520)

The Procedure Committee assigned its chief care to the former function, with the bulk of its recommendations pertaining to the expeditious despatch of government business, as Chapter 3 demonstrated. Indeed, for those who favoured a move towards a more committee-based approach to parliamentary work, the conclusions of the Procedure Committee may have been disap-pointing (HC 129, 1931–32). Although it recommended the enlargement of the Estimates Committee, it declined to adopt suggestions for more system-atic committee work (Jogerst 1993: 44).

Nevertheless, the kinds of concerns expressed to the Procedure Committee about the limited effectiveness of the House of Commons persisted into the 1930s, as did advocacy of a committee system to address those limitations. Ivor Jennings (1934: 22–3), for example, explained that, if the central function of the Commons was to provide a forum for the scrutiny of government and for the discussion of policy, then it was clear that parlia-ment had to play a much greater role in 'checking administration'. Government activity had expanded to such a degree that it was only logical that the House required a dedicated committee system, organised on an all-party basis reflecting the composition of the chamber, in order properly to shadow and scrutinise government activities. Jennings perceived roles for these committees in obtaining information, debating policy, gathering evidence, publishing reports and advising government departments (1934: 142–52).

By the mid-1930s, however, as Johnson (1979: 445) notes, 'the mood of criticism of Parliament was quickly modified under the impact of the threat stemming from the success of political extremism' throughout Europe, and the focus shifted to ensuring the existence of a strong and 'vigorous' executive to deal with the prospect of war. While those committees that already existed, such as the Public Accounts Committee and the Estimates Committee, continued to work away quietly in the background, the calls for a structured select committee system were effectively silenced as the prospects of yet another war began to darken the political horizon. Some commentators did of course press on with their case outlining the need for serious parliamentary reform: Harold Laski (1938), for example, on the very eve of war, outlined the failures of the Commons, and regretted its subservience to government. Furthermore, the eventual experience of the Second World War, and the subsequent victory, contributed to a vastly improved status of parliament, and the House of Commons in particular, in the eyes of the public (Butt 1969: 147; Johnson 1979: 446). In addition, in the decade following the conclusion of war, committees were anyway used more fully for enquiring into government activities (Chester 1966: 423), most notably the Committee on Nationalised Industries (Jogerst 1993: 45–6). Pre-existing committees also continued to play a part in the work of the Commons, with the Public Accounts Committee and the Estimates Committee seeking to push the boundaries of their inquiries (Johnson 1979: 451–4). Nonetheless, calls for the creation of a system of specialised Commons committees did eventually resurface, prompted by the re-emergence of the concerns in the mid-1950s about the performance of parliament and the House of Commons.

The decline of parliament

In truth, although there was widespread admiration for parliament following the end of the Second World War, concerns about the effectiveness of the House of Commons had not entirely disappeared. In 1946, for example, a group of Conservatives published a tract outlining a number of constitutional reforms, based in part on concerns about the quality of MPs (no doubt prompted by the election of the Labour government in 1945), and advocating the creation of pre-legislative scrutiny committees (Group of Conservatives 1946: 47). In 1949, Christopher Hollis asked, somewhat apocalyptically, *Can Parliament Survive?*, and regretted the decline of Commons influence over the government as a consequence of the accretion of executive powers during the war.

These complaints continued to bubble up during the 1950s. Keeton (1952) lamented *The Passing of Parliament* in the face of expanding executive powers which bordered on the dictatorial. Bromhead (1959) based his discussion of the need for parliamentary reform on what he perceived to be the crucial issue, which was the acceptability of the electoral system. He argued that, while the system contributed to the maintenance of a two-party system, that system was acceptable only in the short term, because it enabled 'the electorate to do no more than choose periodically between two self-perpetuating oligarchies' (Bromhead 1959: 274). Part of his solution was to institute a committee system capable of scrutinising the government more effectively. Similarly, Wiseman (1959: 240) observed the existence of two different approaches to the 'problem of parliament':

> One is concerned with everything which may affect its working as the central point of our governmental system. It assumes the continuance of the parliamentary cabinet system but is prepared for changes which might radically alter its working in practice. The other is concerned only with the relatively narrow question of parliamentary procedure and is liable to reject even moderate proposals for change if they appear even remotely likely to alter the balance of power in the Constitution or the traditional functions and attitudes of Parliament.

This important observation came at an important time. In the 1920s and 1930s, those who advocated Commons reform did not flinch from making radical suggestions, such as those concerning devolution or electoral reform. However, by the 1960s, the emphasis had shifted categorically towards the opportunities for reforming the Commons internally. The question of the utility of specialised committees had already gained considerable currency by the end of the 1950s, and it was this issue that dominated discussion concerning House of Commons reform in the following decades. As Wiseman (1959: 240) noted, the idea of specialised committees lay at the centre of the two extremes he discussed. Nevertheless, a 1959 report from the Procedure Committee entirely rejected the notion of a move towards specialised committees. It examined the issue with reference to the creation of a committee to examine colonial policy, but argued that this would be a 'radical constitutional innovation' (HC 92, 1958–59, para. 47). It concluded that such a committee would endeavour to control policy, rather than simply criticise it, and thus 'arrogate' to itself powers that should only be exercised by the executive.

The establishment of Commons committees: 1961–97

Until the 1960s, the question of Commons reform continued to exercise the minds of some academics, but it was not an issue at the top of the political agenda. In the early 1960s, however, concern emerged once more about the condition and future direction of Britain politically, socially and economically. The 1950s had been an apparent 'golden age', but as a new decade began, such views were 'drowned out by a wave of negative assessments of British economic performance' and the golden age was replaced by a discourse of 'declinism' (Tomlinson 2003: 202). By the 1960s, Britain seemed to be a receding actor on the world stage. Relinquishing her vast empire may have been viewed as essential by the British governing elites after 1945, but the imperial humiliation endured over Suez was harsh, and it led to serious questioning about Britain's ability to manage her role as a strategic global actor (Douglas 2002: 73–86). By the early 1960s, Britain's empire had been liquidated, and the nation was in a pseudo-limbo, uncertain of the long-term potential worth of the Commonwealth, and hesitant about participating in the emerging European Community (Douglas 2002: 142; Tomlinson 2003: 208).

These concerns fed into contemporary analyses of British institutions and their performance, and much of the resulting discourse focused on a perceived loss of 'purpose' in Britain (Tomlinson 2003: 203). With retrospect, these analyses were perhaps more alarmist than was merited, and they did not accurately reflect the true economic condition of the nation. For example, while many accounts pinpoint a number of concerns, particularly a low growth rate, a balance of payments problem, and a decline in manufacturing exports (Cairncross 1994: 134–7; May 1995: 431–2; More 1997: 254; Robbins 1994: 302), most do not fully corroborate the descriptions offered by the declinist narratives of the early 1960s (Tomlinson 2003: 203). Nonetheless, there was little question that the British economy did not seem to be keeping pace with its main rivals (Jeffreys 1997: 111), and these economic concerns provided a 'backcloth' to broader concerns about Britain more generally (Morgan 1990: 209). In the 1960s, the notion of a Britain that was in perpetual decline and lacking in purpose 'became a national preoccupation, stimulating wide-ranging debate and creating intense pressure in favour of reform' (Jefferys 1997: 111).

Early analyses of the source of decline pointed to 'deep structural obstacles rooted in British history which prevented dynamism or innovation' (Morgan 1990: 197). Andre Shonfield's *British Economic Policy Since the War* (1958) and Michael Shanks' *The Stagnant Society* (1961) both focused on this issue of a lack of purpose, and located specifically economic reasons for Britain's post-war decline (Tomlinson 2001: 22). In contrast, Anthony Sampson's *Anatomy of Britain* (1962) argued that British society and politics were reliant on an incompetent elite. Such texts belonged to a collection of work emerging at that time, which expressed concern about the 'state of the nation', and which comprised 'a motley collection of books and articles by people often with axes to grind but united by the common belief that something was indeed "wrong" with Britain' (Grant 2003: 30). A substantial portion of this literature was disseminated through the Penguin Specials range, which comprised texts that inquired into what was wrong with British industry, hospitals, unions, the church, as well as one entitled *What's Wrong with Parliament?* Although the declinist discourse may not have impacted directly upon popular opinion, 'amongst "opinion formers" declinism became the norm' (Tomlinson 2001: 25). On the whole, such texts called for the wholesale modernisation of British institutions, and the British approach to government and politics (Jefferys 1997: 122).

The problem with parliament

The Penguin Special on *What's Wrong with Parliament?* (Hill and Whichelow 1964) became a benchmark piece in the analysis of all that was problematic with Westminster at the start of the 1960s. Parliament had adopted 'a hangdog air' and a 'down-at-heels appearance', which contrasted sharply with the golden image it enjoyed when Britain stood victorious in 1945 (Hill and Whichelow 1964: 11). The central argument presented by this particular Penguin Special was that government activity had greatly expanded, but parliament had not engaged in any structural adaptation or innovation to keep up with that expansion, and executive scrutiny was consequently suffering. The pressure on parliamentary time because of the increased workload placed upon it by government, and the reluctance of the House to function at the level of specifics instead of the level of generalities, 'conspired to strengthen the hand of Government and weaken that of Parliament' (Hill and Whichelow 1964: 36).

These themes were also explored more systematically and thoroughly by Bernard Crick, in his seminal text *The Reform of Parliament*, first published in 1964. Crick categorically rejected the notion of a 'golden age' of parliament that reformers should aspire to recreate, and instead corroborated the argument made by many before him that the problem lay with the fact that, while government had expanded its powers and spheres of competence, parliament had failed to update its 'own instruments of control, scrutiny, criticism and suggestion' (Crick 1970: 12). Crick (1970: 81) characterised the purpose of parliamentary oversight and scrutiny in these terms:

> Parliamentary control is not the stop switch, it is the tuning, the tone and the amplifier of a system of communication which tells governments what the electorate want (rightly and wrongly) and what they will stand for (rightly and wrongly); and tells the electorate what is possible within the resources available …

Parliament's role was not continuously to challenge and defeat governments, but to provide mechanisms of control that would facilitate enhanced governmental responsiveness to public opinion (Crick 1970: 79). The kind of parliamentary control Crick had in mind was that where '[c]ontrol means *influence*, not direct power; *advice*, not command; *criticism*, not obstruction; *scrutiny*, not initiation; and *publicity*, not secrecy' (Crick 1970: 80; original emphasis). The key solution for Crick was the introduction of structured committee systems – both standing and select – redesigned as mechanisms that would facilitate the kind of parliamentary control he described. Heretofore, committees had lacked resources and were undervalued, even by MPs (Crick 1970: 88–92). Specialisation had to be encouraged and fostered through the creation of a system of scrutiny committees that would shadow government departments.

In the early 1960s, parliamentary scholars in general were becoming increasingly interested in the potential for investigative committees to enhance the effectiveness of the House of Commons. A 1963 *Political Quarterly* editorial entitled 'The decline of parliament' set the character of the debate, arguing that MPs were not of a sufficiently high quality, that party influence was too great inside the Commons, and that parliamentary discussion was stunted by isolation from the outside world. It also advocated a number of solutions, including an expansion of committee work, a proposal the journal endorsed again in a subsequent editorial two years later (*Political Quarterly*, 1963, 1965).

Furthermore, while Crick's *The Reform of Parliament* is often cited as the benchmark piece of the period, many other academics also weighed in on the debate, both in terms of the broad 'problem of parliament' and the specifics of how that problem could be solved. Walkland (1960) championed the case for scrutiny committees with particular reference to how they would assist the House in financial scrutiny. He also argued that such committees would only be of use if MPs changed their perceptions about their individual roles within the Commons (Walkland 1964: 402). King-Hall (1962) similarly recommended a committee system to enhance scrutiny, along with a total re-engineering of the party system. Hanson (1964) explored the difficulties parliament experienced in fulfilling its purpose in an era of mass democracy, and advocated a total rethinking of its function, suggesting that it should no longer be viewed as a tool to control the executive, but as an advisor to it, not least because this would provide a good rationale for a comprehensive select committee system and make it more palatable to government. Robson (1964) identified part of the problem in the assumption that every issue before the House was a question of confidence in the government, which necessarily restricted the independence of the House. Like many of his academic colleagues, he recommended the creation of a committee system that would scrutinise individual government departments. Ryle (1965) assessed positively the various ways in which existing committees already aided the Commons in its task of executive scrutiny, and argued for an expansion of the system, an approach also adopted by Marshall (1965) on the grounds that a system of scrutiny committees would greatly aid the way that parliament held the government to account, without actually impeding the ability of government to govern.

The Procedure Committee view in 1965

Academic thinking on the question of committee scrutiny did, to an extent, begin to impact on parliamentary circles and shape Commons responses to the increasingly urgent question of how to improve effectiveness, as evidenced by the Procedure Committee report of 1965 (HC 303, 1964–65). As part of its investigation, the Committee took extensive oral evidence from

Professors Hanson, Wiseman and Bromhead, who had written on the issue of parliamentary reform, and were members of the embryonic Study of Parliament Group. Wiseman later noted the significant shift that had occurred in Procedure Committee thinking on this subject, given that in the 1958–59 session, it had not even published the written evidence the he and Hanson had submitted, let alone asked them to provide oral testimony (Wiseman 1970b: 198). In their evidence, the professors pointed to the inequality between government and parliament in access to information, and suggested that a move towards specialisation, and specialist committees in particular, would address those inequalities in a significant and meaningful way. They did not see any difficulties in finding MPs to serve on the proposed new committees, and suggested that an informal relationship between the Selection Committee and the whips would suffice. Nor did they foresee partisanship as a problem, arguing that previous committees had simply avoided those contentious issues that were likely to cause party divisions, and that the committees would anyway be examining matters of administration, not policy. The memorandum submitted to the Procedure Committee by the Study of Parliament Group argued that:

> Strong government needs critical opposition; it can benefit from such criticism and stand up to it. Political control, thus conceived, does not directly hinder governments; sometimes it can even help them to anticipate trouble. (HC 303, 1964–65)

Just six years after having rejected these same arguments, the Procedure Committee endorsed proposals for an expansion of committee work. Part of this Damascene conversion lay in the Committee's acceptance that parliament had indeed experienced a real decline in its ability effectively to scrutinise government (Jogerst 1993: 53). Nonetheless, the Committee still found it problematic to couch its proposals in the language of enhanced executive accountability, and maintained that the purpose of reform was to 'increase the efficiency of the House of Commons as a debating chamber' (HC 303, 1964–65: v).

The Crossman reforms

Despite a Commons debate on the Procedure Committee report of 1965, there was little movement towards implementation of its recommendations. Following the 1966 general election, however, the new Labour government under Harold Wilson became interested in the idea of using specialist committees to enhance parliament's role in the governing process, partly as a way to placate those new MPs who were uneasy about the state of the economy and the mechanics of Westminster politics, and thus perhaps more likely candidates for inciting rebellion (Butt 1969: 367–8). Richard Crossman was appointed Leader of the House, a move intended to appease backbenchers and ensure that calls for parliamentary reform could be filtered through, and thus managed by, the government (Jogerst 1993: 59). Nonetheless, Crossman, if his later *Diaries* are to be believed, viewed himself as a serious reformer (Baines 1985: 20). In a rudimentary way, therefore, Norton's conditions for parliamentary reform, as outlined in Chapter 2, were fulfilled in this instance at least to a minimal degree. A reform agenda existed thanks to the Procedure Committee report of 1965. Political leadership was in place in the person of Richard Crossman. A window of opportunity existed thanks to the start of a new parliament and the addition of new MPs to the governing party. Significantly, however, what was somewhat less in evidence was real political will to see reform proceed, and this disabled the reforms before they had even been set in motion.

Following cross-party discussions, a cautious government approach emerged, which rejected the idea of a system of committees shadowing government departments (Butt 1969: 368). Six committees were established during the 1966–70 parliament: Agriculture, Science and Technology, Education, Race Relations and Immigration, Overseas Aid and Development, and Scottish Affairs. Despite enjoying a degree of support upon their creation, the committees subsequently endured considerable difficulties, partly attributable to the scale of the operations they were undertaking (Baines 1985: 21), and also to the reductions in the numbers of MPs serving on them (Jogerst 1993: 21). The committees also faced long delays between the publications of their reports and Commons debates on them (Jogerst 1993: 67), a problem that has plagued committees ever since. Both the Agriculture and Nationalised Industries Committees subsequently published reports criticising the attitude of government towards them, which Jogerst (1993: 71) argues suggested 'an embryonic change in the perceived duty of MPs in the policy process'. A significant problem faced by the committees was that the proposals which led to their creation prevented them from examining policy matters, which arguably did much to emasculate them, and significantly constrained them in their purpose of scrutinising government and its activities (Butt 1969: 371–4).

A few years into its existence, the Procedure Committee returned to the issue of the specialised committees, and advocated that the system be restructured (HC 410, 1968–69). Academic observers were also aware of the limitations of the committee system that had been created, and also of the questions the simple existence of the system raised with regards to how the Commons organised itself. Wiseman (1970a) wondered if the specialised committees might function better if they formed the core of standing committees, and if the legislative and scrutiny systems were somehow combined. These musings were prompted in part by the difficulties the new committees had in securing reasonable levels of attendance at their meetings, exacerbated by the fact that a government career was far more appealing to

MPs than one serving on backbench committees (Wiseman 1970b). For Wiseman (1970b), the committees had at least been successful in improving the knowledge base from which the Commons operated. Yet other observers were less impressed on this point. Johnson (1970), for example, argued that better information was just a small part of the story, and that what was most important was the way in which structures of power and influence at Westminster mediated that flow of information. He judged the results of the new committee system as 'meagre', with little achieved by way of subject specialisation, and argued that there was no real evidence that the executive was being better held to account. Johnson (1970: 243) argued that the committees were wrongly seen as a solution to parliament's problems, and that reformers had placed 'an exaggerated faith' in the likely impact of an increase in information. Scrutiny would only be qualitatively improved if the actual powers of the committees were considerably enhanced (Johnson 1970: 243).

The introduction of the select committee system

Having previously been opposed to a systematic Commons committee system, the Procedure Committee (HC 410, 1968–69) was clear that considerable reform of the specialised committees was required if effective parliamentary scrutiny was to be achieved. The Conservative Party elected to government under Edward Heath in 1970 published a green paper (Cmnd 4507, 1970) which drew on recommendations made by the Procedure Committee as well as the outgoing Labour government's review of the committee process, and which noted that the full potential of the specialist committee system had not been reached. Despite this, no significant efforts were made to reform the system, and this status quo persisted when Labour returned to power in October 1974, even although the new government advocated the strengthening of the committee system as a way to assist government in its various activities. By the mid-1970s, however, committee advocates were once more arguing for them to engage with a broader range of functions, particularly in relation to the scrutiny of government (Jogerst 1993: 85). In light of continuing concern about the functioning of the committees, and the obstacles documented by the Nationalised Industries Committee in particular, the Procedure Committee in 1978 published recommendations for the creation of a departmental select committee system (HC 588, 1977–78). The Committee's report was the result of two related concerns: first, that parliament had failed to keep up with the expansion in government activity; and, second, that the public held parliament in low esteem because it did not hold government effectively to account (Jogerst 1993: 93). The Committee believed that the creation of the departmental select committee system would address these twin concerns, thus improving the quality of parliamentary scrutiny and enhancing the status of parliament.

Of course, it is also possible to view the pressure for, and creation of, the departmental select committee system as part of a response to wider concerns about the state of Britain. These concerns had antecedents in the 1960s, explored earlier, in the context of alarm about British economic decline. Such concerns continued to prompt alarm in the late 1970s, although by that time there was considerable disagreement among observers regarding the causes of these problems and their extent (Hay 1999: 87). The press in general still obsessed about the state of Britain, and an observer noted that 'there is a general mood of malaise and stagnation on the one hand, and on the other the growth of unrest, discontent and disorder' (Kramnick 1979: 12). Economic worries remained at the top of the agenda, particularly since entry into the EEC in 1973 had not apparently had the positive impact that had been anticipated (Buller 1999: 113–4). Levels of social and political tensions were mounting, not least due to the demands of the unions and the events of the winter of 1977 (Dorfman 1979: 55; Nairn 1979: 234). Some put the problems down to 'overload' and 'ungovernability', whereby the capabilities of the political and economic systems were simply inadequate to meet expectations (Blank 1979: 69; Hay 1999: 93–7). Contemporary observers argued that the nation's economic problems were symptomatic of deep-rooted political problems, rather than their causes, and argued for the reinvigoration of political institutions, such as parties and parliament, in order to stave off further 'institutional disintegration' (Blank 1979: 73–80). If 'modernisation' had been the remedy in the early 1960s, it continued to be the solution of choice in the late 1970s. As Johnson (1999: 63) comments, 'a dominant theme within the literature on Britain's relative economic decline is an alleged political failure to modernise the state in order to meet the demands of a highly competitive and increasingly globalised capitalist economic system'. A crucial part of the solution, therefore, was finding exactly the right kind of institutional innovation to address the problem at hand. Consequently, the idea that a system of select committees could help contribute to 'better governance' and more 'modern governance' must be taken into consideration when examining the way in which this particular parliamentary reform unfolded.

The Procedure Committee recommended the creation of twelve select committees that would each scrutinise particular government departments (HC 588, 1977–78). Committee chairmen were to be paid, and opposition MPs would be allowed to chair some of the committees. A Committee of Selection would choose those to serve on them in order to remove any malign party influence. The committees would have permanent Standing Orders and fixed memberships for the duration of a parliament, and would have access to full-time expert staff. Certain days would be dedicated in the chamber for debate on committee reports, and the government would be expected to reply to reports within a specified time. The Procedure

Committee also attempted to define the powers and organisation of the committees so as to avoid some of the problems endured by the Crossman committees. In particular, they would be able to send for persons, papers and records to aid their investigations, a recommendation borne directly from the difficulties experienced by the Nationalised Industries Committee during its investigation of the British Steel Corporation (Poole 1979: 268). Significantly, as Leader of the House, Michael Foot was utterly opposed to any committee system that would detract from the work of the chamber or foster cross-party collaboration. As a member of the Procedure Committee, he objected to its 1978 report and recommendations, and prevented debate on the report from taking place (Jogerst 1993). This particularly highlights the potential for an individual in a pivotal position to impact upon the course of reform: as the recommendations had the support of the overwhelming majority of the Procedure Committee, it also demonstrates how one individual can thwart the wishes of many by exploiting the institutional role he occupies.

The Procedure Committee report came at the end of the parliament, which made it harder for the Conservatives to renege on their commitment to support and implement the reform package if elected to government, particularly in the face of obvious Labour hesitation on the matter. Norman St John-Stevas, as Shadow Leader of the House, committed his party to the Procedure Committee recommendations, on the grounds that the primary function of parliament was to hold the executive to account. However, in the February 1979 debate on the report, St John-Stevas made plain that he did not want to 'exaggerate the case for reform and emphasised that he saw the report as radical rather than revolutionary' (Baines 1985: 29). When he became Leader of the House in the new Conservative government elected in 1979, St John-Stevas 'displayed a dedication to procedural reform that was significant in maintaining the momentum for change in the first session of the 1979 parliament' (Jogerst 1993: 108). Yet we might well ask why a new government dedicated to a range of policy commitments would indeed proceed with parliamentary reform, rather than simply ditch the pledge like so many others before it. For Jogerst (1993: 109), the answer is that the Thatcher government, and Thatcher in particular, rationalised the select committee system on the grounds that it was consistent with the aims of rolling back the state: vigorous committees could be useful in checking bureaucracy and controlling departments, and thus helpful in addressing some of the main concerns outlined by those who expressed alarm about the economic and political state of Britain in the late 1970s.

The pattern of developments that resulted in the establishment of the departmental select committee system in 1979 fits well with Norton's views of the conditions required before parliamentary reform can take place, and seems to suggest the existence of a critical juncture away from institutional path dependency (Collier and Collier 1991) and towards a quite new kind of internal organisation. There was a clear and workable report from the Procedure Committee that formed the basis for a reform package. The new government had already accepted the need for change and committed to it in opposition, and the prime minister and Cabinet were at least willing to acquiesce in the reforms, although it is not clear that this condition would have long persisted had St John-Stevas not acted quickly. Backbench pressure for change had been building for some time, and a leader was in place in the person of St John-Stevas to take reform forward. It seems that the window for opportunity at the start of the 1979 parliament was a narrow one, but one that was nevertheless successfully exploited.

However, in their government-adapted configurations, the reforms did not significantly upset the constitutional status quo (Baines 1985: 33), and, when scrutinised carefully, do not seem to suggest a complete critical juncture from the pre-existing path of institutional development. The committees were not allocated all of the powers recommended by the Procedure Committee. Committee chairmen were not paid, thus obstructing the creation of an alternative parliamentary career path to that of government. The committees were not given powers to force witnesses, such as ministers, to attend hearings, and thus the operation of the ministerial responsibility convention was not significantly transformed. No appreciable time was allocated for report debates in the chamber, which thus restricted the visibility and impact of committee work. Furthermore, the way that MPs would be selected for committee service was evaded. The Procedure Committee's suggestion of an independent selection committee was ignored, and nomination remained in the power of the whips, which meant that parliamentary scrutiny continued to be structured with reference to partisan considerations. So, although the emergence of the departmental select committee system was an important development as far as the enhancement of parliamentary scrutiny was concerned, it was by no means an unqualified victory for the advocates of reform. The change was made palatable to the dominant elite inside the Commons precisely because many of the most radical of the Procedure Committee recommendations formed no part of the package that was finally adopted. The norms and values of the elite thus remained as significant obstacles to effective parliamentary scrutiny of the executive.

The impact of the departmental select committees

Assessment of the select committee system in the 1980s produced mixed conclusions about its effectiveness, and raised questions about its fundamental design and structure. The committees did not, for example, attempt to achieve a co-ordinated approach to public expenditure scrutiny. Indeed, the decision to abolish the Expenditure Committee in favour of the new system resulted in the arrested development 'of a systematic, critical approach to public expenditure scrutiny which was just starting to evolve towards the end of the 1974–79 Parliament' (Robinson 1985: 307–8). The committees broadly shied away from detailed financial scrutiny work, mainly because they lacked information and expertise in such matters. Furthermore, as select committees served as extensions of parliament itself, they also shared in its weaknesses: in their endeavour to produce cross-party reports, they were accused of only examining non-controversial subjects that would not ignite party conflict, and thus of failing to grasp the mantle of serious and difficult executive scrutiny (Drewry 1985a: 349).

Other observers, however, were encouraged by the changing attitudes of MPs towards their work. Giddings (1985: 372) argued that 'inter-party dissent can connect with inter-party consensus'. The evidence pointed to a new vision held by MPs of themselves, one in which they were controllers of the executive rather than 'simple' party supporters (Giddings 1985: 372). Nonetheless, the effect of the new committees on government policy-making seemed a more complex matter. The process through which ministers and witnesses gave evidence before the select committees apparently served to 'concentrate the mind', with the possibility that government changed its policies in advance of, and in expectation of, detailed select committee scrutiny (Giddings 1985: 373).

Some observers noted a change in the chemistry of the House of Commons as a result of the 1979 reforms, and a changing attitude towards the utility of select committees (Drewry 1985b: 383). The 1979 reforms were couched in the arguments of those new MPs with professional backgrounds who believed the House of Commons should be more professional in its business (Judge 1981: 197). Although the reforms did not affect constitutional arrangements, they did have an impact as 'an important evolutionary step in the modernisation of a House of Commons that has been slow to adapt to the realities of a complex and highly diversified polity' (Drewry 1985b: 391). Select committees thus enriched debate and facilitated specialisation, and served to produce information for public consumption (Drewry 1985b: 392).

Others were less persuaded by these arguments. Judge (1989: 400–1), for example, called into question the entire basis on which reform had proceeded, noting the 'fundamental but too often neglected distinction between Parliament as an institution and parliamentary democracy as a mode of government'. In this respect:

> It is possible to reform one, the institution, without necessarily affecting the other, the system. 'Internal' reform of the procedures and organisation within the Palace of Westminster neither automatically nor necessarily impacts upon the wider 'external' system of parliamentary government. (Judge 1989: 401)

Judge also took issue with the argument that a select committee system could help parliament fulfil its function of disseminating information to the electorate, because it was one which ignored the realities of power and control at Westminster:

> If the theory of parliamentary procedure was 'anti-specialist' in the 1960s, it remains so in the 1980s. Despite the movement towards greater specialisation ... the House and its Members remain essentially amateur. That this is so reflects the institutional values of a parliament dominated by the executive. The organisational logic of reform is subverted by the very political configuration to which the reform is a response and to which it is directed. (Judge 1989: 409)

Parliamentarians did not necessarily share this pessimism, as demonstrated by the Liaison Committee report on the workings of the select committee system published in 1985 (HC 363, 1984–85). The Committee did note a number of concerns about some aspects of the system, such as too few formal debates on committee reports, excessive delays in establishing select committees at the start of new parliaments, and problems with poor attendance on some committees (HC 363, paras 21–7). However, its main conclusion was that the departmental select committee system 'can now be seen as a major, successful, Parliamentary reform' (para. 1). The government nevertheless rejected a number of its recommendations, suggesting that additional sub-committees would put too much pressure on departments, and that delays in establishing committees were not the fault of government (HC 225, 1985–86). The Liaison Committee's optimism about the impact of the system seemed increasingly misplaced as time went on. The Committee, along with the Treasury and Civil Service Committee and the Defence Committee, became embroiled in a long-running dispute with the government regarding how ministerial accountability should be interpreted within the new committee system (HC 92, 1985–86; HC 519, 1985–86; Cm 78, 1986; Cmnd 9841, 1986; Cmnd 9916, 1986; HC 62, 1986–87; HC 100, 1986–87). Even at that point, the Liaison Committee seemed remarkably forgiving of the government's attitude towards the scrutiny capacity of the select committees. It declared that the government's advice that civil servants should not answer questions about their own conduct was an 'aberration' and the result of the political heat generated by the Westland affair then under Defence Committee investigation (HC 100, 1986–87, para. 19).

This line of thinking was also adopted by the Procedure Committee in its 1990 evaluation of the select committee system (HC 19, 1989–90). While accepting that there were concerns about the functioning of the system, its central conclusion was that there were few serious problems with the effectiveness of the committees. Most of those who gave evidence to the Procedure Committee testified that there was better scrutiny of the executive as a result of the creation of the select committees. However, Judge (1992) outlines a number of problems with this analysis. For example, the Procedure Committee failed to take into account the full implications of departmental reluctance to disclose information to the select committees, not least because the committees themselves under-emphasised the extent of the problems they had endured (Judge 1992: 94). The purpose of the 1978 Procedure Committee recommendations had been to redress the imbalance in access to information between executive and legislature, but many of the powers that would have secured this redress had never been granted. This affected the committees because it 'constrain[ed] their ability to secure information from a reluctant executive' (Judge 1992: 98). Yet, for Judge, the fundamental impediment to the ability of the select committees to function effectively was 'the ethos and mentality of the British executive' and 'the adversarial nature of party politics which helps to sustain this mentality in the first place' (1992: 99). For example, some select committees reported whip interference in the selection process that placed MPs onto select committees, yet the Procedure Committee failed to acknowledge the breadth or depth of this problem, instead describing it as 'exceptional' (Judge 1992: 99). For Judge, the entire Procedure Committee approach to assessing the select committee system seemed complacent and ignorant of the political realities at Westminster (1992: 99–100).

Other commentators were also reluctant to offer a ringing endorsement of the impact of the select committee system. Tivey (1995: 282) argued that it did not matter whether select committees did good work or not, because their reports would 'attract attention only if they provide ammunition for the opposition'. Giddings (1994: 680–2), while acknowledging that the system had extended parliamentary scrutiny, deepened parliamentary accountability and widened public debate, nevertheless noted that 'the committees have not radically altered the balance between government and Parliament'. The committees' success depended on them being more fully involved in parliamentary work, although Giddings (1994: 684–5) believed that pressure for such involvement would eventually emerge, largely because of the growing perception of overload in the Commons and also because of the need to overhaul the legislative process, both of which might offer opportunities for an expansion in the committees' remits. Indeed, select committees themselves soon became more vocal in expressing concerns regarding their functioning. In the 1995–96 session, both the Trade and Industry Committee (HC 87, 1995–96) and the Public Service Committee (HC 313, 1995–96) pinpointed problematic issues such as access to information and publication of government replies that impeded their scrutiny work. As the next chapter demonstrates, the Liaison Committee also came to join the ranks of those with serious concerns about the capabilities and powers of the select committees.

Conclusion

In the 1920s and 1930s, advocates of reforms to enhance the effectiveness of the House of Commons promoted 'external' reforms such as devolution and electoral change that would bring about effectiveness by altering fundamentally the nature of the Westminster political system. Such reforms aimed to change the structured institutional context in which the Commons operated, and thus also the norms and values that maintained the position of the executive as the dominant actor at Westminster. These proposals were responses to the perceived ineffectiveness of parliament after the First World War and its subsequent inability to help solve the economic crisis of the depression years. However, following the Second World War, these kinds of reform suggestions gave way to those that focused on 'internal' solutions based on specialised investigative committees. They were partly prompted by concerns about a decline in British international standing, largely associated with the withdrawal from empire, and by economic under-performance and a resultant concern about a lack of national purpose. Academics in particular channelled these concerns into designing mechanisms aimed at improving the way the Commons scrutinised government, and the Commons itself eventually approved the plans for specialised, and later departmental, select committees.

The reason why the executive permitted the creation of these innovations in the first place essentially involves broader questions about why institutions change. The events surrounding the emergence of both these committee systems seem to be in keeping with Norton's conditions for parliamentary reform: that there must be a window of opportunity, a reform agenda, political leadership, and political will all in place before significant reform can proceed. The evidence with respect to the emergence of the departmental select committee systems in the late 1970s, which had the potential to deliver considerable institutional reconfiguration, suggests that these conditions for reform were almost entirely met. From a historical institutionalist perspective, what emerged in the late 1970s was a critical juncture in the developmental path of the Westminster parliament. More crucially still, this critical juncture was not wholly the result of exogenous force for change. Part of the problem with the historical institutionalist perspective is that it perhaps too often relies on explanations for change which lie outside the institution in question. In the case of the emergence of the departmental select committee system, the analysis suggests something quite different. There were, to be sure, exogenous concerns about national economic and political performance, but these in many ways provided the background, rather than the foreground, for institutional change. The main force for change came from within parliament itself, and, as historical institutional theory predicts, emerged as a result of internal problems and inconsistencies thrown up by previous institutional development. That development, which had favoured changes designed to improve the legislative efficiency of parliament, eventually forced an institutional correction to address other aspects of parliament's functioning, in this case, its executive scrutiny capacity, which had remained underdeveloped throughout. And that shift in focus emerged because parliamentarians themselves acknowledged that something had to be done, and more importantly, that something *could* be done, a conclusion MPs had up until that point failed to draw. Furthermore, the ideas which underpinned the logic of specialised committees grew in their persuasive power in the 1960s, and by the 1970s, the previously dominant idea that such committees would impede the ability of governments to govern had been challenged successfully.

However, also in keeping with the predictions of historical institutional theory, the dominant actors who would be detrimentally affected by these reforms at first resisted them, and then proceeded to implement them in a much pared-down form. Both the specialised committees and the departmental select committees were not composed as the respective Procedure Committees had intended, and were deprived of a number of important powers. Although the conditions for reform were almost entirely met, what was not in supply was sufficient political will to ensure that the changes could take full effect, and be implemented in the way the Procedure Committee had originally envisaged. The reason for the absence of adequate political will can be explained by the lessons generated by institutional theory. The structured institutional context at Westminster favours some strategies for change over others, and the strategies that are not favoured are those which significantly enhance the abilities of parliament to hold the executive in check. Such reforms, from the perspective of the executive as the dominant actor at Westminster, would result in unwelcome and unacceptable interference with the ability of the government to govern. Reforms designed to enhance the effectiveness of the Commons have therefore been infrequent, and, more importantly, have been implemented by government in a diluted format. Consequently, we must on the one hand acknowledge that the departmental select committee system was an important institutional innovation, with the potential to reconfigure executive-legislative relations at Westminster. On the other hand, we must also acknowledge that this potential for reconfiguration was managed and constrained by the government, so that the resulting committee system did not impact significantly on the operation of either of the central norms of ministerial responsibility or strong government.

Crucially, however, what this episode means is that the historical institutionalist perspective can explain change without total recourse to exogenous events, and it can do so if we are willing to accept the merits of the idea of a critical juncture from path dependent development as it has been recounted here. Yet, what it also means is that the nature and degree of divergence from institutional path dependency has an important bearing on how that institution develops thereafter. In this respect, it is not unlike the notion of a ship at sea, which, by deviating from its course by just a small degree, will eventually end up in a very different place from where it would have been had that deviation not occurred. So, too, with the long-term impact of the departmental select committee system. As it was originally implemented, the select committees had nothing even approaching the kind of powers that had been anticipated, and in their first decades of existence, their impact in terms of holding the executive to account was undoubtedly limited. Yet, the very fact that the committees were created in the first place has perhaps more significance than does short-term concerns about their utility. The experimental specialised committees of the 1960s, hopelessly ineffective though they were, marked the first, tentative branching away from the existing path of parliamentary development, a branching which eventually led to the departmental select committee system some years later. The path branched again with their creation, even although it may not have looked like a particularly promising offshoot at the time.

In this respect, when it comes to reforms designed to enhance parliamentary effectiveness and rebalance executive-legislative relations at Westminster, the important lesson is that, in the long run, process matters more than outcome. It is very easy to be cynical about the 'real' effects brought about by reforms such as the select committees, and there is indeed good cause to be sceptical about their role and impact. But, if one of the lessons of historical institutional theory is that we must take a long-term view of institutional development, and not focus simply on individual episodes of change, then a key conclusion must be that the process of institutional change, in the long term, matters more than the short-term outcome of those changes. That this is so is demonstrated in part by the next chapter, which charts the continuing process of institutional change through the development of the select committee system in the post-1997 era.

6
Effectiveness in the House of Commons since 1997

Introduction

In the period after 1997, the debate surrounding the need to improve the effectiveness of the Commons select committee system assumed a new tone with the creation of the Modernisation Committee. Examination of the events surrounding the Committee's attempt to reform the system provides a valuable opportunity to explore the attitudinal and contextual approaches noted in Chapter 2, and to probe further the explanatory utility of historical institutionalism.

Norton (2000) outlined three conditions that must be met before effective parliamentary reform may proceed, and these conditions are worth restating in detail. The first necessary condition is a window of opportunity in which reform can take place. Second, there has to be a coherent reform agenda in place that provides a package behind which MPs might organise. Third, leadership must exist to exploit the window of opportunity and promote the reform agenda. Central to all three conditions, there must be political will for successful reform to take place. These reform conditions only apply to efforts to secure effectiveness reforms. As Chapters 3 and 4 demonstrated, governments are able to use their Commons majority to secure efficiency reforms with relative ease. Effectiveness reforms, by contrast, are not likely to originate from government, and so the particular conditions outlined by Norton need to be met in order to secure government acquiescence. From the historical institutionalist perspective, the fulfilment of these reform conditions may facilitate a critical juncture and provide the opportunity for departure from a historically dependent pathway.

As Chapter 4 illustrated, the Modernisation Committee proved to be a useful conduit through which government was able to secure a range of efficiency reforms after 1997. In the early years of the Committee's existence, however, there was a degree of frustration at the nature of the work undertaken.

Mounting dissatisfaction with the pace of reform

In the summer of 1998, Charter 88 complained of the 'disappointingly slow' pace of reform and the 'extremely cautious' nature of the Modernisation Committee's recommendations (Charter 88, 1998). Senior MPs of all parties soon came to state their own concerns. In a Commons modernisation debate in late 1998, Conservative George Young noted his hope that the Committee would soon come to focus its attention on scrutiny issues (HC Debs, 16 December 1998, col. 1004). Similarly, Liberal Democrat Paul Tyler regretted the time the Committee had already dedicated to matters such as sitting hours, and urged that the House should 'be debating the wider issues' (col. 1010). Labour's Robert Sheldon also described concerns about sitting hours as 'a minor matter', and argued that changes to the select committee system were a higher priority (cols 1014–18).

MPs had in fact been asking if the Modernisation Committee would examine the effectiveness of the select committee system since June 1997, when the Committee was first established (HC Debs, written answers, 17 June 1997, col. 129), but the responses were not especially encouraging (HC Debs, written answers, 6 April 1998, col. 35; 25 January 1999, col. 13). Furthermore, the two ministers who first held the post of chair of the Modernisation Committee – Ann Taylor and Margaret Beckett – were criticised for their approach to modernisation, and to issues of scrutiny in particular. A Labour member of the Committee in 2002 argued that Taylor had 'lacked the political clout to really drive the agenda forward' (interview, 15 May 2002), while another Labour colleague described the reforms instituted by Taylor as 'tame and mere tinkering' (interview, 16 April 2002). Indeed, Taylor herself accepted that many of the reforms she helped to introduce were 'not exactly earth shattering' (HC Debs, 13 November 1997, col. 1065). Things seemed bleaker still under the stewardship of Beckett, with MPs of all parties who served on the Committee at that time commenting that 'we made no progress whatsoever', that the process was 'stalled', and that she 'was not at all convinced of the need for modernisation and nothing was achieved in her reign' (interviews, 23 April 2002, 22 May 2002, 16 April 2002, 15 May 2002). One Conservative member of the Modernisation Committee described Beckett's attitude towards it as 'fairly Stalinist' (HC Debs, 14 May 2002, col. 688).

The emergence of a reform agenda

During the first few years of its existence, then, the Modernisation Committee did not examine the issue of enhancing the effectiveness of the House of Commons, as effectiveness has been defined here. This not only prompted dismay amongst some MPs, like those just noted above, but also prompted other groups to investigate such matters on their own terms. In particular, the potential for reforming the select committee system soon emerged as a key issue.

The Liaison Committee and views in the Commons

In the mid-1990s, the Trade and Industry Select Committee (HC 87, 1995–96) and the Public Service Select Committee (HC 313, 1995–96) both expressed concerns about the operation of the select committee system as a result of problems experienced while conducting inquiries. Consequently, the Liaison Committee, under the chairmanship of Sir Terence Higgins, used its 1997 report on the work of the select committees as an opportunity to explore the issues in greater depth (HC 323, 1996–97). The report drew attention to a range of serious problems associated with the functioning of the select committee system. These problems included the inordinate length of time taken at the start of a new parliament in establishing the select committees and agreeing their membership, difficulties in securing co-operation and information from government and civil servants, and a lack of committee resources. The report also pointed to a poverty of discussion about committee work, and to the need for greater select committee involvement in the scrutiny of executive agencies, the legislative process and departmental expenditure. The committee chairman also specifically pointed to the problem of availability of MPs for committee service as a result of the greater attraction of government employment (HC 323, 1996–97, Appendix 1).

In March 2000, under the chairmanship of Robert Sheldon, the Liaison Committee returned to the question of the select committee system and its relationship with government in its report *Shifting the Balance* (HC 300, 1999–2000). This had been partly prompted by ongoing concern about the issues raised in the 1997 report, but also by a meeting held by the Liaison Committee with the then fledgling Hansard Society Commission on Parliamentary Scrutiny. This Commission was established in September 1999 under the chairmanship of Lord Newton of Braintree, a former Leader of the House, and was at that time initiating evidence-gathering sessions. On 19 November 1999, the Commission met privately with members of the Liaison Committee at the London School of Economics as part of that investigative process (HC Debs, 9 November 2000, col. 476; Hansard Society 2001: 127). One Hansard Society Commission member later explained how the Liaison Committee members present had:

> beat their breasts about how difficult it was for the select committees to be effective, because there was such frequent rotation in their membership, and ... because they were controlled by the whips in terms of nominations. [I]t apparently became a sort of exercise in group therapy, and I think it was an important contributing factor to the Liaison Committee then publishing the

quite unprecedented report which it did in March 2000 [*Shifting the Balance*].
(Interview, 28 November 2001)

Several members of the Hansard Society Commission, as well as a range
of MPs, expressed the view that, prior to the summer of 1999, the main
purpose of the Liaison Committee had been to divide the overseas travel
budget among the select committees (interviews, 28 and 29 November
2001, 12 June 2007). One Commission member noted his belief that 'it was
not a Committee … which had systematically had any discussion about the
effectiveness of select committees', and that the Hansard Society Commission
had 'by accident … found itself facilitating a discussion in which the select
committee chairmen, possibly for the first time, discussed with each other
some of the fundamentals of what was wrong with the select committee
system' (interview, 28 November 2001). Another Commission member
described the Liaison Committee has having been 'sparked into life' by its
private, off-the-record meeting with them (interview, 29 November 2001).
Yet another Commission member described the meeting as 'a kind of release
for them [the Liaison Committee]' because 'they were actually talking about
their problems' (interview, 17 April 2002). Robert Sheldon, chair of the
Liaison Committee, confirmed the impact this meeting had on his
committee. He explained that, prior to that meeting, the Liaison Committee
had attempted to canvas opinion amongst the select committee chairs
regarding the problems they had encountered, but that it had not attracted
much of a response: the subsequent meeting with the Hansard Society
Commission had, however, focused minds and 'brought everything to a head'
(HC 224-II, 2001–2, Q. 21).

The Liaison Committee report on the relationship between the executive
and the select committees, *Shifting the Balance*, observed that 'in practice governmental power has always outstripped parliamentary control' (HC 300,
1999–2000, para. 1). It acknowledged 'that the performance of the select
committee system has not been consistent, and its success not unalloyed' not
least because 'on occasion the government has been too ready – and has
found it too easy – to thwart a committee's legitimate purpose' (para. 6). The
report maintained that the time had come for 'further reform and modernisation' (para. 8).

The first set of concerns related to select committee membership. It was
noted that when the committees were originally established in 1979, the
Committee of Selection was designed to be independent of government. The
report concluded, however, that the Committee of Selection, 'itself heavily
influenced by the Whips', had nominated MPs for committee service
'primarily on the basis of lists supplied by the Whips' (para. 11). This, the
Committee believed, led to three 'unwelcome results': delays in setting up
committees at the start of a new parliament; delays in replacing MPs who
leave committees; and deliberate obstruction of MPs, and their being kept off

committees, on account of their views (para. 12). The report remarked that 'it is wrong in principle that party managers should exercise effective control of select committee membership' (para. 13). It proposed that the Liaison Committee should be renamed the Select Committee Panel, and that the chairmen and deputies of this Panel should put forward to the House the select committee membership nominations (paras 14–17).

Another aspect of the matter was that 'able and effective select committee members ... are so easily tempted by the lowliest of government and opposition appointments' (para. 29), which underlined the need for a better balance between government and parliamentary service. The Liaison Committee hoped that select committee service would be perceived as a proper career path with associated rewards in terms of status and influence, and that the status of committee chairmanships might be improved by way of remuneration (paras 30–4). Concerns were also raised about the status of committee reports, with the Committee arguing that debates on such reports had to be both timely and effective, and that they should avoid having committee members simply restate the arguments already made in writing. The Liaison Committee also highlighted the 'patchy' standard of government replies to committee reports (para. 47). Analysis of these matters inevitably led to broader issues, such as those about the staffing and resources enjoyed by select committees. The report concluded that, as far as the select committees were concerned, 'their full potential has still to be realised' and argued that the recommendations forwarded by the Liaison Committee would help with that realisation. The final words of the report threw down the gauntlet of reform, stating that 'there are some who see the House of Commons as a toothless adjunct of an all-powerful Executive. We aim to disprove this' (para. 106).

The publication of the Liaison Committee report was accompanied by an Early Day Motion (EDM 476, 1999–2000), which supported the main arguments and recommendations made, and which attracted 245 signatures, 146 from Labour MPs, 41 from Conservatives, and 40 from Liberal Democrats. Significantly, half the membership of the Modernisation Committee also signed the EDM (3 Labour, 3 Conservative and 1 Liberal Democrat). Yet despite this relatively high level of Commons support, the government rejected almost every recommendation made by the Liaison Committee (Cm 4737, 2000). The Committee responded immediately to this comprehensive rejection in another report entitled *Independence or Control?*, in which it described the government's position as 'disappointing and surprising', particularly because 'a Government which has made so much of its policy of modernising Parliament should apparently take so different a view when its own accountability and freedom of action are at issue' (HC 748, 1999–2000, para. 3). Such was the Liaison Committee's dissatisfaction with the government's response that it held an evidence session on the matter to which it summoned the Leader of the House, Margaret Beckett. The report concluded that it was 'strange that the expressions of support for increasing the effectiveness of Select Committees are not matched by things that might make a real difference' (para. 77). The Liaison Committee also put the discussion into the broader context of work undertaken by the Modernisation Committee in these critical terms:

> There has been much discussion about shorter sitting hours, and more family-friendly scheduling of business in the House. This may be all very well; but any real modernisation of Parliament must provide better accountability and tougher scrutiny of the Government of the day. (para. 78)

The issue of the Liaison Committee's position on select committee reform remained on the agenda thereafter: for example, it was referenced during ministerial questions to the Leader of the House (HC Debs, 27 June 2000, col. 717; 25 July 2000, cols 897–8), and during an Opposition Day debate on parliament and the executive on 13 July 2000. Much of the focus throughout rested on the extent to which any vote held on the report would be a free one. Crucially, however, early signs that the parties themselves might move to resolve this essentially parliamentary issue in a party context came when Margaret Beckett indicated that the Parliamentary Labour Party might adopt internal party nomination procedures that would remove the need for a change in House procedure. Beckett's statement that 'the procedures that we [the PLP] are to adopt, which will produce the list put forward by the Whips, are in many ways similar to those proposed by the Liaison Committee' (HC Debs, 25 July 2000, col. 899).

The *Shifting the Balance* report did eventually come before the House for debate on 9 November 2000, some eight months after it was published. The debate immediately followed controversy in the Commons on 7 November 2000 surrounding the nature of the Modernisation Committee's recommendations for programming of legislation. The juxtaposition of the two debates could hardly have been more illustrative of the friction then emerging over the future direction of Commons reform. Furthermore, the *Shifting the Balance* debate was accompanied by another Early Day Motion tabled by Robert Sheldon (EDM 1135, 1999–2000), which restated the case made in the report, and although it attracted just 74 signatures, far fewer than the EDM of March 2000, it was signed by all 30 select committee chairmen (except the Modernisation Committee chairman who was, of course, also a government minister).

The debate on the Liaison Committee report provided an opportunity for MPs not only to support the recommendations made, but also to vent some frustration about the direction of Commons reform taken thus far. Robert Sheldon, for example, argued that the legislative programming plans agreed two days previously had emanated from a divided Modernisation Committee which had failed to produce a unanimous report. The Liaison Committee report, by contrast, was unanimous, and Sheldon argued that this 'entitled [the Committee] to ask for substantive motions on it to be put to the House' (HC Debs, 9 November 2000, col. 480). On the broader issue, Labour's Tony Wright asked 'who owns the scrutiny system we have created?' and urged MPs to decide whether it should be owned by the government or by the House (col. 511). Yet, Leader of the House Margaret Beckett argued that the Liaison Committee's proposals were not 'modest' and would lead to a situation in which select committees would 'substitute their own judgement for that of the Executive' (col. 481). Since the debate was held only on the adjournment, no substantive motions were voted upon.

The impact of the *Shifting the Balance* report was dealt a hard blow on 12 February 2001, when the Conservative Party tabled an Opposition Day motion which supported the Liaison Committee recommendations, and which used wording very similar to that of the *Independence or Control?* report. Since this was the way in which the Liaison Committee report came to be substantively debated, Labour MPs were subject to a three-line whip: had it been debated as a House matter, no such formal strictures would have been placed on them. Although the Liaison Committee had generated a degree of cross-party support for its proposals, the debate in February 2001 was inherently partisan because it was an Opposition Day debate: the motion was defeated by 170 votes to 280, and a government amendment which applauded the progress made by the Modernisation Committee was approved by 276 votes to 164.

One month after the Liaison Committee's work apparently lay in tatters as a result of the Opposition Day debate, it published yet another report, *Shifting the Balance: Unfinished Business* (HC 321, 2000–1). This rejected the idea that the Committee's original proposals had been radical, and stated that its suggestions for reforming the nomination process had not 'deserved the somewhat apocalyptic tone' in which it had been received by the government (para. 12). The report outlined alternative ways of reforming the nominations process, and restated the Liaison Committee's belief that the executive had to view select committee work as an opportunity for co-operation between government and parliament, rather than as a threat (para. 151). The idea that effective scrutiny would benefit both government and parliament became a growing theme amongst those interested in parliamentary reform.

The Commission to Strengthen Parliament

Shortly after the Liaison Committee published *Independence or Control?*, the dynamics of the reform agenda changed with the publication of the report of the Commission to Strengthen Parliament. This was a Conservative Party Commission chaired by the parliamentary scholar Professor the Lord Norton of Louth, and appointed by Conservative leader William Hague in July 1999.

The Norton Commission was instructed 'to examine the causes of the decline in the effectiveness of Parliament in holding the executive to account and to make proposals for strengthening democratic control over the Government' (Conservative Party 1999a).

The Commission emerged from a growing interest inside the Conservative Party in the workings of parliament, in part consolidated by two years in opposition (interview with Norton Commission member, 29 November 2001). The Commission was small, and deliberately included a mix of experience (interview with Commission member, 29 November 2001), with the membership comprising Peter Brooke (who has since become a peer), Lord Forsyth of Drumlean, Lord Waldegrave of North Hill (all three former ministers), Matthew Parris (journalist) and Gillian Peele (academic). The first publication to emerge from the Commission was a consultation document, published in September 1999, which made clear its intention to focus analysis on the ability of parliament to scrutinise and influence the executive, which 'had not kept pace with the growth in the size and the changing nature of the executive in Britain' (Conservative Party 1999a). The small size of the Commission, and shared party outlook of the members, meant that proceedings were fairly consensual, and a report emerged quite quickly (interview with Commission member, 19 March 2002).

The Commission report argued that it is not only citizens who require an effective parliament, but government too. Because government derives its authority from parliament, 'the more it distances itself from Parliament, the more it undermines popular consent for the system of government'. In particular:

> An effective Parliament ensures that government engages in rigorous thinking, is able to argue convincingly for what it proposes, and that its proposals emerge after robust probing ... In essence, good government requires an effective Parliament. (Conservative Party 2000: 5)

The report distinguished between the different types of parliamentary reform that might be undertaken. It noted that 'there may be a clash between seeking to allow a government to get its business more expeditiously and seeking to strengthen Parliament as a scrutinising body' (Conservative Party 2000: 7). Nonetheless, the report recommendations contained a mix of both effectiveness and efficiency reforms, and the Commission endorsed a 'big bang' approach to parliamentary reform (Conservative Party 2000: 20). It also acknowledged the difficulties inherent in trying to secure effectiveness reforms, asking, 'Why should a government support, or acquiesce in, changes designed to make it more accountable to Parliament?' The answer for the Commission was quite clear, and lay in the observation that 'government ultimately benefits from an effective Parliament' (Conservative Party 2000: 9).

As far as specific proposals for enhanced effectiveness were concerned, the Commission focused on the need to reform the select committee system, and endorsed many of the proposals previously made by the Liaison Committee. The Commission recommended the removal of whip influence from the nomination process, arguing that this would 'allow more free-thinking and able members to join the select committees' (Conservative Party 2000: 29). It supported the idea of creating an alternative career path to that of government, and advocated payment of committee chairmen. It also recommended an increase in the size and composition of select committees, the creation of clear work remits, the granting of power to create sub-committees, as well as enhanced and increased resources. Changes were also suggested aimed at improving the reception of committee reports and government responses to them.

The Hansard Commission on Parliamentary Scrutiny

The question of enhancing the effectiveness of the select committee system remained on the agenda with the publication of the report of the Hansard Society Commission on Parliamentary Scrutiny in June 2001, three months after the Opposition Day debate on the Liaison Committee's *Shifting the Balance*. The Hansard Society Commission report was entitled *The Challenge for Parliament: Making Government Accountable* (Hansard Society 2001). The report was the result of nineteen months of work on a brief that required it to examine 'how Parliament carries out its role as scrutineer of the words and actions of the Executive and assess whether the structure and processes are in need of change' (Power 2001:1). The Commission was chaired by Lord Newton of Braintree, a former Leader of the House of Commons, and comprised eighteen members. The driving force behind setting up the Commission came from David Butler, then chairman of the Hansard Society, whose view was that, in light of the government's large majority, the time had come to examine mechanisms of accountability (interviews with Hansard Society Commission members, 28 and 29 November 2001, 13 May 2002). Lord Newton was chosen as chairman because he was perceived as a heavyweight public figure, and although a Conservative Party member, was not partisan (interview, 28 November 2001). The two Commission vice-chairmen were also substantial figures: Robert Hazell, a former civil servant, was director of the Constitution Unit, and Peter Riddell was a columnist for *The Times* who published extensively on the subject of parliament. The Commission met as a whole every two months, and worked in three sub-groups that met monthly and which focused, respectively, on the role of the chamber, the role of select committees, and financial accountability (Hansard Society 2001: vii).

A core group of Commission members did the bulk of the work, and the aim was to publish a report that did not have dissenting views, with Newton playing a key role on that point (interviews, 12 and 19 March 2002, 17 April 2002). The Commission evidence was taken in private, mainly because the members wanted ideas drawn out without party considerations dominating, and in order to secure a frank exchange of views (interview, 12 March 2002). The Commission published interim reports on its progress along with preliminary conclusions, which impacted upon the positions then being taken by the Liaison Committee in its own work on the select committees. The Commission also interacted informally with the Norton Commission, as their lifetimes overlapped and there was shared membership between the two in the Hansard Society Council (interviews, 28 and 29 November 2001). One Hansard Society Commission member remarked that it was 'quite humbling for the Hansard Society Commission, which was a big body which had eighteen months and a big budget, getting on for £100,000, that Philip Norton almost single-handedly in the space of only some nine months, and with a budget I think of less than £10,000, produced a report which is I think very well argued and very clear and very forceful' (interview, 28 November 2001).

The Hansard Society Commission report argued that '[p]arliament has been left behind by far-reaching changes to the constitution, government and society in the past two decades' and that, despite reforms instituted by the Modernisation Committee, 'the central question of Westminster's scrutiny of the executive has not been addressed' (Hansard Society 2001: x). The report outlined a number of issues that the Liaison Committee and the Norton Commission had already highlighted:

> Scrutiny of Government by MPs and peers is neither systematic nor rigorous. The quality of information provided to Parliament is variable. Parliamentary inquiries have a poor record in locating responsibility for failures by the Executive, ensuring that the Government acts upon them and in following up recommendations for improvement. A survey of MPs' views ... showed that Members themselves are sceptical about Parliament's ability to hold the Government to account. (Hansard Society 2001: x)

The report also outlined the Commission's vision for a reformed parliament:

> Its central theme is that Parliament should be at the apex of a system of accountability – drawing more effectively on the investigations of outside regulators and commissions, enhancing the status of select committees and clarifying the role of Parliament and its politicians. The various activities of MPs and peers in the committees and chambers of both Houses should be better co-ordinated so that they complement each other in the pursuit of accountability. (Hansard Society 2001: x)

The report outlined seven principles for reform: parliament must be at the apex; parliament must develop a culture of scrutiny; committees should play a more influential role within parliament; the chamber should remain central to accountability; financial scrutiny should be central to accountability; the House of Lords should complement the Commons; and parliament should communicate more effectively with the public.

The crucial recommendation from the Hansard Society Commission with respect to our study here was that there had to be a culture of scrutiny in the House of Commons, a point which endorsed much of what the Liaison Committee had already said in this area. The report argued that parliament 'should become a more committee-based institution' (Hansard Society 2001: 19–20). The Commission made the case for select committees forming an alternative career path to that of government, and went as far as to recommend that every backbench MP should serve on one. Correspondingly, the number of MPs on the government's payroll vote was to be reduced, and select committee chairmen were to be paid a ministerial salary (Hansard Society 2001: 21–2). The report recommended that the reformed select committee system should derive its effectiveness from 'bringing added value to other forms of scrutiny, making all other structures of accountability relevant, by identifying the public interest and linking it into the parliamentary process' (Hansard Society 2001: 30). Committee core duties were to be more clearly specified, and should incorporate performance indicators against which their work could be judged (Hansard Society 2001: 31–7). Increased use of sub-committees, new methods of reporting, and better integration of the work of committees into the general work of parliament was also suggested, along with improved resources and staffing (Hansard Society 2001: 38–42).

The Commission had little to say about the issue of select committee nomination, arguably the most pressing issue at that time. Subsequently, when Hansard Society Commission members gave evidence to the Modernisation Committee, Leader of the House Robin Cook described its views on nominations as 'almost a dog that did not bark' (HC 224-II, 2001–2, Q. 49). Lord Newton explained that, despite the existence of views that supported the removal of whip influence from the nominations process, the Commission had no clear view on what should replace the existing system. Peter Riddell was more direct, remarking that '[t]he frank answer is we slightly copped out on the details', but also confirming that he did not think the Liaison Committee recommendations were workable (HC 224-II, 2001–2, Qs 49–50). In interview, one Hansard Society Commission member argued that it was only feasible to pay chairmen if the appointment process was reformed, because it would be wrong to pay chairmen while the nominations process remained in the hands of the whips (12 March 2002). Another Commission member argued that the method of appointment was the real problem facing select committees, and gave several examples of how whips had interfered previously in this process (interview, 12 March 2002).

Clearly, Commission members were not unaware of the problems with the nominations process, but were constrained in terms of what they could say because of the tensions associated with providing alternative solutions.

The reform agenda in the balance

By the summer of 2001, a select committee reform agenda was beginning to emerge due to the work done by the Liaison Committee, the Norton Commission and the Hansard Society Commission. The Commission reports in particular contained a variety of both efficiency and effectiveness reforms that were designed to complement each other. As far as creating a more effective Commons was concerned, all three reports had focused on the need to reform the select committee system. Many of the ideas they promoted had already been aired in the Commons during debates, primarily as a way to criticise the Modernisation Committee for not taking a more radical approach to reform. In terms of Norton's framework of conditions for reform, therefore, the reform agenda was partially in place by the summer of 2001, thanks to the persistent focus on the shortcomings of the select committees.

Political leadership in favour of reform

Following Labour's re-election in June 2001, Robin Cook was appointed Leader of the House. The appointment was a slightly risky one for the government. Cook had spent four years as Foreign Secretary, a job he enjoyed and had not expected to lose. Cook was also a reformer as far as parliament was concerned. Several of those interviewed at the time indicated that Cook's reform instincts made him a strange choice for the job from the government's perspective (interviews, 12 and 20 March 2002). The only conclusion may be that, once he was removed from the Foreign Office, and once the reshuffle had taken place, there was no other obvious ministerial post for him. At any rate, Cook's relocation from the Foreign Office undoubtedly served as a useful lever in his new role. For example, in his memoirs, Cook explains how Number 10 'meekly submitted' to his request to have Stephen Twigg as his junior minister, an appointment Cook was sure would 'send out all the right signals on [his] commitment to modernisation of the Commons' (Cook 2003b: 9).

Cook's first time before the House for business questions, on 21 June 2001, gave a taste of what was to come during his time as Leader of the House. He was immediately pressed on whether the select committees would be set up prior to the summer recess, a question based on the experience of previously long delays in securing their establishment. Cook agreed that the committees should be set up as quickly as possible, 'and that the House should have the ability to use them for effective scrutiny' (HC Debs, 21 June

2001, col. 155). Cook also agreed that there was 'unfinished business' with respect to modernisation (col. 157), an allusion to the language of the Liaison Committee report which marked out his reform intentions. These intentions were underscored when, on 5 July 2001, Cook brought recommendations to the House that would enable the select committees to be established quickly, and which drew on collaboration with three senior Liaison Committee members from the previous parliament. The changes included some of the proposals endorsed by the Liaison Committee, such as enabling the creation of sub-committees and joint committees (HC Debs, 5 July 2001, cols 480–1). Cook contextualised his approach to future select committee reform when he commented that:

> Many complex and thoughtful proposals have of course been presented by the Liaison Committee, the Hansard Society and the Norton Commission ... We should reflect on many of these proposals, and see whether we can find ways of making incremental improvements to the system. (col. 484)

Cook also highlighted the conflict inherent in any reform programme when he explained that 'we should obtain the right balance between the Government's ability to secure the legislation on the basis of which they were elected, and the House's right to scrutinise that and other Government legislation' (col. 484). He also made his own assessment of the dilemma clear, when he stated that 'scrutiny of Government does not necessarily constitute an adversarial relationship between Executive and Parliament' (col. 485).

A window of opportunity

Cook's commitment to ensuring the House was quickly able to vote on select committee nomination proposals itself contributed to the opening of a window of opportunity for effective Commons reform. Nominations lists were brought before the House on 16 July 2001, and some MPs complained that the names had been 'plucked out of the air' without proper discussion (HC Debs, 16 July 2001, cols 21–6). It soon became clear that there was much discontent about the proposals agreed by the Committee of Selection. For example, when the chairman of the Committee of Selection, John McWilliam, was asked how many changes had been made to the proposals made by the political parties, he responded:

> None. I reasonably thought that the representatives of the various political parties had sorted the recommendations out with their members before they put them to the Committee. (col. 35)

This prompted Tony Wright to ask '[i]f the Committee of Selection does not select, what does it do?', while Sir Patrick Cormack wondered '[i]s there

really any point in having the Committee?' (cols 35–6). McWilliam emphasised that '[t]he duty of the Committee of Selection is to ensure that the
balance of the House is kept in terms of membership of Committees, that the
motions for nomination are properly made and that the procedures are
properly adhered to' (col. 38). Douglas Hogg rejected this analysis:

> Does the hon. Gentleman understand the dismay with which his remarks are
> being greeted? In fact, he is saying that the sole function of the Committee of
> Selection is to rubber-stamp the nominations made by those on the Front
> Benches of the respective parties. Surely, that is not the function of the
> Committee. The function of the Committee of Selection is genuinely to select
> names. (col. 38)

Sir George Young, a former member of the Committee of Selection, explained
the way in which it reached its decisions, and highlighted aspects of his own
experience:

> There is a convention among Whips that they do not challenge the nominations
> of other parties. If the other side wants to put someone on a Committee or to
> keep someone off whose interests may be relevant but unhelpful that is not
> challenged. It is no secret that I recently proposed an amendment in the
> Committee … I was shot down in flames. (col. 56)

The central concerns of those who contributed to the debate of 16 July 2001
not only revolved around the principles along which the Committee of
Selection worked, but also around the practical effects of those principles,
which included the exclusion from the Committee's nomination lists the
names of two senior backbenchers, Gwyneth Dunwoody and Donald
Anderson. Dunwoody had been chair of the Transport sub-committee in the
previous parliament, and Anderson chair of the Foreign Affairs select
committee, and both had presided over the publication of reports that were
highly critical of government policy and administration. Many of those who
took place in the debate argued that both MPs should have been returned to
committee service, and the failure of the Committee of Selection to ensure
their names appeared on the nominations lists merely highlighted the inade-
quacies of the nomination process.

Robin Cook had already received intimations of potential problems over
the select committee nominations on 9 July 2001, during a meeting with the
Chief Whip, Hilary Armstrong, who explained that she was 'under pressure'
from Number 10 to exclude Dunwoody and Anderson from the nomination
lists (Cook 2003b: 19, 23). Cook emphasised that 'it would look like the
worst kind of government authoritarianism for the whips to deprive them of
their Chairs by the devious device of leaving them off their committees'
(Cook 2003b: 19). On 11 July 2001, Cook learned that the names had
indeed been kept off the nomination lists, and that 'all hell had broken loose

at the PLP, which had approached a near riot when they were told that the [party] standing orders did not allow them to amend the lists, but only to swallow them whole or not at all' (Cook 2003b: 20).

In the 16 July 2001 debate, then, Cook accepted that 'the events of the past few days have given greater urgency to the search for a more transparent system [of nomination]' and also committed the government to reform the PLP procedures (Cook 2003b: 21). He explained that the Modernisation Committee's starting point would be the Liaison Committee report *Shifting the Balance: Unfinished Business*, and underpinned his approach to reform with the notion that 'good scrutiny makes for good government' (HC Debs, 16 July 2001, cols 48–9). Cook hinted at the window of opportunity then opening, remarking that 'if there has ever been a moment when we are likely to achieve consensus it is now', and stated the need to 'ensure that future nominations to Select Committees are seen to be fully in the hands of Members of this House' (col. 49).

Consequently, the motion to reconstitute the Transport, Local Government and the Regions select committee without including Gwyneth Dunwoody was defeated by 308 votes to 221, while the motion to reconstitute the Foreign Affairs select committee without including Donald Anderson was defeated by 301 votes to 232. The House was presented with revised nomination lists from the Committee of Selection on 19 July 2001, which included Dunwoody and Anderson, and which met with House approval. Cook later commented that he 'could not have hoped for a clearer illustration of the case for modernising the proceedings of Parliament than the debacle into which we tumbled over membership of the select committees,' describing it as 'a classic example of the tussle between Parliament's right to scrutiny and the Executive's power of control' (Cook 2003b: 23). In Cook's opinion, Number 10's interference in the nominations process 'sharpened the question why the government should decide who it was that sat in on scrutiny of them', and as far as he was concerned, the matter boiled down to one simple question: 'if Parliament cannot control the membership of its own committees, what real power is left to it?' (Cook 2003b: 23).

The parliamentary network of reformers

Cook may have firmly taken the reins in terms of providing effective leadership to drive forward reform, but he also helped create a second layer of leadership inside the Commons by assisting a process of organisation amongst concerned backbenchers. The All-Party Group on Parliamentary Reform, chaired by Labour MP Anne Campbell, was created 'to promote the reform of Parliament in order to improve the effectiveness of the work of Parliament'. The Group was established partly as an outpost of the Hansard Society, and designed to promote the Hansard Society Commission's report on parliamentary scrutiny amongst MPs, with many of the Group's members having some involvement with the Hansard Society (interviews with All-Party Group members, 22 and 23 April 2002, 15 May 2002). Robin Cook was instrumental in the creation of the Group: he took the initiative in approaching Anne Campbell and requesting that she bring together a group of reform-minded MPs in order to demonstrate, mainly to the government and the whips, that Commons reform had broad-ranging support and a firm leadership base (interview, 30 April 2002). The group successfully reflected a reasonably broad range of members, incorporating individuals such as Sir George Young, a former Modernisation Committee member and Shadow Leader of the House, as well as those who were Modernisation Committee members at the time, such as Helen Jackson and Joan Ruddock. Indeed, these two latter MPs explained that their membership of the All-Party Group assisted them in disseminating wider Commons opinion on reform to the Modernisation Committee (interviews, 16 and 18 April 2002).

The comments of those involved in the All-Party Group at that time offer an interesting insight into how MPs conceptualised reform more broadly. One MP, for example, referred to the frustration felt 'amongst a number of the newer intake of MPs, particularly the 1997 intake, about the whole way in which this building operates' (interview, 14 May 2002). This MP had welcomed the creation of the Modernisation Committee, but this had soon been followed by the 'realisation that that was full of dinosaurs as well, and that the pace of change was so slow that it needed the All-Party Group to try and push the agenda a little quicker'. Nonetheless, most of the members had a realistic idea of the potential impact of their Group. While one MP admitted that such groups are 'more form than substance', another confirmed that not all Group members were agreed on the way forward for parliamentary reform (interviews, 15 May 2002, 23 April 2002). Yet there was agreement that the Group did function as a useful network of like-minded reformers, and that it could work as a 'useful vehicle for MPs who can't necessarily be on the Modernisation Committee' as well as providing a forum for unofficial communication channels (interviews, 14 May 2002, 23 April 2002). Yet another MP also believed their had been 'a slight crowding of the field' in terms of reform, 'with Hansard, the All-Party Group, some of the select committees, the Modernisation Committee, Charter 88 – the ground is quite full of people who want to modernise here, but co-ordination of activities isn't quite as well thought out as it could be' (interview, 14 May 2002).

The field was arguably crowded further still when we consider the existence of the Parliament First Group, formed at the end of the 1997 parliament, and chaired by Labour MP Mark Fisher. This Group was also borne out of dissatisfaction with the pace of reform, with Fisher explaining that he and others were 'becoming increasingly frustrated by modernisation of the

House, and felt that, welcome though that was in principle and sensible though some of its changes were, nevertheless they were not getting to the political meat of what was wrong with the relations between parliament and the government' (interview, 30 April 2003). Parliament First helped to underpin the drive for reform by providing 'a sharper cutting edge to reform' than did the All-Party Group, which had to be 'more understanding of what the present government could or could not do' (interview, 30 April 2003). Yet, the Parliament First Group maintained a relatively broad membership, with much overlap with the All-Party Group, and incorporated many past and (at the time) present Modernisation Committee members. Furthermore, the Hansard Society were also involved in this group, assisting with organisational matters, and subsequently helping them to publish their 2003 pamphlet about parliamentary reform, Parliament's Last Chance, which was researched and drafted by the Hansard Society's Alex Brazier, who had also been clerk to the Hansard Society Commission.

In this way, a network of highly inter-linked reformers emerged, with each group operating at a different level of parliamentary influence, yet intimately connected to the others around it. Crucially, the Hansard Society was central to these groups. The Society had not only published its own clear programme for reform, but it was also central to the functioning of both the All-Party and the Parliament First Groups. Its work not only gained public commendation from Robin Cook: he also appointed Greg Power as his special adviser, who had worked previously with the Hansard Society, and had been secretary to its Commission on Parliamentary Scrutiny. In order to appreciate the events that unfolded around select committee reform in 2001–2, it is necessary to bear in mind the high degree of connection between the key actors involved.

The Modernisation Committee and a consolidated reform agenda

By the summer of 2001, the conditions required for effective reform to proceed were almost met. Robin Cook was in a position to provide the leadership required in the reform process, and was able to utilise the All-Party Group on Parliamentary Reform and the Parliament First Group to provide additional backbench leadership. A partial reform agenda existed, thanks to the reports published by the Liaison Committee, the Norton Commission and the Hansard Society Commission. A window of opportunity had opened as a result of the controversy surrounding the select committee nomination lists. What remained to be secured was a specific reform package that could be presented to the House of Commons.

Cook was eager to proceed with reform by way of a comprehensive package, and to jettison the 'piecemeal' approach that had characterised the Modernisation Committee in its first parliament (Cook 2003b: 46–7), and the memorandum that eventually emerged from the Committee encapsulated just that sort of approach (HC 440, 2001–2). The memorandum proceeded from the assessment already espoused by Cook that '[g]ood scrutiny makes for good government', and attempted to persuade MPs of its merits by stating its aim as to 'create a modern and effective Commons' (paras 2, 4). The need to focus particularly on reform of the select committees was made clear: the memorandum described the committees as 'the most developed vehicle through which MPs can carry out detailed scrutiny of Government policy and Ministerial conduct' and therefore emphasised that they should be a 'priority for consideration' by the Modernisation Committee (para. 5). This new focus for the Modernisation Committee received a warm endorsement by the Liaison Committee (HC 590, 2001–2).

The Modernisation Committee published its report on reform of the select committees in February 2002 (HC 224, 2001–2). The Committee heard evidence from many of the advocates of reform, such as Robert Sheldon, Lord Norton, Lord Newton and Peter Riddell, all of whom emphasised the issue of the nomination process as a key problem to be tackled. In turn, the nominations issue was the first aspect of the committee system that the report addressed. The Modernisation Committee agreed that '[t]he Committee of Selection has come to interpret its role as limited to confirming the proposals put to it by the front benches on both sides' and that '[a]ny new method of nomination needs to be independent, authoritative, transparent and able to command the confidence of the House on both sides' (para. 9). It explained that 'what is required is not an alternative to the party process [for making nominations], but a fail-safe mechanism to ensure fair play and to provide a court of appeal' (para. 12). The difficulty lay in designing such a fail-safe mechanism, although, as the report appendices demonstrate, there were no shortage of proposals, all with their own supporters and detractors. The Modernisation Committee was not swayed by the idea of direct election to select committees by the House (para. 10), but nor was it persuaded by the Liaison Committee's proposal for a three-member body to make nominations, on the grounds that it would place too much power in too few hands (para. 13).

The Modernisation Committee finally endorsed the idea that, at the start of each parliament, the chairman of Ways and Means should chair a Committee of Nomination, on which he would have no vote, with the Committee membership drawn from the Chairman's Panel, which is itself appointed by the Speaker (para. 16). The Committee of Nomination would therefore comprise the chairman of Ways and Means, along with the four most senior Chairman's Panel members from the governing party, the two most senior members of the official opposition, and the most senior member of the second largest opposition party. The Committee would also include the most senior backbencher on the government and opposition sides respectively (para. 17). The chairman of Ways and Means would initiate the nomination process by issuing a form for parties to circulate amongst their members, who would indicate the committees on which they wished to serve, and the parties would then process those forms and submit names to the Committee of Nomination. The Modernisation Committee had set ideas about the anticipated role for this new committee:

> We start from the presumption that the political parties will wish to submit nominations which fairly reflect the preference, gender and experience of their Members. We therefore would not anticipate that it would be necessary for the Committee of Nomination to vary the party nominations other than exceptional circumstances where it was clear that a fundamental problem had arisen. In those exceptional circumstances the Committee of Nomination would have access to all the relevant forms returned by Members. In the event that the Committee of Nomination remained concerned we would expect it in the first instance to refer back the nominations to that specific committee for further consideration. If that failed to produce a satisfactory explanation or solution the Committee of Nomination would have the power and authority to make any amendments it thought fit before submitting that list of nominations to the House. (para. 19)

The final decision regarding select committee membership would still rest with the House (para. 21). The Modernisation Committee believed this new procedure would provide 'an independent mechanism which will place nominations to all select committees in the hands of an independent author-itative body' and ensure nominations were 'in the hands of the Commons' (para. 23).

Cook's memoirs detail the gathering storm over the Committee of Nomination before the recommendations were laid before the House. On 29 January 2002, he met with the Chief Whip, Hilary Armstrong, who, having seen a draft copy of the report, became 'particularly worked up' over the Committee of Nomination proposal, which she perceived to be 'an affront' to the new nominations mechanisms already settled inside the PLP (Cook 2003b: 93). Armstrong wished to see a system that enabled the parties to put nominations to the House and which prevented the House from making changes to them. Cook explained that it was impossible to draft Standing Orders for such a scenario, and that even the Committee of Selection was entitled to make changes if it so wished. Cook believed 'the real problem' was that 'the old Committee of Selection was controlled by the whips and this new committee will not be' (Cook 2003b: 93–4). Cook was, however, forced to make changes to the report, removing 'any prejudicial reference to whips or political parties', but refused to change the substance of the Committee's report (Cook 2003b: 94).

Although the most controversial aspect of the report was its approach to the nominations issue, it also said a great deal about how to get the select committees working more effectively. The Modernisation Committee recommended that the House begin funding a central unit of specialist support staff dedicated to assisting the select committees, and that sufficient staff be made available to them to deal with their administrative workloads (paras 28–30). It suggested that the select committees adopt a statement of core tasks in order to clarify their objectives and achieve more consistency in their work, and that they each produce annual reports that charted their performance in these tasks (paras 33–5). It recommended that the committees experiment with rapporteurs on specific projects, and that there be a review of the committees' abilities to compel witnesses to give evidence before them (paras 34–6). The report also suggested that there be a clearer split between the domestic committees of the House of Commons and the departmental select committees (paras 37–9). The Modernisation Committee also explored the idea of using the select committees in order to create an alternative career structure for MPs, and recommended that committee chairmen be paid an additional salary (para. 41), while also suggesting that chairmen should not serve in the chair for more than two parliaments (para. 43). It advocated an increase in the size of select committees, to fifteen members, and that the Committee of Nomination be empowered to remove those MPs with poor attendance records (paras 44–8). The report also made recommendations for how committee reports are debated in the Commons, suggesting that they should also be debated in Westminster Hall under certain circumstances (para. 57). The Liaison Committee broadly endorsed the Modernisation Committee's proposals, and welcomed its alternative nominations framework as 'sensible new machinery, which is worth trying' (HC 692, 2001–2, para. 4).

The progress of select committee reform

By spring 2002, therefore, all three of the conditions outlined by Norton (2000b) had been met. From the varied reform agendas emanating from the Liaison Committee, the Norton Commission and the Hansard Society Commission, the Modernisation Committee produced a single package of select committee reforms to present to the House. Political leadership was in place with Robin Cook as Leader of the House, supported on the backbenches by the All-Party Group on Parliamentary Reform and the Parliament First Group. The window of opportunity was opened as a result of the controversy surrounding the select committee nominations of the previous summer. The fulfilment of these conditions seem to suggest the existence of a critical juncture that could facilitate meaningful reform and mark some kind of restructuring of the norms that shape the House of Commons, by facilitating a reduction in the powers of party whips and, by extension, the parties on select committee functioning. The key unknown right up to the final moments, however, was whether there truly was sufficient political will to carry through the reform package.

On 14 May 2002, the Modernisation Committee proposals for select committee reform came before the House of Commons in a debate that was generally in favour of change (Kelso 2003: 64). MPs seemed hopeful that reform might well be secured. Tony Wright, for example, noting his long-standing pessimism regarding the likelihood of reform, remarked that 'this is the first time I can say with honesty that we may just have turned the corner' (HC Debs, 14 May 2002, cols 687–8). Archy Kirkwood made a similar observation, declaring that 'I have not seen such an opportunity for change in my time in the House' (col. 701). Nonetheless, a good deal of the debate was preoccupied with discussion about the likely impact of the proposed Committee of Nomination, and whether it would genuinely be a better mechanism than the one already in place. In addition, there was anxiety about the whether the whips' offices would acquiesce in a free vote or intervene to obstruct it. Tony Wright's comments once more serve to sum up the concerns of reformers:

> This is the kind of modernisation that deserves the name. It is the kind of modernisation that begins to shift the balance and to point the House in the right direction. I just hope – if I can put it this way – that the dark forces that inhabit this place do not want to prevent this package of reforms from continuing. (HC Debs, 14 May 2002, col. 688)

Indeed, despite the absence of any dissenting report within the Modernisation Committee, it also became clear that some of its members, particularly on the opposition side, had reservations about supporting the reforms being proposed, as Greg Knight indicated when he cautioned Robin Cook as follows:

> I must advise him that he needs to watch his back, because it is clear that not all his ministerial colleagues share his enthusiasm for what he is seeking to do. Indeed, the Modernisation Committee is still reflecting on whether all his proposed changes are necessary in the interests either of modernisation or of scrutiny. (col. 664)

If consensus was vital to the success of the reform package, the criticisms aired by Knight and others during the debate did little to help secure it. Consequently, the House divisions on the various aspects of the Modernisation Committee's recommendations come as no real surprise. Although the House approved the proposals to employ core tasks for select committees and to pay select committee chairmen, the recommendation to create a Committee of Nomination was defeated by fourteen votes. The House debate intimated the difficulties surrounding this particular proposal, and analysis of the vote provides further evidence of those problems (Kelso 2003: 65). Of the four Conservative MPs on the Modernisation Committee, only one, Nicholas Winterton, voted for the Committee of Nomination proposal: two others voted against while a third was absent. Two members of the Modernisation Committee subsequently indicated that the whips had been far from supportive of this proposal (interviews, 15 and 23 May 2002), and the voting record supports the observation: while the Chief Whip (Hillary Armstrong) and the Deputy Chief Whip (Keith Hill) voted for the proposal, nine junior whips voted against it. Of Cook's ministerial colleagues who participated in the vote, twelve voted for the Committee of Nomination proposal, while fifteen voted against.

The Hansard record of the night's proceedings demonstrate just how controversial was the Committee of Nomination vote: at its conclusion, Labour MP Gordon Prentice asked whether 'on a free vote, is it in order for the Government whips to point to the No Lobby saying "PLP this way"?' (HC Debs, 14 May 2002, col. 720). This impression of whips guiding Labour MPs into the 'wrong' lobby was substantiated in interview with several members of the Modernisation Committee (Kelso 2003: 65). One Labour MP, for example, indicated that at least six MPs may have inadvertently voted the wrong way as a result of the whips' actions (interview, 22 May 2002), which is notable, bearing in mind the small margin on which the vote was lost. Another Labour MP remarked that the vote was lost 'because the government whips and the opposition whips were in collusion together because they don't want to see the power of the whips office diminished' (interview, 15 May 2002). A Conservative Modernisation Committee member claimed that:

> The matter was supposed to have been decided on a free vote: I have to tell you it certainly was not a free vote. While the chief whip and the deputy chief whip of the government voted with Robin Cook and myself, the rest of the whips in the Labour whips' office voted against, I think clearly [they] had been asked to do so, I have no proof, its my opinion and an opinion shared by other Labour members. (Interview, 23 May 2002)

This MP was also certain that 'a majority of the Conservative parliamentary party voted against on the urging of the Conservative whips' office'. Robin Cook later confirmed these allegations about the whips' voting behaviour:

> If that had been all they'd done [vote against the proposal] we would still have won, but they also led an operation to persuade others to join them. Several recent ex-whips staying outside the 'No' lobby crying, 'Labour lobby this way', and pointing to the door just inside which stood several of the existing whips. Habit alone ensured that a large number of Labour MPs followed orders. (Cook 2003b: 153)

Even Cook's own informal whipping operation – designed to ensure that like-minded reformers successfully voted the 'right' way – failed to muster enough support to secure success. As one Labour member of the Modernisation Committee commented, 'I think that the forces of conservatism in this place are better organised than the forces of modernisation' (interview, 22 May 2002). This MP explained that those who were against the changes to the nomination procedures had operated a 'really quite clever campaign that targeted specific people and their own specific needs and grudges'. Tony Wright, who had earlier warned against the 'dark forces' at work inside the Commons, was later forced to ask:

> Where were the massed ranks of parliamentary reformers last night? It [the motion] was lost, and it was lost because all the whip fraternity organised to vote it down, and the forces of progress, where were they? (Interview, 15 May 2002)

The failure to reform the select committee nominations system

As the House of Commons voted down the proposed changes to the select committee nominations system, there was, by definition, an absence of political will to secure reform. If the events in the months leading up to May 2002 did constitute a critical juncture in the path of House of Commons development, it was clearly not a sufficiently robust critical juncture. According to Norton's (2000b) approach, the three conditions – reform agenda, political leadership, window of opportunity – must be underpinned by political will. Despite the apparent fulfilment of these conditions, the lack of political will meant the reform was doomed.

However, blaming the absence of political will for the failure is too simplistic. We must first acknowledge the fact that the PLP reformed its own internal procedures for select committee nomination, which removed much of the sting from the issue. This in itself demonstrates how intra-party dynamics can undermine a 'House' approach to reform. However, charting the course of events prior to May 2002, and the rationale behind the various reform proposals, illustrates an inherent contradiction in the attitudinal approach. Reformers themselves have stated the contradiction: why would government acquiesce in reforms that would undermine its position within parliament? Why would the dominant elite choose to exercise political will and enact reforms that infringe upon its governing capability? The answer provided by the attitudinal approach – that they would acquiesce because this contributes to better government – is deeply unsatisfactory. It assumes that the dominant elite agree with that analysis, and agree that such reforms benefit government because they produce a more balanced political system. In other words, it assumes, in Beattie's (1995) language, that they operate from a Whig approach to the constitution. The reality, and the evidence from the application of the institutional lens, is that they do not, and that they actually operate from a Peelite approach. The attitudinal approach is flawed because it makes unsound assumptions about the conditions under which, and the reasons why, political will is exercised. Moreover, despite acknowledging the conflict between MPs parliamentary and party roles, the attitudinal approach concludes that MPs can, under certain conditions such as those outlined above, set aside the latter role in favour of the former.

Ultimately, the reform attempt of May 2002 failed in significant ways. The most important part of the reform package geared towards improving the effectiveness of the Commons by removing the power of the whips from the nomination process was defeated. Select committees were, however, reformed in terms of their working practices, with the introduction of core duties and some pre-legislative scrutiny, which were welcomed by the Liaison Committee (HC 558, 2002–3; HC 446, 2003–4). The proposal to pay select committee chairmen was also approved, which may be viewed as a substantial step towards creating an alternative career path to that of government, and thus eventually contributing to a more effective House. However, as one Liberal Democrat MP pointed out, payment of select committee chairmen is only a truly effective reform if whips no longer control the nomination process (interview, 12 March 2002). Another Liberal Democrat MP, who was also a Modernisation Committee member, endorsed this view, explaining that paying select committee chairmen while not reforming the nominations process 'could just be a licence for old fogies, because it's also about who actually gets to be the chair of select committees' (interview, 23 April 2002). As one Conservative MP on the All-Party Group for Parliamentary Reform remarked, 'payment [of chairmen] alone won't work, but must proceed in conjunction with other reforms' (interview 23 April 2002).

The dilution of the select committee reform package proposed in 2002 bears considerable similarities to the dilution of the select committee package of 1978–79. On both occasions, many of the powers and capabilities proposed for the select committee system were subsequently thwarted by the dominant elites inside the House of Commons, who would have been detrimentally affected by them. The select committee system was supposed to improve the ability of the Commons to hold the executive to account. However, more than twenty years after they were created, one member of the Hansard Society Commission nevertheless felt compelled to describe the select committees as 'amateur' and as 'not terribly relevant' (interview, 12 March 2002). That this might be so is testament to the structured institutional context into which the select committee system was born and developed. As one Liberal Democrat member of the Modernisation Committee explained, 'the main barrier to reforming the House is the government, which ever government, because the last thing an executive wants is an effective parliament' (interview, 23 April 2002).

The central problem with the attitudinal approach is its reliance on the existence of political will. Beetham et al (2002: 135) offer this analysis of the logic of appropriateness that confronts MPs of the governing party, and which helps illuminate the sheer complexity of this idea of political will:

> In constitutional terms, Labour MPs are asked to fulfil conflicting roles: they must first sustain their government in power; they must act as guardians of the manifesto on which they were elected; and they must make government accountable. But [Tony] Blair believes that Labour MPs should act neither as the government's conscience nor as watchdogs for the public, but rather as the government's ambassadors.

To understand the reasons why the attempt to reform comprehensively the select committee system failed in 2002, we must better appreciate the role of the norms and values of the dominant elite in the structured institutional context of Westminster. The events can best be discerned by taking into consideration the implications of historical institutionalism. The norms and values that maintain the structured institutional context at Westminster can only be substantially changed if those who currently benefit from them assert the political will to change them. The attitudinal approach does not adequately account for how this paradox can be resolved: it argues that MPs can secure reform if they have the political will to do it, but fails to explain properly how and why that political will can be generated. Political will does not only underpin the conditions of a reform agenda, political leadership and a window of opportunity: it is itself an entirely separate condition, and is also arguably the one that is most difficult to fulfil. The logic of the historical institutionalist approach suggests that it is extremely unlikely that the dominant elites would ever choose to foster and exercise the political will required to substantially reduce their capabilities inside the House of Commons. Critical junctures may well emerge at Westminster, but they are only ever partially, not fully, exploited.

Effectiveness beyond the select committees

This chapter has so far focused almost exclusively on one particular aspect of effectiveness, that is, the role of the House of Commons select committees in holding the government to account. Given the way in which some observers argue that the select committees could form a key part in any shift in the balance of power between government and parliament, it is right that they have been afforded such attention here. Nonetheless, there are other sides to the effectiveness debate. The aim in this book is not to provide a comprehensive account of every aspect of parliamentary reform ever undertaken, and so some reform issues have necessarily been omitted. Yet, it is worthwhile saying a few brief words about some of these other aspects of reform.

For example, in the second New Labour parliament, the Modernisation Committee under Peter Hain undertook a comprehensive enquiry into how parliament might become better connected to the public it serves, and produced a range of recommendations designed to improve the effectiveness of the representational role performed by the Commons broadly (HC 368, 2003–4). This report reveals much about how MPs perceive their relationship with the public, and how they think Commons effectiveness can be improved in this regard (Kelso 2007a). MPs do not exist only to pass legislation and scrutinise the executive: they are also representatives, and this part of their role, and how it is performed, has drawn increasing attention, as the first paragraphs of this book indicated. The effectiveness with which MPs perform their representational duties is, however, distinct (although not entirely separate) from the effectiveness with which parliament holds the government to account, and, indeed, issues concerning the democratic effectiveness of parliament more broadly is perhaps suited to an entirely separate volume.

In a different vein, the Modernisation Committee has also engaged in a reasonable amount of work in order to enhance how the Commons deals with scrutiny of European matters (HC 791 1997–98; HC 465, 2004–5), which is an important issue considering how poorly the House has done in this area historically. Again, although this is an important topic, it does not arguably fall within the parameters of the issues examined here, and, again, more usefully forms part of a debate about how national institutions carve a relevant role for themselves in the context of supranational government.

However, it is useful to close this chapter on Commons effectiveness reform since 1997 with a comment on two reports published by the Modernisation Committee at the close of the Blair era, both of which very clearly signalled a marked change in the Committee's approach to these matters, and, perhaps also, a certain maturation in its collective thought processes. In September 2006, the Committee published a report on the legislative process (HC 1097, 2005–6), which, unlike many of its predecessor reports on this issue, contained just one page on legislative programming. Far from being another attempt to enhance the efficiency of the House of Commons by increasing the speed with which government secures its legislation, the report was instead a remarkable exploration of the ways in which the House could become more effective in the legislative process. It explored the process in its entirety, with the aim of improving its effectiveness in terms of parliamentary input, and in terms of how the public interacts with the process, demonstrating the continued effects of the *Connecting Parliament with the Public* enquiry of the previous year. The report said much about ways to extend and enhance prelegislative scrutiny, which had been done only patchily and poorly in the previous decade, and was billed as a way not only to improve the quality of government legislation, but as a mechanism to encourage government to consider publishing more bills in draft form in the first place. Crucially, however, one of the most interesting aspects of this particular report was its focus on the committee stage of the legislative process. This was a key aspect of the enquiry, as the committee stage has long been viewed as almost entirely ineffective, and as providing almost no genuine parliamentary scrutiny whatsoever. The Committee recommended the use of special standing committees for this stage, which would provide for the ability to take evidence about bills as well as to deliberate in the traditional fashion over each clause. Evidence-gathering in the style of select committee practice was viewed as a means not only to involve the public more usefully in the legislative process, but as a way to improve the knowledge of MPs working on such committees about the bills before them, and therefore as a way to create more meaningful, and possibly more effective, legislative scrutiny. Although this aspect of reform of the legislative process is still in its infancy, it has the potential to alter radically the way that the House of Commons approaches its legislative role, and to improve significantly the effectiveness of the House in scrutinising government legislation in terms of the questions it asks of it and the way it approaches the process. Consequently, after so many years fixated on the efficiency aspects of the legislative process, and of tinkering with legislative programming, the Committee's ability to produce a report which enabled the emergence of legislative committees of this sort – something that governments have largely resisted – is testament not only to the role of the Leader of the House in convincing ministerial colleagues of the utility of the reforms, but also to the institutional development of the Modernisation Committee itself, and its growing ability to tackle such matters in a more independent and capable way.

This maturation of the Modernisation Committee is further underlined by its report on revitalising the role of the backbencher, published in June 2007 and overseen by Jack Straw (HC 337, 2006–7). Again, while this report ranged widely across the whole spectrum of the working life of a Commons backbencher, many of its most interesting recommendations relate to the role of backbenchers in the chamber, and ways of enhancing the contribution that they may make. Its key suggestions involved better incorporation of backbenchers into the work of the Commons through the creation of topical debates, improvements to the practice of urgent questions and urgent debates, the creation of opportunities for short debates, and more opportunities for backbenchers to initiate business. With time, such developments may well enhance the effectiveness of the Commons more generally by creating more pockets of space within the parliamentary schedule that belong to backbenchers, rather than government or opposition, and thereby facilitate the further improvement of backbench scrutiny capacity.

Conclusion

The work which characterised the Modernisation Committee agenda in the years after 2002, following the failure to reform the select committee nominations process, was very different from that which characterised it previously. There is no question that much of this is down to the role of the Leader of the House, and, in attitudinal-speak, the political will he or she possesses to pursue the cause of creating a more effective House of Commons. Prior to Robin Cook's time in the chair, no one at the helm of the Modernisation Committee was sufficiently motivated to pursue an agenda geared around effectiveness issues. Yet, this changed after 2001, with the presence in the chair of individuals such as Robin Cook, Peter Hain and Jack Straw, each of whom had very different views of parliament compared with someone like Margaret Beckett. The role of the Leader of the House was universally acknowledged by many different members on the Committee. As one Labour member commented, 'it depends on who is the Leader of the House, but the Shadow Leader of the House is also on the Committee' (interview, 19 June 2007). The presence of both of these important House figures is highly relevant: as this same Labour Committee member acknowledged, 'that keeps us away from pointless enquiries that aren't going to lead us anywhere, because they are part of the apparatus of the business of the House, and they know what the Whips' office is going to say'. A senior Conservative Committee member made a similar observation, noting that, 'in terms of controversial issues, it does depend very much on who is in the chair and the extent to which they are willing to work to ensure that their colleagues in government are going to take on board what the committee says' (interview, 19 June 2007). Yet, at the same time, this same member also remarked that:

> Having a cabinet member chair the committee is both an advantage and a disadvantage. The disadvantage is that there is a cabinet member chairing the committee. The advantage is that there is a cabinet member chairing the committee. And if you have a cabinet member chairing the committee, by definition they're not going to want the committee to come up with something the government isn't willing to accept. That can be an advantage, in that if they can sell committee proposals to government, then they will happen. The disadvantage is that, sometimes, more radical and interesting suggestions will come up, that won't become part of the committee's recommendations because it would be too far, and the government wouldn't accept it.

Nonetheless, after 2002, the battles of the early years of the Modernisation Committee – over legislative programming and sitting hours in particular – receded into the background, and what emerged was a far more sophisticated view amongst Committee members about their role within the Committee, and the role of the Committee within the House of Commons. In many ways, it is almost impossible to imagine the Modernisation Committee in its early years pursuing the kind of agenda which it did after 2002. The afore-mentioned Conservative Committee member remarked of its development 'there is a positive direction to it' (interview, 19 June 2007). This member added that:

> It has taken time for it to work out that it is a strategic committee, and that's partly because, when it was first set up, issues like sitting hours were at the forefront of everybody's mind, and it was seen as a modernisation issue, and that was what made its name, if you like. Once it had gone through that, and the programming issue, there was a sense to my mind of, well, what is its role? It has taken time for it to take these more strategic views.

While noting the role of the Leader of the House in this, we should also note the institutional maturation undergone by the Committee itself. Such maturation is different from saying that the Committee has evolved – the notion of evolution is not particularly helpful either descriptively or analyti-cally. In a strict biological sense, evolution happens because of accidental genetic transformations. Nothing accidental happened to the Modernisation Committee – it has not so much evolved as it has learned, and matured as a result of that learning. Although the members of the Committee change with each parliament, there remains a repository of institutional knowledge and experience which is unique to the Modernisation Committee, just as it is to any select committee. We cannot, of course, underestimate the role of the Leader of the House in this process. Yet, after Robin Cook, the Modernisation Committee was chaired by very different individuals to those who chaired it in its initial phase, and by those who possess very different perceptions of the roles of parliament and the parliamentarian. Kelso (2007b) argued that the government needs the Modernisation Committee far more than does the House of Commons, and this was certainly true of the Committee during the first five or six years of its existence. Yet, the reports from the Committee in 2006 and 2007 on the legislative process and the role of the backbencher respectively point to a far more complex institutional position than has perhaps been acknowledged thus far.

That is not to say that the later Modernisation Committee reports somehow radically alter the balance in power between government and parliament, nor that they are likely to produce sudden and remarkable improvements in the effectiveness of the Commons in holding the executive to account. They do not, and they will not. Indeed, they may even be described as enhancing the scrutiny capacity of the House without actually impacting on the operation of executive government (Flinders 2007: 178). While this may then lead us to suggest they are not therefore effectiveness changes as we have described them here, the fact is that things are rather more complicated than this. Indeed, these kinds of reforms lead to something which is more profound and, from an academic perspective, more inter-esting. They reveal that, as far as effectiveness reforms are concerned, process matters more than outcome. In the 2002 select committee reform episode, the outcome was not what the reformers had hoped for, and the central task of removing whip influence from the select committee nominations process ended largely in failure, even if other important reforms did proceed success-fully. Yet, while that may well have been a blow to reformers, and certainly to Robin Cook, the man who had championed the cause, the process of attempting to secure those reforms ultimately mattered more than the partially unsuccessful outcome. The process itself altered the institutional context in which the reform debate took place, if only modestly, and in so doing, subtly altered the developmental path on which the House of Commons had previously been travelling. This is true of the entire history of the select committee system, dating right back to the time of the specialised committees created in the 1960s. While each reform episode may not secure all the goals attached to it, the very existence of the process itself affects the institutional context in which it occurred, and weaves into the institutional fabric the threads of a future reform tapestry. This is not to say that change is necessarily incremental at Westminster – observers too casually claim this, because it means that we do not have to work too hard to explain change when it occurs. The creation of a departmental select committee system may well seem incremental against the background of a previous specialised committee system, but it is far from incremental against the background of an executive which has historically resisted such innovations.

What is clear from the story recounted here about select committee reform after 1997 is that, by adopting a historical institutionalist framework, we do not necessarily disadvantage ourselves in terms of explaining institu-tional change. Critics claim that the problem with the perspective is that it has to resort to exogenous events to explain change when it occurs. This is demonstrably not the case with select committee reform, which was prompted in the first instance by concerns voiced by senior backbench MPs on the Liaison Committee about the constraints placed on the committees, and which prevented them from scrutinising the executive effectively. The trigger for change in this respect was entirely endogenous to the institution concerned, and emerged as a consequence of the growing awareness of the deficiencies caused by the historical development of parliament. The Norton Commission and the Hansard Society Commission certainly played a key role in agenda-setting, but both came after the Liaison Committee had already demarcated the relevant issues and resolved to act. To the extent that these two groups were exogenous to parliament (and this if far from clear anyway, given their origins and personnel), they simply restated concerns that MPs had themselves already acknowledged. Furthermore, the key political leader during the reform episode, Robin Cook, was clearly embedded within the institution that was the object of change, and used the select committee he chaired to engineer a reform agenda for action. There is no question, in other words, that the parliamentary reform pursued in 2002 can be accounted for by anything other than endogenous reasons.

As with the emergence of the select committee system in the first place, the 2002 episode also prompts some rethinking of the whole notion of critical junctures in explaining institutional change. A critical juncture emerged in 2002, of that there can be no question. What does need refining from a historical institutional perspective, however, is what we expect to result from such a critical juncture. The wording of the term itself seems to invite the idea that institutional change will be immediate and substantial. The lessons from both 1979 and 2002 are that critical junctures do not always result in critical change, and that the implications of those changes that are secured are not felt immediately but are instead played out across a longer time span. The executive and the respective party leadership of both the government and opposition were successful in 2002 in preventing the most important parts of the reform programme from being implemented. Yet, in 1979, the government was successful in preventing payment for committee chairmen and other aspects of the embryonic committee system, which subsequently met with approval in 2002. So, too, may it be the case in time with the issue of select committee membership selection.

We can, therefore, understand change more fully if we appreciate that, at Westminster at least, the process of institutional change is more important than the outcome, because of the way it affects the institutional context in which it occurred. The consequences of what seem initially like minor, perhaps even cosmetic, changes only become apparent once the institutional ship has had sufficient time to sail further along its subtly deviated path and towards what eventually becomes a quite different institutional context from the one it departed. This is not only the case as far as House of Commons reform is concerned – it is also true of House of Lords reform.

7
Reform of the House of Lords 1900–97

Introduction

Throughout the twentieth century, arguments regarding reform of the second chamber were traditionally portrayed as concerning a battle between the House of Lords and the House of Commons, and discussions were frequently predicated on the assumption that the pre-eminence of the latter had to be preserved in any restructuring of the former. When executives wished to curtail the capabilities and powers of the second chamber, they argued that such restrictions were necessary in order to ensure the continued pre-eminence of the House of Commons. Generally, governments were drawn into Lords reform as a way to ensure that their ability to enact legislation was not impeded by the second chamber. During the twentieth century, successive governments argued that, due to the undemocratic nature of the House of Lords, it should not be able to restrain unduly the will of the popularly elected, democratic House of Commons: certainly, these were the arguments that underpinned the passing of the Parliament Acts in 1911 and 1949. However, when reformers then attempted to alter the undemocratic basis of the second chamber, and to deal with the question of the unelected membership, it was always the issue of democratic legitimacy that impeded them. Those who were against comprehensive changes to the composition of the House of Lords argued that any kind of democratic election for the second chamber would bestow legitimacy on it, and thus enable it to challenge the will of the Commons: such arguments were heard repeatedly in the reform 'episodes' of 1968–69 and again in 2002–3, the second of which is covered in the next chapter.

Historical institutionalism provides a useful lens through which to view the events surrounding reform of the House of Lords in the past century. The norms and values of the dominant elite inside Westminster have enabled executives successfully to argue for the restriction of the powers of the Lords in order to preserve their own position inside parliament. They have done so by reference to the argument concerning a lack of democratic legitimacy in the Lords, and the need to ensure the pre-eminence of the Commons. Simultaneously, these same norms and values have helped foster the belief among a number of interested actors that any reform of the composition of the Lords will ultimately weaken the strength of the Commons and compromise its status as the supreme parliamentary chamber. The democratic legitimacy argument, therefore, has been inverted in order to prevent reforms designed to make the Lords a more effective chamber, and discourse surrounding the reform debate has been underpinned by the normative argument regarding the pre-eminence of the Commons. That this is so is testament to the particular way in which the two Houses of Parliament developed through the centuries, as detailed in chapter two, and to the fact that the historical development of Westminster has hinged on executive authority residing in one particular chamber. The pre-eminence argument therefore reflects the norms and values of the executive in particular, rather than the Commons in general. The case is frequently made that reform of the second chamber constitutes a battle between Commons and Lords: this characterisation suits the purposes of successive governments, because it neatly obscures the real fault-line, which has always been drawn between parliament and the executive.

The norm of the pre-eminent Commons shaped the course of House of Lords reform throughout the last century, and it is this issue of pre-eminence that shapes both this chapter and the next. Nevertheless, the issues of efficiency and effectiveness explored in the context of House of Commons reform still have a significant role to play here. As this chapter demonstrates, when executives have made the case for maintaining the pre-eminence of the Commons, they have argued that the unelected second chamber should not be able to interfere with the will of the elected first chamber. However, due to executive dominance in the Commons, this is simply another way of saying that the unelected second chamber should not interfere with the will of the elected government. From this perspective, then, arguments about upholding the pre-eminence of the Commons are also arguments about securing an efficient parliament in which an allegedly illegitimate House of Lords does not frustrate the will of the executive and hold up its programme of business. Similarly, arguments for reforming the House of Lords have tended to proceed on the basis that a better constituted second chamber would be regarded as more legitimate, and therefore better able to contribute to parliamentary work. A second chamber whose composition was considered 'legitimate' would be perhaps then be considered a 'more equal' House, and consequently positioned to work in tandem with the House of Commons with the goal of holding the executive more fully to account. Overwhelmingly, those arguments in favour of a 'more legitimately' composed House of Lords are essentially arguments for a more effective parliament. As we shall see, efficiency reforms proposed for the House of Lords have often been initiated and secured by government, while effectiveness reforms have largely been opposed by executives, as well as by considerable numbers of MPs who adhere strongly to the norm of the pre-eminent Commons.

The battle joined: 1900–30

At the start of the twentieth century, the House of Lords 'was, above all else, a hereditary and partisan assembly' (Adonis 1993: 17). Contemporary observers of the British political system, such as Sidney Low, provide a useful insight into the position of the second chamber at that time, and into the kinds of reform packages being aired. He declared, for instance, that '[t]he strength of the House of Lords is in its weakness' (Low 1906: 217). The central problem with the Lords was that it possessed a not inconsiderable amount of power, but was restricted from using it because that power existed in convention alone: actually using those powers might provoke the Commons into removing them altogether. This political reality was compounded by the hereditary composition of the second chamber, which influenced the role of the Lords within the political system, and delineated any discussions about potential reform, as Low (1906: 218) explained:

> It is sometimes urged that while the House of Commons represents everybody, the House of Lords represents nobody. This is one of the reasons why, on the whole, the two Chambers get on so well together. Everybody and Nobody ... must find it hard to quarrel. But if a Second Chamber were established, which represented somebody, the case would be different. Everybody could quarrel with Somebody easily enough.

Low was nonetheless convinced that some compositional reform was required, and he advocated the introduction of life peers into the second chamber (to sit alongside the hereditary peers), who would bring valuable experience from different professions and walks of life, and thus enhance its representational credentials (Low 1906: 236–7). He was naturally aware that altering the basis upon which individuals sat in the House of Lords would have ramifications for its relations with the House of Commons, and that reform might convince the former that it was able legitimately to challenge the latter. Yet, Low considered this to be a valuable addition to the political system, on the grounds that there were already difficulties in securing effective accountability in the Commons, and he thought it no bad thing for the Lords to become the supreme 'ventilating chamber' (Low 1906: 247–9). For Low, reforming the composition of the second chamber was an important way to enhance the effectiveness of parliament as a whole.

Yet, even an unreformed House of Lords was more than able to perform its main function, which Low (1906: 223) considered to be ensuring 'that time is given for mature reflection on matters of importance.' Unknown, however, was the specific lengths to which the peers would go in order to fulfil this function:

> Might they throw out a first-class political measure after an ad hoc election? It depends on the real strength of ministers, and the extent to which they can be supposed to carry public opinion with them. The leaders of the Peers have to consider whether they are defying a popular sentiment, sufficiently intense to make itself felt decisively at the polls. They can act freely when they believe that the Government would be bound to 'take it lying down' and that it is in no condition to go to the country. (Low 1906: 223–4)

Although Low had a previous clash over Irish home rule in mind with this outline, he was scarcely to know that a similar confrontation between Commons and Lords was just around the corner, one which would test fully the conditions under which the Lords would oppose the Commons. Fundamentally, the crisis that ensued between 1909 and 1911 demonstrates exactly how parliamentary reform may be entertained as a mechanism to enhance executive power at Westminster. Stripping the second chamber of its powers – which is what happened – is a useful strategy for any executive that wishes to secure its legislation with the minimum of parliamentary interference. Furthermore, the episode highlights how that aspect of the Lords that most agitates reformers – its composition – is also that aspect which governments are reluctant to tackle.

The Liberal government and the 1911 Parliament Act

The Parliament Act of 1911, and the events surrounding its enactment, explains how the House of Lords was successfully stripped of much of its remaining powers in relation to the House of Commons. Reform was pursued as a means to secure a parliamentary context which ensured the efficient processing of government legislation, and in order to remove the ability of the second chamber to prevent the executive governing as it saw fit. The passing of the Parliament Act 1911 is one of the best examples of how governments can use their dominant position at Westminster to adapt the structured institutional context in a way that further consolidates that dominance.

When the Liberal Party was elected to government in 1906 with 400 seats, conflict with the Conservative-dominated House of Lords seemed likely (Shell 1988: 9). Despite their reduced numbers in the Commons, the Conservatives were dominant in the Lords, and it was from that chamber that they intended to thwart the new government (Wells 1997: 206). The Liberals were, however, unwilling to restrict their legislative goals in order to avoid confrontation with the House of Lords, and so the peers soon rejected a number a major bills on education and plural voting in 1906, and land valuation in 1907 (Rush 1999: 8; Jenkins 1989: 37–63). In 1907, the King's Speech issued a vague threat of constitutional reform if the Lords persisted in their behaviour, and a cabinet committee was established to examine the relationship between the two houses in more detail (Jenkins 1989: 48, 51). Campbell-Bannerman went on to issue a House of Commons resolution, which declared that 'it is necessary that the power of the other House should be so restricted by law as to secure that within the limits of a single Parliament the final decision of the Commons must prevail' (Jenkins 1989: 54). This veiled threat had little impact, and in 1908 the Lords rejected the government's Licensing Bill, knowing 'that this course would make a collision between the Houses unavoidable' (Smith 1992: 173–4).

In order to circumvent the possibility that something along the lines of the Campbell-Bannerman resolution might well be implemented, the peers got to work on their own proposals for reform of the second chamber (Lowell 1912: 429). A Lords select committee was established in June 1907 under the chairmanship of Lord Rosebery, and reported the following year. The committee based its reform proposals on three central axioms. First, admission to the Lords should not be based only on the hereditary principle. Second, members of the reformed chamber should be qualified by means of their experience. Third, reform should proceed on the basis of utility, not by comparisons with other second chambers elsewhere. The committee aimed to shift the emphasis of the debate away from the question of powers – then the preoccupation of the government – and towards the issue of composition. Yet, the committee members had difficulty detaching themselves from the hereditary principle (McKechnie 1909: 110), and the proposals were not dissimilar to those already outlined by Conservative peers at the end of the nineteenth century (Adonis 1993: 61–2). The reformed House proposed by the committee would still have been predominantly hereditary, and it was not entirely clear why they would be any more 'qualified' to sit there than they had been previously. Moreover, the committee failed to answer what was anyway the most pressing question at the time: how their reform plans would help improve the relationship between the two chambers (McKechnie 1909: 199).

By 1909, circumstances had worsened for the Liberal government: it was losing popular support, and more revenue was required to meet Exchequer commitments than had been anticipated. It was these considerations, rather than a desire to make a profound constitutional point, that led the government to the inevitable conclusion of a difficult, and controversial, budget package (Smith 1992: 174). Indeed, Jenkins (1989: 69) even argues that the aim of the 1909 budget was to avoid a protracted struggle with the Lords, rather than seek one out by delivering a package that the second chamber was forced to reject. The aim of the budget was not to precipitate constitutional mischief, but to secure the funds required by the government for its social legislation and restore its credibility (Adonis 1993: 144).

Yet, although the Lords had not rejected a Finance Bill in over 250 years, the Conservative leaders in the second chamber, Lansdowne and Balfour, eventually advocated rejection on the grounds not only that the budget discriminated against property, but that it would force a general election from which the Liberals would emerge dependent on the Irish in order to govern, leading to an Irish Home Rule Bill that would also be rejected by the Lords, leading to another general election that the Conservatives would win (Smith 1992: 175). The Lords consequently attached an amendment to the Finance Bill which indicated that their approval would only be forthcoming if the public endorsed the Liberal plans in a general election. The House of Commons passed a resolution (by 349 votes to 134), declaring the actions of the Lords to be unconstitutional, and parliament was quickly dissolved (Jenkins 1989: 108). Yet, the resulting election focused on the merits of the budget, not on the constitutional impasse (Jenkins 1989: 111), and the Liberals were returned to government, albeit relying on Labour and Irish support.

The January 1910 election, held directly because of the peers' rejection of the budget, served to make it more likely that the veto power of the second chamber would be removed. Once it became clear that reform would proceed, the Conservative peers once again began forwarding their own proposals for compositional restructuring, all of which were rejected by the Liberal government, who believed the election gave them the authority to deal specifically with the issue of powers (Smith 1992: 172). In March 1910, therefore, the government moved three resolutions in the House of Commons which were designed to form a basis for a future Parliament Bill. These stated that the Lords could not amend or reject money bills; that they would have a power of delay of two years over 'ordinary' legislation, with bills becoming law if they were unsuccessful after three attempts in the Lords; and that the maximum duration of a parliament should be five years, instead of seven (Jenkins 1989: 130). These resolutions were passed in April 1910, and a Parliament Bill was subsequently introduced, containing this much-quoted preamble:

> Whereas it is intended to substitute for the House of Lords as it at present exists a Second Chamber constituted on a popular instead of a hereditary basis, but such a substitution cannot immediately be brought into operation: And whereas provision will require hereafter to be made by Parliament in a measure effecting such substitution for limiting and defining the powers of the new Second Chamber, but it is expedient to make such provision as in this Act appears for restricting the existing powers of the House of Lords. (Quoted in Jenkins 1989: 135–6)

Much political manoeuvring took place in the summer of 1910, the bulk of which need not detain us here. A second general election in 1910, which again returned the Liberals to government, was taken (rightly or wrongly) as a vindication of the principles of the Parliament Bill. However, when the bill reached the House of Lords, it was all but eviscerated by the peers: the King then accepted the advice of the prime minister, Asquith, that new peers had to be created in order to enact the will of the people expressed at the ballot box (Shell 1988: 9). With this understanding reached with the monarch, the government was able convincingly to inform the Conservative leadership that continued truculence over the Parliament Bill would result in their number being diluted in the second chamber. Consequently, when the final Lords debate on the Parliament Bill was held in August 1911, the Conservative leadership succeeded in persuading a sufficient number of peers to abstain, rather than vote against it, and it passed by 131 votes to 114 (Southern 1986; Weston and Kelvin 1986).

Lowell (1912: 433) makes an important observation with regards to the Parliament Act:

> The act bears the marks of the conditions under which it was passed. It is an effort by the dominant party in the nation to remove a political grievance, not a methodical attempt to confer on a second chamber the powers appropriate to such a body in the parliamentary government of England. The Liberal majority could hardly suffer their policy on important questions to be thwarted by a house permanently under the control of their opponents, and if a referendum to be applied equally to the bills of both parties were not adopted, they curtailed the powers of the House of Lords no more than was necessary to secure the enactment of their measures within a reasonable time.

The lesson of the 1911 Parliament Act, and the events surrounding it, is that parliamentary reform almost always occurs as a means to an end, and is rarely ever the end in itself. Moreover, the decision of the Liberal government to ignore the question of composition was testament to the practical approach taken: the aim was to ensure that legislation could be passed be the government in the face of opposition from a traditionally Conservative-dominated House of Lords, and so was, above all else, about securing legislative efficiency at Westminster.

The Bryce Conference

The preamble to the Parliament Act indicated that the changes introduced were only intended to be temporary, and, in 1917, the Bryce Conference was established to consolidate reform. Lord Bryce, the Conference chairman, was a respected academic lawyer and politician, who organised the thirty-two leading political figures who worked alongside him so as to produce a report in 1918 (Cd 9038, 1918).

The Conference members agreed that the 1911 Parliament Act did not provide an adequate settlement in the long-term (Shell 1988: 10). They advocated a solution that bore many similarities to the scheme offered by the Conservative peers during the crisis years of 1909–11. The Conference report outlined four key functions performed by the second chamber (Wheeler-Booth 2003: 639). First, it should examine, and if necessary revise, bills coming up from the House of Commons. Second, it should initiate legislation of a non-controversial character. Third, it should inflict a degree of delay on bills in order to ascertain the opinion of the nation. Finally, it should facilitate the discussion of significant issues of the day, particularly when the House of Commons is prevented, for whatever reason, from having those discussions itself.

Yet, while the Bryce Conference was in agreement about these functions, it struggled to agree on how to reform the second chamber, and while recommendations were included in the report, these were not unanimously approved. The proposals hinged on there being two different bases for the composition of the Lords (Bromhead 1958: 261). First, there would be 246 members elected by the House of Commons. These would be based on geographical areas, and elected using the single transferable vote. Second, a joint committee of both Houses would elect eighty peers, with the membership being replaced on a rolling basis every four years. It was this principle of election by MPs that was rejected by the peers on the Bryce Conference, and which effectively hamstrung the entire report. The failure of the Conference to find consensus on the question of composition served to reinforce the outcome of the 1909–11 crisis, that any attempt to rationalise the membership would likely be detrimental for the Commons, and by extension, the executive that resided there.

The Coalition government pledged to persevere with Lords reform in its 1918 manifesto, and to create a chamber 'based on direct contact with the people' (Wheeler-Booth 2003: 639). However, as the Conference had failed to provide a solid plan to reform the chamber's composition, and in light of other pressures emanating from the end of the First World War, the impetus for change was decidedly lacking (Rush 1999: 9). However, the Conservatives continued to be interested in second chamber reform as a way of counteracting the effects of franchise extension (Close 1977: 909). The Commons debated the prospects for reform in 1922 and 1927, and even endorsed the tentative plans outlined by the Bryce Conference (Rush 1999: 9). However, there was still little progress, 'the basic reason being that the motivation for any change lay too transparently in the Conservatives' desire to enhance the legitimacy of the Lords so as to enable it to block the sort of legislation which a majority Labour government might introduce' (Shell 1988: 11). At any rate, the Conservatives were, in the 1920s, split regarding both the need for reform, and over the specific content of any reform package

(Close 1977: 911). On the Labour side, clear partisan motivations existed against reform. As the Lords had a natural Conservative majority, it would be difficult for it to use what powers remained to it, because this would leave it open to attack for its hereditary basis, and for opposing the will of the people (Wheeler-Booth 2003: 639). At any rate, although the Liberal Party was in steep decline by the 1920s, Labour failed to secure a clear majority at the elections of either 1924 or 1929, and so was unable to pursue radical legislation anyway (Shell 1988: 11).

The battle advanced: 1931–60

The general principles for reform, as outlined by the Bryce Conference in 1918, were still being debated in the 1930s, which proved to be a fertile time for discussions about institutional reform, as previous chapters have demonstrated. In the spring of 1934, there was a second reading debate in the House of Lords on a package proposed by Lord Salisbury, although the government refused to engage with it, claiming that only the executive had the authority to bring forward such constitutional measures (Bromhead 1958: 263–4). In late 1935, Lord Strickland urged piecemeal reform of the Lords, and the introduction of life peers, to avoid the abolition then being contemplated by the Labour party, although the government again remained uncommitted (Bromhead 1958: 264). In 1946, a 'group of Conservatives' outlined plans for reform, which were predicated on the assumption that the second chamber 'must not be the political rival of the House of Commons' and on the need to improve its representational credentials without introducing elections (Group of Conservatives 1946: 48). The Group fell in line with what many others had been arguing for some time, which was that life peers had to be created for the second chamber, mainly because this would help make it more representative of the nation as a whole, and because such peers would greatly aid the chamber in its scrutiny functions.

The Labour government and the 1949 Parliament Act

When Labour came to power in 1945, its aim was to enact the legislative commitments it had made in its manifesto, rather than engage in significant constitutional reform. Despite the new government's radical agenda, conflict with the second chamber was not as likely as it had been in the past, largely due to the Salisbury convention, which advised that the House of Lords should not block legislation that had formed part of the governing party's manifesto (Shell 1988: 11; Lascelles 1952: 206). Nevertheless, the government became increasingly concerned that the peers might oppose its legislation as the parliament neared its end (Morrison 1964: 184). It was particularly concerned about its Iron and Steel Bill, which, as a radical piece of socialist legislation, seemed certain to provoke opposition from the Conservative peers (Walters 2004: 229). In order to maximise the chances of securing this nationalisation legislation, the Labour government resolved to bring forward a second Parliament Bill that would reduce the Lords' delaying power from two years to one (Bromhead 1958: 265). Prior to the introduction of the bill, the Conservative peers, led by Lord Salisbury, succeeded in securing informal discussions with the government to explore how more comprehensive reform might proceed, including reform of the composition of the second chamber.

Consequently, representatives of both government and opposition from both chambers met between February and April 1948. In a reversal of the outcome of the Bryce Conference, these meetings found agreement about a reformed composition, but disagreement about the question of powers (Wheeler-Booth 2003: 641). The two main parties failed to agree on the length of the delaying power of the Lords, although they were only three months apart in their views (Morrison 1964: 201). Remarkably, everyone attending managed to agree on nine principles for a reformed composition: reform of the existing chamber was better than creating a new one; no party should have a majority in the Lords; hereditary status was an insufficient basis for membership; women should be permitted to sit in the House; peers should receive payment; peers who refused their seat in the Lords should be able to seek election to the Commons; and members should be subject to disqualification from the House under certain circumstances (Bromhead 1958: 267; Shell 1988: 12). Despite this wide-ranging agreement, the failure to agree on the question of powers meant that no working proposals for reform emerged from the informal discussions.

Thereafter, the government proceeded to use the 1911 Parliament Act to secure the new Parliament Bill, which became law in 1949. The decision further to restrict the delaying power of the second chamber was primarily aimed at safeguarding the ability of the Labour government to secure its legislation. As was the case in 1909–11, the nature of second chamber reform reflected the values of the dominant elite at Westminster. Although there had been agreement on the issue of composition, the fact that this facet of reform never really got off the ground is testament to the fact that the predominant concern at the time was simply to constrain the delaying power of the Lords, rather than explore ways of reforming it that might make it even more politically active. It was also indicative of the 'innate constitutional conservatism' of the Labour leadership, and that, on the whole, the government had been broadly successful in working with the upper house to secure its legislation (Thorpe 2001: 114).

Yet, the question of the composition of the second chamber did not necessarily go away: a Hansard symposium which looked at the matter extensively in 1954, drew the conclusion that there had to be a far more representative second chamber (Bailey 1954a). Furthermore, when the Conservatives returned to government between 1951 and 1964, they implemented several of the changes proposed through the inter-party talks of 1948. They introduced expenses payment for peers, for example, a relatively minor reform which nonetheless brought about a change in the way the Lords approached their parliamentary work (Shell 1988: 13). More significant was their decision to enable women to sit in the upper house, and to allow peers to seek election to the Commons. These were piecemeal changes, but they did help strengthen the status of the chamber. Furthermore, instituting these changes meant the party did not have to engage too vigorously with the issue of the hereditary principle, the abandonment of which would significantly impact on Conservative numbers in the upper house (Wheeler-Booth 2003: 641). Overall, the kinds of changes pursued by the Conservative government at this time were of a 'modernising' sort, which did not dramatically enhance the effectiveness of the chamber in scrutinising the government in the short or mid-term, but which did contribute to the task of updating Britain's political institutions and infrastructure, which was a key trend of the time. With these gradual changes, and the subsequent improvement in the ability of the House to fulfil its various functions, the argument was increasingly heard that there was no need to reform the upper house at all (Lascelles 1952: 212). The Lords were sitting longer than ever before in the period 1951–64 (Punnett 1965: 85), and with the chamber apparently performing well, the only substantial criticism that could be levelled at it was the principled one that it was composed on a hereditary basis and dominated by one party (Lascelles 1952: 213). The former was an argument that the Conservatives soon attempted to extinguish.

The 1958 Life Peerages Act

The Lords themselves had been promoting the idea of life peerages prior to 1958. Aside from the general championing of the idea by some senior peers, bills had even been introduced unsuccessfully to establish life peers by Viscount Elibank in 1929, Lord Rockley in 1935, Lord Strickland in 1937, and Viscount Simon in 1953, that latter of which secured a government commitment to further reform discussions (Bailey 1954b: 119). The goal of the government in introducing life peers was to enhance the legitimacy of the second chamber without actually removing the hereditary peers which were so important to their dominance of the upper house. The reform was pursued for very strategic reasons of political expediency, rather than because of a principled approach to reform worked out along constitutional lines. The politics of the manoeuvre were not lost on the Labour Party, and its leaders 'made clear their suspicion that the Government's main intention was to enhance the prestige of the Lords, while retaining the hereditary principle' (Shell 1988: 14). Once the bill was enacted, the Labour Party view changed, particularly once it was returned to office and able to reinforce the Labour ranks in the House of Lords through the creation of new life peers (Wheeler-Booth 2003: 641). Although the introduction of life peerages did not impact upon the party balance in the Lords in terms of divisions, it did help 'to enhance the administrative and party usefulness of the House to the Labour party' (Vincent 1966: 476).

The Conservative gamble undoubtedly paid off, and in the years following the Life Peerages Act, a profound change took place in the ethos and status of the House of Lords (Rush 1999: 11). The Conservatives lost their substantial majority over time, but remained the single largest party in the Lords. The pay-off was that the House became a far more professional place, particularly when coupled with the previous changes, such as the payment of expenses. As the House became more professional in its outlook, its workload increased, and the expertise of the chamber expanded thanks to the influx of new members from a broad range of professions (Wheeler-Booth 2003: 641). The Life Peerages Act therefore served to enhance the overall effectiveness of the second chamber, to improve the effectiveness of its participation in parliamentary work, and, over time, it served to improve the ability of parliament to scrutinise the executive, even if it did not lead to a significant rebalancing of executive-legislative relations. Yet, the original Conservative aim of preserving the hereditary peers was also fulfilled: the contribution of the new life peers enabled the House to perform its various functions with greater ability, and, over time, its obvious contribution to the effective functioning of parliament made it increasingly difficult to argue for a comprehensive reassessment of the powers and composition of the chamber.

A new front in Lords reform: 1961–97

Consequently, despite the promises of the 1911 Parliament Act, there had been no attempt to tackle together the issues of the powers and composition of the House of Lords. The hereditary peers remained, and the 1958 Life Peerages Act simply supplemented their number, and did not intimate a wholesale reassessment of the basis on which the second chamber was constituted. For academic observers, the problem with reforming the House of Lords was quite clear:

> No lasting solution to the resulting set of anomalies, contradictions, privileges and inefficiencies will be achieved until both political parties are willing to look, not just at the question of powers and composition of the Chamber, either separately – which has been foolish enough – or even together, which has been deliberately avoided, but at the basic questions of the function and utility of the Second Chamber in the context of the work of Parliament as a whole, indeed of the whole framework of British government and administration. (Crick 1963: 174)

Yet, the 1960s became the decade in which British institutions were examined and found wanting. As Chapter 5 explained, Richard Crossman, as Leader of the House of Commons, had already embraced the demand for reform in the lower chamber. As a contemporary observer noted, '[a]lthough the [Labour] government would doubtless prefer not to be involved in radical reconstruction of the Second Chamber, there is a mounting demand for modernisation of all Parliamentary institutions' (Weare 1965: 432). The constitutional situation of the House of Lords left it almost ripe for reform:

> On one side, it can be said that the continued possession of even these powers by a House so constituted is inherently objectionable; on the other hand that, because the powers are unsatisfactory and unlikely to be used, there is no really worthwhile role for the House to perform in modern government (Bromhead and Shell 1967: 337).

The Labour government and the Parliament (No. 2) Bill

Despite, or perhaps even because of, such 'ripeness', there nevertheless followed one of the most remarkable disasters in the history of British constitutional reform, expertly chronicled by Morgan (1975). The new Labour government elected in 1964 was largely unenthusiastic about second chamber reform, although it had formed an exploratory committee to examine the specific case of removing the Lords' delaying powers. Rumours of this committee and its work concerned Conservatives in both the Commons and the Lords, and the party stated its commitment to pursuing reform on an inter-party basis. Labour proponents of reform became convinced that the Conservatives might well abandon the hereditary membership, and the possibility of a reform package that dealt with both powers and composition began to seem a real possibility. Senior Labour MPs, such as Richard Crossman, who believed that a genuine cross-party endeavour might be feasible, convinced their more sceptical cabinet colleagues that any future Lords reform had to encompass both powers and composition (Morgan 1975: 171–4).

On this highly speculative basis of senior party figures trying to second-guess the intentions of their colleagues across the Dispatch Box did this particular episode of Lords reform begin. The Labour cabinet committee already in existence had very restricted terms of reference, which did not include compositional issues, but Labour reformers had successfully expanded the party's chosen sphere of action on the grounds that the Conservative party might well be willing to work with them, and it was on this basis that a window of opportunity opened up across the two parties for reform. An inter-party conference was established in the autumn of 1967, which had by the following spring reached agreement on the proposed delaying powers of a reformed second chamber as well as its composition (Morgan 1975: 183). The chamber should not be allowed to delay legislation for more than six months, and the new composition would be based on a two-tier approach of voting life peers and non-voting hereditary peers, with the latter gradually being erased from the House over time by preventing heirs taking up their seats. Yet, although the conference had reached these agreements, it was not guaranteed that the parties as a whole would accept the proposals, nor was it clear that even the conference representatives from both houses were willing to act together as far as reform was concerned: indeed, '[f]or Commons' delegates, reform was not a central part of their legislative lives; for the Lords it had become a vital and urgent duty' (Morgan 1975: 189). Sensing that the moment for reform may quickly pass, the pro-reform conference delegates quickly drafted a white paper based on the conclusions thus far reached, in the hope that it could pass through parliament before the political climate changed.

Political expediency then intervened to shatter the inter-party conference altogether. The Conservative leadership in the Lords, under pressure from their backbenchers who could sense the legislative difficulties that the Labour government was getting itself into, was compelled to allow the defeat of the Southern Rhodesia (United Nations Sanctions) Order in the summer of 1968 (Wheeler-Booth 2003: 641). The government consequently announced the demise of the conference, and pledged to proceed unilaterally with its own plans for Lords reform (Morgan 1975: 194). Yet the government was already locked into a reform path from which it could not escape: it had been unwilling initially to examine the issue of composition, but it was now compelled to do so. The defeat of the Southern Rhodesia Order served to confirm to the Labour leadership that their biggest problem was not the delaying powers of the second chamber, but its hereditary, Conservative-leaning composition.

The government published its own white paper in November 1968 (Cmnd 3799, 1968), which outlined four principles on which reform should be based. First, the second chamber should not rival the Commons. Second, the composition and powers of the Lords prevented it performing its various duties. Third, reform had to be geared towards creating a more efficient parliament in general. Finally, a reformed second chamber should be able to work in a more co-ordinated and integrated way with the Commons. These principles informed five key objectives of reform, which comprised the elimination of the hereditary membership, the removal of a permanent majority for any party, the creation of a working majority for the governing party, the restriction of the power of delay over legislation, and the removal of the veto over subordinate legislation. The government supported the two-tier system of voting and non-voting peers agreed by the inter-party conference, and also rejected arguments for direct or indirect election to the Lords because, with such a membership base, it would 'inevitably become a rival to the House of Commons' (para. 22).

Despite these apparently determined government views on the future path of second chamber reform, many Labour backbenchers and cabinet ministers were either completely indifferent to the proposals or actively disliked them (Morgan 1975: 203). Indeed, it is likely that the reform package was doomed even before the introduction of the Parliament (No. 2) Bill:

> Though it was no fault of the reformers, the breaking off of talks had been a major mistake. And to proceed with the 'agreed' non-partisan measure in an atmosphere of party rancour, without the declared support of the whip on both sides of the Commons, was indeed imprudent. Furthermore, whether in unconscious escapism or remote preoccupation, or even sheer failure of political sensitivity, the reformers were unaware of the strength of backbench hostility. Their scheme was itself incredibly complicated and, to those who had not created it, probably bizarre. To many members of the Commons, the Lords might have been inhabitants of some other planet; a similar separation now seemed to exist between the world of the reformers and that of down-to-earth backbench MPs. The career of the Parliament (No. 2) Bill had brought two worlds into collision and every tactical error reached fruition. (Morgan 1975: 208)

The bill was eventually undone on the floor of the House of Commons, where it had to take its committee stage because of its constitutional ramifications, by an unlikely political alliance between Enoch Powell and Michael Foot. The filibustering orchestrated by these two MPs provided a platform for every critic of the bill, ranging from those who opposed any rationalisation of the Lords composition on the grounds that it would allow the peers to challenge the House of Commons, to those who worried that a fully appointed chamber would be little more than a tool of prime ministerial patronage (Longford 1999: 172; Shell 1988: 19). Aware that the derailed Parliament (No.2) was playing havoc with the rest of its legislative programme, the government eventually withdrew it.

In this particular attempt at parliamentary reform, then, the conditions required for success were never really met. There was initially a small window of opportunity, opened by the overtures of the Conservative party and exploited by Labour reformers, but it never opened wide enough. Political leadership was sporadic, and while there was a key group of reformers, they were mostly peers who were divorced from the realities of party politics in the Commons, and the key Commons' figure, Richard Crossman, was no longer Leader of the House by the time the bill was introduced. There was a reform agenda, but it seemed complex and irrational to those who had not been involved in constructing it. Most importantly, there simply was not enough political will to take reform forward, and as a consequence, when the bill did come before the Commons, it did so without any group of reformers really championing it, rendering it an easy target for its opponents.

A new functional legitimacy in the House of Lords

Despite the fact that the attempt to reform the second chamber at the end of the 1960s ended in total failure, the House of Lords had at least welcomed the proposed changes: the continued unreformed state of the Lords was not due to the peers themselves, but to the total inability of the House of Commons and of the government to act in a decisive way. Yet the episode also neatly underlined the peers' impotence with regards to the composition issue: if there was to be any reform of the second chamber, it was clear it would not come as a result of the activism of the Lords. The result was that the House of Lords began a gradual process of examining its functions and procedures. The failed white paper of 1968–69 had included the suggestion that the Lords may in future institute select committees and engage with detailed law reform, as part of an attempt to rationalise the work of parliament as a whole. Therefore, as the contributions of the life peers expanded over time as their numbers grew, the ambitions of the House broadened accordingly, and the idea became more attractive of engaging proactively with its scrutiny function in the ways suggested by the failed white paper. The UK's membership of the European Community offered a particularly good opportunity for the House of Lords to become more skilled in its scrutinising functions (Shell 1988: 186). Over time, the House of Lords European Community Committee, in its various manifestations, served at least partially to correct the absence of Commons work in this area (Shell 1988: 191). Its expansive use of sub-committees enabled many peers to be involved in scrutiny work, and committee reports were successful in informing and influencing ministers (Shell 1992a: 281). The Lords Science and Technology Committee similarly succeeded in providing scrutiny in an area that was traditionally overlooked by the Commons, and has published reports which have influenced government policy and set the political agenda (Grantham 1992: 295–8). The establishment and expansion of Lords select committees contributed to the effectiveness of parliament overall, and illustrate the way that institutions can change and innovate as a way of addressing their various limitations, in this case, the limitation being that the existence of the Lords always be predicated on its inferiority to the Commons. Consequently, the House of Lords has engineered for itself a crucial role within the political system, and its scrutiny capacity is such that governments increasingly rely on it to perform those aspects of legislative scrutiny for which the House of Commons simply does not have time (Shell 1999: 2000). Yet there is a paradox: at the end of the twentieth century, the House of Lords remained 'a blatant contradiction of democratic principle' but nevertheless performed an indispensable role in British politics (Shell 1999: 200). It became an effective part of Westminster in response to the persistent reluctance of successive governments to tackle the composition of the second chamber because they feared that to do so would enhance the status of the Lords to the detriment of the Commons.

Conclusion

The twentieth century witnessed a shift in emphasis in the House of Lords. It shifted from what was, to modern eyes at least, a strange appendage at Westminster, to a chamber that sought to complement the work of the House of Commons and to challenge the government when the lower chamber did not seem to be properly doing so. These shifts occurred as a consequence of the desire of the House of Lords to ensure it remained a significant part of the institution of parliament despite its archaic composition. As Baldwin (1999: 41) summarises:

> [The House of Lords] is a product of history. It has not been made; it has grown. Herein lies the key to why the House of Lords, this curious institution which has been the subject of a protracted, often ritual, campaign of abuse, is still in existence; the key to why it has not only remained, in essence, untouched by the hand of whole-scale reform, but also to why it has not fallen victim to inward decay; they key to why the House of Lords can correctly be depicted as the perennial survivor. It is because it has an inherent evolutionary adaptability.

The role of the Conservative membership of the Lords in securing the success of this evolutionary adaptability is noteworthy. The growth and development of the upper chamber into a *functionally* legitimate part of the political system was not the result of good fortune on the part of the peers. Rather, it was the outcome of a clear Conservative strategy, dating back over one hundred years, to counteract the fact that the chamber is not *democratically* legitimate.

Moreover, this approach benefited from the relative failure of attempts to address simultaneously the powers and composition of the House of Lords. In 1911 and 1949, the central concern of the executive was to remove the ability of the Lords to impede its governing capacity, and thus to secure maximum parliamentary efficiency and strengthen executive sovereignty. This was done with reference to the undemocratic basis of the second chamber, and its illegitimacy in challenging the Commons. From the perspective of the executive, leaving the composition of the Lords, and its democratic illegitimacy, well alone, constrained the ability of the chamber to use what powers remained to it, thus creating a smoother path for government legislation to traverse. A lack of compositional reform also meant that the effectiveness of the second chamber in holding the executive to account remained curtailed. In 1968–69, the government attempted to reform both powers and composition, yet it was the latter of these on which MPs fixated: backbenchers objected to the proposed reforms for a variety of reasons, but most were underpinned by the argument that any change to the composition of the second chamber would inevitably impact on the pre-eminence of the first. The structured institutional context at Westminster, predicated as it is on defending a strong executive, helped rationalise the idea that a more effective House of Lords would belittle the status of the House of Commons, and with it, the executive that resides there. What is perhaps most remarkable is that the 1969 bill did not advocate any kind of democratic election to the Lords, proposing instead a system of nomination by the prime minister. It was therefore hard to argue that a second chamber reformed on such a basis would be any more democratically legitimate than it had been before. Certainly, some MPs did reject the idea of a wholly appointed chamber because of the opportunities it would afford in terms of patronage, and the power that it would give to the prime minister and the whips. Yet, the failure of the bill to progress as a result of concerns that reform would provide a basis for the House of Lords to challenge the pre-eminence of the House of Commons is testament to the strength of the norms and values that structure the political realities of Westminster and which define the parameters within which MPs engage with reform debates.

By the 1990s, there were two clear 'obstacles' in the way of reformers who wished to rationalise both the powers and the composition of the House of Lords. First, the continued strength of the pre-eminence argument appeared difficult to surmount. Executives had used the absence of democracy in the Lords as grounds for reforming its powers, but had also used the democratic basis of the Commons as grounds for *not* reforming the composition of Lords. This inversion of the democratic legitimacy argument, in order to defend the norm of a pre-eminent Commons, therefore made Lords reform a conceptually difficult issue. Second, the Lords were aware of their problematic composition and how it inhibited them from using their powers fully. They therefore embarked on a process of functional renewal, and, by the early 1990s, the chamber attracted applause for its work, its expertise, and the independence provided by the cross-bench members. By the end of the century, therefore, the Lords still attracted criticism for the same reasons as at the start of the century: their hereditary composition and their dominance by one party. However, the newly found functional legitimacy of the chamber, and the continued strength of the pre-eminence argument, meant that the way forward for reform remained unclear.

How does a historical institutionalist perspective help us analyse House of Lords reform prior to 1997? Its main strength in this instance is its emphasis on institutional persistence: despite attempts to remove them, the hereditary peers remained, and so a key aspect of the institutional make-up of the second chamber also remained. There was, in other words, insufficient political will in the House of Commons generally and in the executive specifically to do anything about composition. There were actors (or agents) in both Houses who did want reform, and there was an abundance of ideas about what reform should accomplish. However, these agents of reform ultimately stumbled, particularly in 1969, because the ideas about reform which they promoted were not compelling to those around them. By contrast, the significant changes secured in both 1911 and 1949 not only had the support of actors who were the dominant elite in parliament, they managed to convince others of the merits of the ideas that they promoted – namely, the idea that the powers of the second chamber should not be such that they could impede the capabilities of the Commons. The idea of restricting the powers of the Lords always seemed more convincing than the idea of overhauling the composition of the Lords, mainly because the outcome of the former could be predicted more easily than could the latter. The main obstacle to pursuing reform of the Lords composition has always been the multitude of unknowns associated with the various plans that have been forwarded in terms of their impact on the House of Commons. Consequently if the outcome of these reform ideas is unclear or contested, the persistence of this institutional feature is far more likely than is change. The idea that the Commons must remain pre-eminent was always more valued than any reform plans that might undermine it. Indeed, the contested nature of ideas about reforming the Lords composition, and controversy about the likely impact of reform plans, continued to characterise the debate once the Labour Party gained power in 1997.

8
Reform of the House of Lords since 1997

Introduction

The Parliament Acts of 1911 and 1949 successfully curtailed the powers of the House of Lords in order to ensure that the executive could secure its legislative programme, and thus enhance the efficiency of parliament. The failed attempt at reform in 1968–69 served to underline the extent to which MPs equated compositional reform of the Lords with a threat to the pre-eminence of the House of Commons, and in turn contributed to the second chamber undergoing a process of functional renewal in the absence of more comprehensive reform. The notion that the House of Commons must remain pre-eminent is an institutional norm derived from the structured institutional context at Westminster, and there has consequently been a path dependency inherent in the development of the second chamber with respect to the principle that it must be subordinate. The pre-eminence argument was used by the Liberal and Labour governments in order to defend the Parliament Acts which reduced the powers of the second chamber. Furthermore, the pre-eminence argument was utilised in order to thwart reform in 1968–69, and to remove the possibility that the hereditary composition of the second chamber would be changed, and thus made (depending on the criteria employed) more legitimate. Other ideas about the reform of the Lords simply lacked the ability to upset the accepted constitutional wisdom about Commons pre-eminence.

This chapter aims to outline the course of House of Lords reform since 1997, and the Labour government's immersion in these often choppy constitutional waters. It again employs historical institutional theory as a lens through which the events may be analysed, and the language of the attitudinal and contextual approaches in order to understand what did and did not happen. The attitudinal approach, while setting out the conditions required for reform to succeed, also places a great deal of emphasis on the presence of political will, which the contextual approach indicates will often be lacking because of the way that institutional norms and values structure political life at Westminster, and shape the logic of appropriateness used by MPs to determine their goals and actions. While the attitudinal approach places great store on the willingness of actors to place a premium on altering their institutional existence, the contextual approach by contrast absorbs the lessons of historical development and its impact on institutional formation to account for why reform does not always proceed as might be expected.

New Labour commits to Lords reform

Despite the creation of numerous Labour life peers, Conservative dominance in the House of Lords had been insufficiently dented by the early 1990s as far as the Labour party was concerned, and the leadership was convinced that some reform of the Lords composition was needed to address the situation. In its 1992 manifesto, the party committed to a directly elected Lords (Labour Party 1992), with Gordon Brown arguing at the time 'for an elected second chamber in place of the anachronism which is the House of Lords' (Brown 1992: 394). The House of Lords scholar Donald Shell, while reflecting on the future of second chamber reform, remarked at that time that the model of the 1958 Life Peerages Act could offer a way forward. The Act was carried through by the Conservatives with almost no cross-party support and, more importantly, as a stand alone measure (Shell 1992b: 350). Shell argued that the government could introduce similar legislation in order to remove the hereditary peers, and only then consider how to build a House containing both life and elected peers. This approach seemed enticing. Publicly, the party remained committed to an elected chamber, but reports of a change in Labour's policy soon attracted attention. Former Labour MP Dick Leonard, for example, worried that a future Labour government 'will shirk the challenge of replacing the House of Lords by an at least partly elected body and will confine itself to the short-term expedient of removing hereditary peers, leaving the House as a wholly appointed body' (Leonard 1995: 287).

The 1997 Labour manifesto commitment on Lords reform is one of political pragmatism, and a testament to the institutional norms already guiding the party as it anticipated entering office:

> The House of Lords must be reformed. As an initial, self-contained reform, not dependent on further reform in the future, the right of hereditary Peers to sit and vote in the House of Lords will be ended by statute. This will be the first *stage* in a process of reform to make the House of Lords more *democratic* and *representative*. The legislative powers of the House of Lords will remain unaltered. (Labour Party 1997, emphasis added)

The manifesto committed to a review of the appointment of life peers, to maintain the presence of cross-bench peers, and to work towards a situation where no one party would have a majority in the second chamber. As far as the second stage of reform was concerned, a joint committee of both Houses was promised 'to undertake a wide-ranging review of possible further change and then to bring forward proposals for reform' (Labour Party 1997). This two-stage approach aimed to combine the political goal of ejecting the hereditary peers with the appearance of working towards a more conclusive settlement.

The attitudinal approach to parliamentary reform argues that there must be a window of opportunity for reform to take place. The start of a new parliament, particularly if there has just been a change of government, is considered prime time to embark on reform, and so the massive Commons majority enjoyed by Labour as it entered government in 1997 marks the opening of just such a window of opportunity. However, Labour came to power with many other constitutional reform commitments, and devolution for Scotland and Wales took precedence. In addition, despite the manifesto commitment to the removal of the hereditary peers, it is not clear that the new government had anything even approaching a firm idea about what it wanted to achieve from any eventual stage two of the reform process, which helps account for why stage one was not immediately embarked upon (Shell 2000: 297). The decision to postpone reform of the House of Lords until a later session had a profound impact on the course of second chamber reform. Not only did it affect the ability of the government to remove the hereditary peers, it threw into turmoil the tentative content of the nascent stage two. The decision to delay reform gave the decimated Conservatives time to regroup and formulate a plan to challenge the removal of the hereditary peers (Wheeler-Booth 2003: 655).

A new approach to Lords reform emerges

In the Queen's Speech of 1998, the government laid out its plans for House of Lords reform. The first stage to remove the hereditary peers would be carried forward, and work would begin also on the second stage. The government pledged to 'publish a White Paper setting out arrangements for a new system of appointments of life Peers and establish a Royal Commission to review further changes and speedily to bring forward proposals for reform' (HL Debs, 24 November 1998, col. 4). The new emphasis was in part the result of the fact the government had relinquished 'the overwhelming political advantage which it had enjoyed in the immediate aftermath of the general election' (Wheeler-Booth 2003: 655), and in part the result of the subsequent rethinking of the merits of a joint committee approach, largely because of the opportunities it might afford for other parties to press for

ical reforms in order to embarrass the government. A Royal
,ion seemed prudent because such a mechanism would permit the
1ent far more control over its scope, work and personnel.

Conservatives fully exploited the political potential of the new
situation. In his response to the Queen's Speech, Conservative leader William
Hague castigated the government for proceeding with 'constitutional
vandalism' by removing the hereditary peers before hearing the conclusions
drawn by the promised Royal Commission (HC Debs, 24 November 1998,
col. 24). He argued that 'the reason the Prime Minister does not want to wait
for the Royal Commission is clear: he has never intended carrying out proper
reform of the House of Lords, but wants to create a house of cronies
beholden to him alone' (col. 24).

Whatever was assumed of the prime minister's attitude towards reform,
the fact remained that the government was divided over the issue. Lord
Richard, Leader of the House of Lords in 1998, was permitted to consult
secretly with Lord Cranborne, Opposition Leader in the Lords, to explore the
possibility of a 'big bang' approach to reform (Cockerell 2001: 120). Several
cabinet ministers consequently became concerned that the discussion was
proceeding on the assumption that there should be an elected element in the
Lords (Shell 2000: 298). Indeed, Lord Richard was himself committed to a
substantial elected membership in the second chamber, as his later publications made clear (Richard and Welfare 1999), and was consequently sacked
in the summer of 1998 in order to avoid a cabinet fracture (Shell 2000: 298).

At the end of January 1999, a white paper was finally published, which
outlined the government's approach to the second chamber, and which
indicated what its reformed composition might ultimately look like (Cm
4183, 1999). Any thoughts of an entirely elected upper house were
abandoned. The white paper pointed instead to a mixed House, which would
contained predominantly nominated members along with either directly or
indirectly elected members. It also pledged to institutionalise the conventions
regulating use of the Lords' powers, and made a commitment to examine
how the second chamber might be linked into the newly devolved assemblies
and with the European Parliament.

The House of Lords Bill and the Weatherill amendment

Work to remove the hereditary peers got underway soon after the Queen's
Speech in November 1998. Baroness Jay, Leader of the Lords, outlined the
reasons why the government had chosen to approach Lords reform in two
stages:

> By trying to do the whole package at once, by saying we will get rid of the
> hereditary peers and then do the long term reform of the House, the short term

reform, getting rid of the hereditary peers, would have got bogged down because nobody could agree about the long term. So what we said right from the start on this occasion was, we get rid of the hereditary peers, we clear the ground. We get rid of that vested interest of people who while they're here will always vote for nothing to change, and then we can have a sensible debate and sensible proposals and sensible action on the long term solutions. (Cockerell 2001: 122)

Although the opposition parties were critical of proceeding with stage one of reform without first knowing what stage two would contain, secret talks had already begun through the usual channels to secure the removal of the hereditary peers. The Lord Chancellor, Derry Irvine, and the Leader of the Opposition in the Lords, Lord Cranborne, bargained to allow some of the hereditary peers to remain in the House, and a deal was concluded allegedly without the consent or knowledge of the Conservative leader, William Hague (Cockerell 2001: 23–5). Lord Cranborne was consequently sacked, yet his successor, Lord Strathclyde, had not only known about the deal, but was instructed to see it through and to save ninety-two of the hereditary peers from expulsion (Shell 2000: 301). Former Speaker of the Commons, Bernard Weatherill, proposed the Cranborne-Derry agreement as an amendment, to lend it a non-partisan appearance (Shell 2000: 300). The announcement of the amendment to provide for the survival of ninety-two hereditary peers in the transitional House was made in December 1998, and the government subsequently indicated that it would accept the amendment so long as the peers did not 'unreasonably impede' its legislative programme (HL Debs, 11 May 1999, col. 1093) or 'frustrate' the progress of the House of Lords Bill (HL Debs, 27 July 1999, col. 1415). The amendment nevertheless caught many Labour backbenchers by surprise, as the retention of any hereditary peers clearly breached the party's manifesto commitment, and for those in favour of a more democratic second chamber, the turn of events did not bode well for the future (Shell 2000: 303).

The House of Lords Bill received royal assent on 11 November 1999, with the Conservatives abstaining from the Lords vote. Elections were held for the ninety-two peers who were to remain, based on rules established by the Lords Procedure Committee (HL 81, 1998–99). In an ironic way, these elections fulfilled the wish of the reformers of the late nineteenth century who wanted to reform the chamber's composition by having elections so that the most qualified peers would remain in the Lords if voted for by their colleagues.

The Royal Commission

The twelve-member Royal Commission on Reform of the House of Lords was appointed in February 1999, with the chairman, Lord Wakeham, chosen to build consensus (Wheeler-Booth 2003: 658). His experience as Leader of the House in both the Commons and the Lords, and as Chief Whip in the Thatcher government, afforded him considerable insight into how both Houses worked and what kind of reform was politically palatable to the parties. The Commission membership drew on members of the main political parties, and also included academics, trade unionists and religious figures. It was given nine months in which to complete its mammoth task.

The Commission report, published in January 2000, explained the way in which the job at hand had been tackled:

> We began our work by looking at the *roles* which the reformed second chamber could play. We then considered the *powers* it should have and the specific *functions* it should perform. Our conclusions on these matters gave us the basis for deter- mining the *characteristics* which the reformed second chamber should possess and it was this assessment that shaped our recommendations on how the second chamber should be *constituted*. (Cm 4534, 2000: 2; original emphasis)

The Commission therefore claimed to start from first principles and ask what is perhaps the most important question lying at the heart of House of Lords reform: what is the purpose and role of the second chamber in the political system? Of course, stating that such an approach was adopted does not mean that is actually what happened: the truth is that taking this first principles approach in fact involves traversing a political minefield. Indeed, the report indicates that the Commission struggled fully to integrate this first principles approach with the criteria that the Commons remain pre-eminent. For example, the report states that the Commission was keen to 'allay fears' that a reformed second chamber 'could undermine the pre-eminence of the House of Commons as the United Kingdom's primary democratic forum' (Cm 4534, 2000: 2), and therefore attempted to address this concern in the context of its approach of looking at roles, functions and powers. The task, indeed, was to build a second chamber 'with the authority and confidence to function effectively and use its powers wisely', but always in the context of institutional norms which prioritised preserving the status of the Commons (Cm 4534, 2000: 3). The parameters of the Commission's work were set out by the government white paper, which emphasised it having 'regard to the need to maintain the position of the House of Commons as the pre-eminent chamber of Parliament' (Cm 4183, 1999). The work of the Commission was therefore underpinned first and foremost, not by a desire to enhance the working relationship between the two parliamentary chambers, but by a desire to ensure that relationship was always couched in terms of superiority and inferiority.

Although the Commission claimed it set out to look at all aspects of the existence of the House of Lords, the fact remains that much of its focus, and most of its recommendations, centred on the issue of composition. The

Commission wished to see a chamber that was 'authoritative, confident and broadly representative of the whole of British society' (Cm 4534, 2000: 6) and its recommendations were largely predicated on the assumption that reforming its composition in particular ways would in turn bring about the authority, confidence and representativeness that it sought. The Commission laid particular emphasis on the value of the expertise, knowledge and skills of the life peers, and on the need to preserve those characteristics as reform proceeded. Debate about the source of authority itself became a key issue for the Commission, and its public evidence session illustrated the variety of opinion that existed about how political authority could be obtained:

> While many who gave evidence took it as an axiomatic truth that political authority flowed from the democratic electoral process alone, others agreed that the ballot box was not the sole valid basis for authority, and that there were other valid justifications for the exercise of political authority, without any basis of election ... A second chamber with an appropriate composition for the performance of its expert, independent and 'value-added' functions pointed away from a House of elected, salaried politicians and instead to a system of choice which provided a different kind of parliamentarian to those in the Commons. (Wheeler-Booth 2003: 659)

The variety of arguments regarding the basis of political authority naturally impacted on the subsequent Commission proposals, which demonstrated the shift that had taken place away from the idea of a reformed second chamber that could only be considered legitimate if it was democratic towards the idea that it could also be legitimate as a result of its functional competence.

Consequently, the Commission report made no mention of the need for a democratic second chamber, despite the fact that the government's election manifesto had made just such a reference, and also despite the fact that a small majority of those who submitted evidence to the Commission enquiry had argued for either a wholly or predominantly elected second chamber (Wheeler-Booth 2003: 659). The Commission instead pointed to what it viewed as the inherently contradictory evidence it had received, noting that while many people wanted to preserve the independence and expertise of the second chamber, they also wanted it to be elected (Cm 4534, 2000: 199). Since the Commission preferred to see a chamber that was free from partisanship, it dismissed both an entirely and a majority elected House. Instead, it recommended a mixed chamber of 550 members, with around 80–90 members selected on a directly elected regional basis, with the remaining numbers selected by an independent, statutory Appointments Commission (Cm 4534, 2000: 8).

Response to the Royal Commission report

The press mauled the Wakeham Commission report when it was published, and the issue of the pre-eminence of the Commons provoked a flurry of criticism. *The Times* (21 January 2000), for example, criticised the Commission for assuming that its terms of reference 'obliged it to endorse in every respect the current crushing superiority nominally held by MPs, which in reality is in the hands of ministers and whips'. The *Daily Telegraph* (21 January 2000) argued that by 'maintaining the position of the Commons ... as the pre-eminent chamber ... the wings of the executive power would remain unclipped' even if the report was fully implemented. Naturally, the press were also disappointed with the Commission's conclusions regarding composition, with many editorials regretting that it had not taken the opportunity to opt for a fully elected chamber.

Yet, parliament itself did not have the opportunity to register its thoughts on the Commission report until the spring and summer of 2000, at which point both the Commission and the government came under attack for their approach to the question of reform. In the Lords, Baroness Jay defended the government's position in favour of a 'subordinate' and 'largely nominated' chamber on the grounds that it avoided the creation of parliamentary 'gridlock', and endorsed the Commission's view that 'any proposal totally to elect a second Chamber under the mistaken view that it would increase the democratic base of Parliament would in fact undermine that democracy' (HL Debs, 7 March 2000, cols 912–4). Similarly, in the Commons, Margaret Beckett argued that 'democracy is not strengthened by adding another body to which people are elected to carry out exactly the same job', and that this 'would produce a different combination of democratically elected Chambers and would lead to conflict' (HC Debs, 19 June 2000, col. 51).

In this way, the arguments about parliamentary efficiency and effectiveness once more emerged. The government's position was that an elected second chamber would not only impede the ability of parliament to fulfil its task in a timely manner, but would also restrict the effectiveness with which it performed those tasks, because the House of Lords would assume it had a democratic basis for challenging the government and the House of Commons. The arguments were, of course, cast in quite different terms by the opposition parties. Lord Strathclyde, opposition Leader of the Lords, explained that a stronger House of Lords would actually aid the effectiveness of parliament, because '[i]f a government carries confidence in a free, independent and respected Parliament ... then that government is the more authoritative and respected' (HL Debs, 7 March 2000, col. 919). Similarly, Sir George Young in the Commons explained that:

> there has been a tendency to represent the debate about Lords reform as a one-dimensional contest with the Commons: if one gains, the other must lose ...

That is the wrong perspective. The real contest today is not between the Lords and the Commons, but between Parliament and the Executive. In that battle, the Houses are not rivals, but partners. (HC Debs, 19 June 2000, col. 56)

The Conservative emphasis on the need for a strong parliament, and a strong House of Lords, reflected the thinking of the Norton Commission recommendations, published in July 2000. The Conservative leader, William Hague, had previously appointed a Commission to examine options for a new second chamber in July 1998 under the chairmanship of Lord Mackay of Clashfern, which reported in April 1999, some nine months before the Wakeham report (Conservative Party 1999b). It suggested two options for the composition of the chamber. The first was for a mixed chamber comprising appointed, directly elected and indirectly elected members. The second option was for a wholly directly elected chamber. The Mackay Commission conclusions were therefore diverse enough to give the party sufficient flexibility for criticism of the Wakeham proposals once they emerged.

A window of opportunity and political leadership

The 1997 Labour manifesto had not promised a Royal Commission, although one had been convened by the time of the 2001 general election, but had promised a joint committee of both Houses, which had failed to materialise. In July 2000, Margaret Beckett informed the Commons that work was underway to establish such a joint committee following the summer recess (HC Debs, 3 July 20000, col. 93W), yet by spring 2001, this had become a touchy subject, with the official line being that inter-party consensus had not been found and that there would be no joint committee before the end of the parliament (HC Debs, 3 March 2001, col. 200W). After the general election, the Leader of the Lords, Lord Williams, confirmed that the government saw no role for a joint committee, and that any future reform of the Lords would be based on the Wakeham Commission conclusions (HL Debs, 10 July 2001, col. 69W).

A government white paper subsequently emerged in November 2001, which outlined the government's plans for the second stage of Lords reform (Cm 5291, 2001). The white paper outlined four principles on which reform would be based: the second chamber should be primarily a revising and deliberating assembly; its membership should suit these functions and not simply clone that of the Commons; it should have a political outlook but not be dominated by one party; and it should be representative of independent expertise in the UK.

Although the government claimed it broadly accepted the Wakeham recommendations, there were divergences in terms of its proposals for composition. The government recommended a chamber of 600 members, 120 of whom would be non-party members selected by the Appointments Commission, 120 would be directly elected, 332 would be nominated by the political parties, and the remaining number would draw on the bishops and law lords. The role of the Appointments Commission was therefore conceived quite differently by the government, who wanted it only to appoint the independent members, and for the political parties to make their own appointments (Cm 5291, 2001, paras 65–8). In addition, while the Commission had recommended that elections for the House of Lords should take place on European election days, the government instead preferred these to be held at general elections. Furthermore, the government planned for the entire elected membership replaced at the same time, unlike the Wakeham Commission, and also endorsed a shorter length of service for both elected and nominated members (paras 54–7).

Much of the content of the white paper was attributed to the influence of the Lord Chancellor, Derry Irvine. However, as early as summer 2001, a difference of opinion existed in the cabinet committee dealing with Lords reform, largely due to the appearance of a new Leader of the Commons, Robin Cook. Insiders were well aware that Cook's preferred option was for the reformed upper house to be at least 50 per cent elected (*The Guardian*, 10 January 2002). In July 2001, the cabinet sub-committee met to map out a way forward from the Royal Commission proposals, and Cook secured an agreement that the elected portion of the reformed composition had to be raised from 11 per cent, where it had been agreed, to the 'marginally less derisory' 20 per cent (Cook 2003b: 32). Cook was not worried that this figure was itself too low, because he 'knew it would be buried in derision the moment we went public' (Cook 2003b: 34). Cook also got the sub-committee to agree to a consultation document on the government's proposals, rather than the rigid white paper that had been designed as a prelude to a near identical bill (Cook 2003b: 32). From Cook's perspective, this provided the time required to come up with 'something better' (Cook 2003b: 32). Cook was certainly in favour of a substantial elected element in the House of Lords, but he was not necessarily in favour of a fully elected second chamber, on the grounds that he could not 'conceive of a wholly elected House of Lords that would not regard itself as having a legitimacy as equal to that of the House of Commons' (HC Debs, 7 November 2001, col. 246).

Yet, while the issue of pre-eminence was integral to Cook's approach, he was not of the view that it needed to hamstring the process of reform, particularly since the reaction to the white paper had helpfully opened up a window of opportunity to engage with more radical reform. Support for a significant elected element in the House of Lords was growing amongst a substantial number of MPs, thanks in part to the leadership provided by Cook in expressing his preference for a higher number of elected peers than did his cabinet colleagues. In September 2001, an Early Day Motion (EDM 226, 2001–2) calling for a wholly or substantially elected second chamber, was tabled by Labour MP Fiona Mactaggart, and by the time the government white paper was debated in the House on 7 November 2001, it had attracted 149 signatures. Hugo Young, writing in The Guardian (8 November 2001), described this development as 'unprecedented', and observed that these MPs:

> seem to be putting the interests of something vaguely definable as democracy ahead of the narrow interests of government. They're a substantial bloc, whose tenacity will now be tested. But in alliance with the Conservatives, committed to more election, and Lib Dems, committed to wholesale election, they could make ministers think again.

By January 2002, the window of opportunity had opened further still, when a two-day Lords debate served to underline further the hostility towards the government's white paper proposals. Most of those who contributed to the debate rejected the pre-eminence argument as fallacious, and many also complained about the continued absence of the promised joint committee (HL Debs, 9 January 2002, col. 566; 10 January 2002, col. 696). The debate highlighted just how many different plans existed for reforming the composition of the second chamber, and the variety of arguments forwarded for and against different proportions of elected members. An additional worry for the government was that Lord Wakeham used the opportunity to attack the white paper proposals, criticising the government for departing from the position of consensus achieved by the Royal Commission, and for proposing that the parties should be able to choose their own appointees without reference to the Appointments Commission (cols 581–2). This condemnation from the chairman of the Royal Commission undermined the argument made by the government that it was implementing its reported proposals.

The options discussed for reforming the composition illustrate the diffi-culties experienced by the parties themselves in reaching settled policies on the matter, particularly the Conservatives, whose senior peer, Lord Strathclyde, worked extraordinarily hard to get the shadow cabinet to agree that 80 per cent of the upper house should be directly elected (The Guardian, 10 January 2002). This decision was largely a political reaction to the diffi-culties the government was getting itself into over the issue, rather than a position reached after weighing up the evidence and arguments from a first principles approach. Problems inside the Labour Party in trying to secure backbench support for the cabinet position were no secret: Derry Irvine had even threatened MPs at a PLP meeting that further progress with stage two of reform would be halted unless they supported the 20 per cent elected option contained in the white paper (The Guardian, 10 January 2002). Clear divisions between the government front and backbenches emerged, with the so-called 'awkward squad relishing the fact that for once they had the PLP behind them and the Cabinet in front of them' (Cook 2003b: 77).

The backbenches had much to encourage them, because in the Commons debate on the white paper on 10 January 2002, Cook once more emphasised that the government's proposals would be changed if there was consensus to do so, noting that '[t]he White Paper is, after all, a consultative paper' (HC Debs, 10 January 2002, col. 702), with this declaration finally removing the possibility that the white paper proposals might well proceed to the legislative stage largely untouched. In case anyone doubted Cook's determination to reformulate the compositional balance outlined in the white paper, he added:

> [t]hat still leaves us with a very difficult judgement – it must be a matter of judgement – about where the balance should be struck between elected and appointed Members ... Many hon. Members have already made it clear to me – some of them on more than one occasion – that they do not think the proposed balance is the right one. I hope that today's debate can take us an extra step beyond that by establishing whether there is an alternative that would command a centre of gravity of opinion in support of reform. (HC Debs, 10 January 2002, col. 709)

In private, Cook was sure that the Lords debate in particular had proved fatal for the government's approach:

> By the end of the debate the White Paper was firmly skewered to the floor with the printer's ink fading from every page. There is simply nobody left who can believe that a bill based on this White Paper will get through the House. It is as dead as Monty Python's famous parrot. (Cook 2003b: 78)

By the middle of January 2002, then, a clear window of opportunity for a different approach to Lords reform had emerged as a result of extensive dissatisfaction with the government's proposals, and firm political leadership was present in the person of Robin Cook as Leader of the House, who played a pivotal role in unstitching the white paper and creating a forum in which more comprehensive change could be discussed. Cook was also liaising closely with the Labour peers and the Lords Leader, Gareth Williams, in order to map out the next steps in the reform process and build consensus for it (Cook 2003b: 82–3). In addition, on 17 January 2002, just a week after the debates on the white paper, Labour backbenchers were in a position to demonstrate that the 'centre of gravity' Cook argued was necessary for reform could be found. Labour MP Graham Allen had circulated a questionnaire to the PLP seeking to identify what proportion of the second chamber should be elected: the results indicated that Labour backbenchers were agreed that not less than half the reformed chamber should be elected, with three-quarters of the respondents favouring a majority elected house (*The Guardian*, 18 January 2002; Cook 2003b: 91).

The government did not take this turn of events lying down, and Derry Irvine remained publicly committed to the white paper position, as demonstrated by his appearance before the Public Administration select committee on 24 January 2002, which was then conducting an inquiry into Lords reform as part of its response to the white paper. Irvine rejected the proposition that the House of Lords was illegitimate on account of its composition, and when asked why, if this was the case, the government had opted for an elected element at all, responded that the aim was not to enhance legitimacy but to ensure regional representation (HC 494-II, 2001–2, Q. 402–13). The session became stranger still when select committee members pressed Irvine about the growing opinion among Labour backbenchers in favour of a substantial elected element, prompting Irvine to respond: 'No, I do not even believe it' (Q. 419). Irvine insisted that when MPs thought more deeply about the need to preserve the pre-eminence of the Commons, they would rethink their positions on election (Q. 465). Such was Irvine's apparent frustration at the turn of events that, when asked about Robin Cook's views on the matter, he seemingly pretended not to know who he was (Q. 437).

By February 2002, there was mounting pressure for substantial reform, endorsed by the existence of EDM 226 which had accumulated over 300 signatures, the majority of which came from Labour MPs. Yet, although a 'centre of gravity' seemed to be coalescing around at least a half-elected house, and although there was a window of opportunity, political leadership and the beginnings of political will for reform, there was still no clear reform agenda in place. The publication of the Public Administration Committee's report on House of Lords reform on 12 February 2002 served to begin constructing the kind of agenda that was required.

An emerging reform agenda

The Public Administration Committee's report title, *The Second Chamber: Continuing the Reform*, was itself a challenge to the government's white paper proposals, which were entitled *Completing the Reform*. The Committee argued that the government had adopted entirely the wrong approach to Lords reform:

> Reform is not a zero-sum game in which advances for one chamber are inevitably threats to the other. That is where the White Paper is fundamentally misconceived, as was the Royal Commission, it its oft-repeated determination to ensure the pre-eminence of the House of Commons. No-one is casting any doubt on that pre-eminence. We believe that the real task is rather to increase the effectiveness of both chambers in holding the Government to account for its actions and policies. The focus should be on the capacities of the institution as a whole (HC 494, 2001–2, para. 36).

The Committee's enquiry incorporated a survey of MPs as well as oral evidence, all of which led it to conclude that a 'centre of gravity' for reform lay with the option of a chamber that was 60 per cent elected, based on the regional constituencies used in European Parliament elections and using a proportional voting system. Elected members would serve a single term spanning two parliaments, by means of staggered elections. The remaining membership would comprise 20 per cent of members nominated by the political parties and 20 per cent independent members, with an Appointments Commission making the final decision on both sets of nominated members, who would serve a term of ten years.

Cook continued to build consensus for a settled reform agenda at this time, and even addressed the Parliamentary Liberal Democrat Party on 6 March 2002, the first Labour minister ever to do so (Cook 2003b: 114). The broad conclusions of the Public Administration Committee were subsequently given an unexpected boost when the government quietly published the responses to its white paper consultation, in which 89 per cent of those responding argued for a chamber that was at least 50 per cent elected (Analysis of Consultation Responses, May 2002, www.dca.gov.uk/constitution/holref/holrefresp/holrefresp.htm – consulted February 2004). Yet, before the publication of the evidence, senior government figures, including Tony Blair, began to refer to mixed models disparagingly as 'hybridity' (even although the government's own proposals had been of a mixed model nature), as part of a new strategy supporting an entirely nominated second chamber. Attempting to head off this new approach at the pass, Cook told the Commons that the, as yet unpublished, responses to the white paper consultation suggested 'that the overwhelming majority of respondents favour a substantially elected second chamber' (HC Debs, 19 March 2002, col. 164), as part of a strategy to get 'another piece of evidence smuggled into the public domain which will increase the pressure on Derry [Irvine] to come to terms with reality' (Cook 2003b: 126).

A surprising turn of events came on 22 April 2002, when Cook met the prime minister to discuss the stalemate on Lords reform:

> He [the prime minister] has a surprise in store for me. 'Can't we put to Parliament different options for the composition of the House of Lords? I'll be frank with you. I just don't see how I can get an agreed position around the Cabinet table. John Prescott won't agree to substantial elections and you won't agree to minority elections. But if we let Parliament decide we do not have to fix an agreed Cabinet line.' He was curiously tentative as he spoke, uncharacteristically looking at the coffee table rather than fixing me with his eyes as he usually does. He seemed relieved, even surprised, when I responded, 'I could make that work. It is what we've just done with the options on hunting. I think it would do a power of good to your own image to be seen to be consulting Parliament.' (Cook 2003b: 138–9)

It would later be rather clearer to Cook why the prime minister had not been able to look him in the eye. Yet at that point, Cook had at least convinced Blair of the need for a joint committee in order to outline a reform agenda, although it was also clear that Blair and Irvine viewed such a committee as a means of tying parliament in knots over the range of options available (Cook 2003b: 146–8), which is more or less exactly what happened.

The Joint Committee and a reform agenda

The Joint Committee on House of Lords reform was established in early July 2002, with terms of reference directing it to 'consider issues relating to House of Lords reform, including the composition and powers of the Second Chamber and its role and authority within the context of Parliament as a whole' (HC 1109, 2001–2, para. 3). It was mandated to consider how any reform would impact on the pre-eminence of the House of Commons, and to consider all options for composition between, and including, a fully nominated and a fully elected house. Each House of Parliament appointed twelve members to the Joint Committee, which was chaired by Labour's Jack Cunningham (in spite of Cook's preference for Sir George Young), a move that was interpreted 'as a clear signal that Downing Street [was] determined to resist pressure for a large number of elected peers' (The Guardian, 18 June 2002).

Early doubts emerged about the extent to which the Committee members would be able to work together. Kenneth Clarke, a senior Conservative member in favour of a substantial elected element, informed Robin Cook that the 'reformers' on the Committee wanted to press ahead with their work, 'while those who want as little reform as possible [were] pressing for delay' (Cook 2003b: 180). Many Committee members in interview confirmed these difficulties, which stemmed from the deliberate inclusion of so many differing viewpoints. Labour MPs on the Committee, for example, confirmed the lack of consensus over composition, but also pointed to general agreement regarding the powers that the Lords should exercise (interviews, 29 April 2003). Most of the Labour peers interviewed pointed to dissatisfaction with the Committee's terms of reference, on the grounds that the wording subtly pointed them towards an analysis of composition only, which one peer argued 'turn[ed] the whole thing on its head' (interview, 30 April 2003). He pointed out that 'if you are running a business or anything else, the first thing you do is see what jobs are required to be done, and once you've decided that then you decide what kind of people you want to fill it'. Another Labour peer concurred, noting that 'most people felt more time should have been spent on powers and roles from which you would have got a better idea of what kind of composition was needed' (interview, 30 April 2003).

The main point of contention was, unsurprisingly, between those who favoured elections to the second chamber and those who wished to maintain a system of appointment. The terms of reference, which simply asked the Committee to present a variety of 'options', were designed to accommodate these differences of opinion. However, the terms of reference also specifically directed the Committee to include the 100 per cent elected and the 100 per cent appointed options in its recommendations. Many on the Joint Committee interpreted this as a reaction against the Royal Commission conclusions in favour of a mixed chamber. One Labour peer, for example, explained that:

> Robin [Cook] wanted to move quickly with a move to direct elections ... Derry Irvine was strongly opposed to direct elections. He had to put forward the government's views from the Royal Commission, but had not basically been in favour of them, and then saw this as an opportunity of introducing an additional option of 100 per cent appointment, which gave him, to use his phrase, the chance to get the genie back in the bottle. (Interview, 30 April 2003)

Indeed, the Joint Committee, according to one Labour MP, 'never actually undertook to reconcile the different views of different members of either House' on the issue of composition (interview, 30 April 2003). As one cross-bench peer noted, the Joint Committee could never have succeeded in taking a position on the 'right option' as far as composition was concerned as a direct result of these differences between the two Houses (interview, 30 April 2003).

The Joint Committee report was published in December 2002 (HC 171, 2002–3). It noted five particular qualities that were 'desirable' in the makeup of a reformed House: legitimacy, representativeness, no domination by any one party, independence and expertise. It accepted that there were different views on the various 'routes to legitimacy', and explained that the House already met the criteria of lack of domination by one party, independence and expertise. The Committee therefore concluded that '[i]f these existing qualities, bolstered by a greater representativeness, can be transferred to the reformed House, we believe that a new legitimacy ... will naturally develop' (para. 43).

Its recommendations were for a chamber of 600 members, who would each serve in office for twelve years, and that a new Appointments Commission be established in line with that already recommended by the Royal Commission. The crucial part of the report lay in its seven options for reform: fully appointed; fully elected; 80 per cent appointed/20 per cent elected; 80 per cent elected/20 per cent appointed; 60 per cent appointed /40 per cent elected; 60 per cent elected/40 per cent appointed; and 50 per cent appointed/50 per cent elected. Each option was accompanied by a set of arguments for and against. The Joint Committee recommended that each

House debate the options before voting on a series of motions on each option, with each motion being moved successively and with members able to vote in favour of as many options as they wished.

The decision of the Joint Committee to place seven options for reform before parliament concerned Robin Cook, who worried that with so many choices before them, MPs would fail to find a clear consensus behind any single one (Cook 2003b: 256). Although both the Conservative and Liberal Democrat parties endorsed the Joint Committee report (Conservative Party 2002; Liberal Democrat Party 2002), and although there remained a substantial group of MPs in favour of a substantially elected option, it remained unclear which of the specific options outlined would command majority support. It was this uncertainty which determined much of Cook's work during the weeks following the publication of the report, when he continued to restate the need to find a 'settled will' and a 'centre of gravity' and for those in favour of a predominantly elected second chamber to ensure they coalesced around it (HC Debs, 7 January 2003, col. 21). The fact remained that the Joint Committee report, comprehensive though it may have been in examining the various composition options, had not demonstrated why a centre of gravity should form around any one option, and it thus failed in the single task with which the Leader of the House had hoped it would find success. If anything, there was perhaps less agreement on reform in January 2003 compared with January 2002. The Public Administration Committee report had at least found a possible point of consensus around a 60 per cent elected option in January 2002. Within the year, however, the Joint Committee had laid additional percentiles onto the table, but had not explained which one might be the obvious 'lowest common denominator.' By early January 2003, the window of opportunity for reform may well have been swinging closed, perhaps given a nudge by the prime minister's decision to make his own anti-election views on reform clear in advance of the vote (Cook 2003b: 268).

Unease amongst the self-confessed reformers was evident in the Commons adjournment debate on the Joint Committee report on 21 January 2003. Several of the pro-election committee members spoke at length against the argument that introducing elections for the second chamber would result in a diminution in the capabilities of the Commons, and many utilised the language of the Public Administration report which emphasised that the relationship between the two chambers was not zero-sum. Yet many other MPs argued that the primacy of the Commons was paramount and thus rejected any elected element. Many of these MPs had already signed an Early Day Motion (EDM 56, 2002–3), tabled the previous November in anticipation of the Joint Committee report, which stated the pre-eminence argument in absolutely unequivocal terms, and which attracted around 84 signatures. The pre-eminence EDM had been followed in January 2003 by EDM 529, which criticised the Joint Committee for not including in its series of options one which provided for the abolition of the second chamber altogether. It argued that the need to reform the Lords stemmed largely from the failings of the Commons, and that it was therefore more straightforward simply to reform the lower house into an effective unicameral parliament. At the time of the adjournment debate on 21 January 2003, this EDM had attracted over ninety signatures, and several members of the Joint Committee confirmed during interview that they had entirely underestimated the strength of the unicameral camp. This strength was made quite clear during the debate, with several MPs speaking in favour of simple abolition of the second chamber.

By the end of the debate, only two things were clear. First, there was apparently no real 'centre of gravity' behind any one of the options outlined by the Joint Committee. Although a number of MPs spoke in favour of elections for the Lords, it remained unclear which specific option attracted most support. Second, a higher proportion of MPs had spoken in favour of a wholly appointed chamber than had perhaps been envisaged. This was partly due to the contribution of the many unicameralists who spoke, who stated that if abolition was not on offer, they would vote for a wholly appointed chamber in order to preserve the pre-eminence of the Commons. The Lords two-day debate on the Joint Committee report was rather more conclusive, demonstrating that while there was a small amount of support for elections, the vast majority of peers favoured a wholly appointed second chamber, which they argued was the only way to preserve the expertise and independence for which the House of Lords was known.

The view of the prime minister was made abundantly clear in the Commons a week later, when, despite the mixed House outlined by the failed government white paper, Tony Blair said that 'I personally think that a hybrid between the two is wrong and will not work' (HC Debs, 29 January 2003, col. 877). He endorsed the essentially monochromatic view of Lords reform, stating that 'I also think that the key question on election is whether we want a revising Chamber of a rival Chamber' (col. 877). Robin Cook described the prime minister's statement in these terms:

> ... Tony slammed a big fat torpedo into our joint strategy on Lords reform. He had an unerring aim and I was left sitting silently beside him for the rest of Question Time contemplating the wreck of democratic reform sinking beneath the horizon. Only last week I had begged him not to express any preference among the options before the House. (Cook 2003b: 274)

One Conservative peer on the Joint Committee provided an interesting analysis of the prime minister's intervention, arguing that the whips had already 'picked up' on a shift of opinion among the PLP regarding support for elections, and that the prime minister was largely reacting to the dominant viewpoint, rather than actively trying to shape it (interview, 1 May

2003). In the language of institutional theory, the 'logic of appropriateness' adopted by MPs was increasingly informed by the norms and values of the Westminster institutional context, which privileged the pre-eminence argument. The prime minister's intervention undoubtedly played a key role in what then occurred.

The vote on the seven options for reform

Both the House of Commons and the House of Lords voted on the seven options for reform on 4 February 2003. In the absence of any clear centre of gravity behind any one single option, Robin Cook declared his intention to vote for the 100 per cent, 80 per cent and 60 per cent elected options, and implored like-minded MPs to do the same. Anticipating that some MPs might only vote for their one preferred option, he urged that '[t]he precise percentage is not important … what is important is the principle that the majority in any parliamentary chamber should be elected by the people for whom it legislates, and I urge the House to vote for that principle' (HC Debs, 4 February 2003, col. 162). The Conservatives adopted a different attitude, with the Shadow Leader of the House, Eric Forth, committing to vote only for the 100 per cent and 80 per cent elected options (the latter being the official Conservative policy), but arguing that the 60 per cent option was 'a step too far' (col. 164). The Liberal Democrat chief whip, Paul Tyler, urged his party to vote for the 100 per cent, 80 per cent and 60 per cent elected options, arguing that '[w]ithout substantial majorities for those options, the forces of reaction will succeed'.

Although the general tenor of the debate was in favour of a substantially elected second chamber, two other key issues were prominent, both of which were intimately linked to the pre-eminence argument. First, those who favoured the abolition of the Lords were unhappy that it was not an option offered by the Joint Committee, and although they urged their colleagues to vote in favour of an amendment tabled in favour of abolition, they resolved to vote for an all-appointed chamber if it was not successful, on the grounds that this was the only way to preserve Commons pre-eminence. The second issue revolved around the argument promoted by the prime minister that the whole idea of a mixed chamber was fundamentally flawed, and that only realistic options were the wholly appointed and wholly elected ones.

Both chambers held simultaneous divisions on the seven options. The Lords voted overwhelmingly in favour of a wholly appointed second chamber. Just 106 peers voted for a wholly elected chamber, and the inter-mediate mixed models attracted only a few dozen votes each. The House of Lords, therefore, was able to state a clear position and a clear centre of gravity around the wholly appointed option. In the House of Commons, by contrast, the voting was entirely inconclusive. The amendment to abolish the second chamber was defeated by 392 votes to 174, with a remarkably high number of MPs voting in favour of abolition. The option for a wholly appointed House was defeated by 325 votes to 247. The options for an 80 per cent appointed, 60 per cent appointed and 50 per cent appointed house were all defeated without division. The option for a 60 per cent elected house was defeated by 318 votes to 255. The option for an 80 per cent elected house was defeated by 286 votes to 283. The option for a wholly elected house was defeated by 291 votes to 274. The Commons failed therefore to support any of the seven options presented by the Joint Committee. The House had consistently argued that the composition of the Lords was unacceptable, yet it proceeded to vote in a way that ensured that this status quo would be preserved. The votes have been fully analysed elsewhere, and a number of hypotheses examined to account for the result (McLean, Spirling and Russell 2003).

What is most important is that the 80 per cent elected option was defeated by just three votes and the wholly elected option by just seventeen votes. McLean et al (2003) point to a 319-strong group of MPs who voted for at least one of the 100 per cent, 80 per cent or 60 per cent elected options, inside which was a sub-group of 134 MPs who voted in favour of all three options. With just a few additional members in this sub-group, the 80 per cent elected option would have been approved. Yet, the picture is more complex than this. The 60 per cent elected option followed the defeat of the 80 per cent elected option, the latter of which was the official Conservative Party position. However, forty-five Conservative MPs who voted for the 80 per cent option then voted against the 60 per cent option. These MPs were ostensibly against a wholly appointed option, but the 60 per cent elected option was the only 'democratic' one remaining, yet they voted against it, no doubt an example of strategic voting designed to embarrass the government with further stalemate (McLean et al 2003: 305). In addition to any strategic voting that may have taken place, some MPs accidentally voted wrongly. There is strong evidence that at least four MPs voted against the 80 per cent elected option by accident, thinking they were voting against the 20 per cent elected option. Without this mistake alone, the 80 per cent elected option would have been approved. There were, then, a number of reasons why the Commons failed to support one option. Significant numbers of Labour and Conservative MPs voted against their official party position, and in the former, against a manifesto commitment. The Liberal Democrat MP Paul Tyler even tabled two EDMs that criticised those Conservative MPs who failed to support the 80 per cent elected option, and the eighteen Labour MPs who had previously signed EDM 226 but who went on to vote for a wholly appointed chamber (EDM 689, 2002–3; EDM 686, 2002–3).

Although the vote was a free one, there is considerable evidence that the whips were active on the day. One Labour member of the Joint Committee confirmed that Robin Cook had an unofficial whip operating in order to shore up support for the elected options (interview, 29 April 2003), and a peer on the Joint Committee stated that the government whips actively whipped against the Leader of the House (interview, 2 May 2003). Cook was himself aware of allegations that the Labour whips encouraged Conservative MPs to vote for the wholly appointed option in order to force him to resign (Cook 2003b: 278). Another Labour peer stated that whips advised any confused or undecided MPs that 'it was safer to vote no to everything' (interview, 30 April 2003). Indeed, out of fifteen government whips, thirteen voted in favour of the wholly appointed option. While one Labour MP on the Joint Committee believed that the Conservative Party had 'went out of its way to make sure there was no majority for any particular option' (interview, 30 April 2003), other Committee members argued that the prime minister's intervention against 'hybridity' had swayed many of those who previously endorsed the mixed options, which was also the reason that Cook himself found most compelling in explaining why so many Labour MPs failed to support those choices (Cook 2003b: 280).

The evidence of the votes and of the feedback obtained from interviews with involved actors casts considerable doubt on the possibility that broad political will for substantial parliamentary reform can be summoned very easily. It endorses the predictions of institutional theory that dominant elites will work to preserve the context that gives them that dominance, and to thwart reforms that might upset the structured institutional context from which they greatly benefit. In this case, arguments pertaining to the need to preserve at all costs the pre-eminence of the House of Commons, and by extension, the government that lies therein, convinced enough MPs to vote against any elected element for the House of Lords. Yet, there is no question that there was a significant number of MPs from all parties who wished to move towards an elected House of Lords. However, whatever will they had to secure such reform was eventually thwarted. For some MPs, the idea that parliamentary effectiveness would in fact be enhanced by an elected Lords was a misguided one, convinced as they were of the pre-eminence argument which indicated that ineffectiveness would be the actual result. Partisan politics also played a role in derailing reform, particularly with respect to the desire of some within the Conservative party to embarrass the government over its policies towards the House of Lords. In the main, however, political will for reform dissipated because MPs had long ago absorbed the norms and values of the Westminster institutional context, and too many were simply unwilling to risk upsetting that context by testing the extent to which the House of Commons would indeed remain pre-eminent in the wake of an elected House of Lords. The idea that an elected second chamber would impede the pre-eminence of the Commons proved far more persuasive than the idea that it would enhance parliamentary effectiveness.

The aftermath of failure

However much we try to account for why the Commons did not support any one option for reform, the fact remains that the endeavour failed because, collectively, MPs did not want to reform the House of Lords. As Cook (2003b: 280) explained, 'no amount of footnotes can obscure the central fact that the Commons had the historic chance to modernise the House of Lords and chose not to do so'. As one Labour member of the Joint Committee commented, 'people came up against the harsh reality ... that whenever we have tried the big bang approach it has failed, and it has failed because the House of Commons is deeply divided on what it wants as an alternative' (interview, 29 April 2003). Indeed, one Labour peer on the Committee argued that the 'muddled' outcomes 'may have been what was wanted' (interview, 29 April 2003). Another Labour MP endorsed this view, stating that 'in a way the government was very smart and very cute to manage to get rid of the hereditaries without completing the second stage of reform' (interview, 29 April 2003).

The failure of the House of Commons to find a centre of gravity around any of the options essentially ended the life of the Joint Committee. Despite the hopes of some Committee members that it might look instead at the issue of powers and roles, agreement could not be found and support for its continued existence was distinctly lacking. The Committee managed to produce one more report in April 2003 (HC 668, 2002–3) which aimed to keep reform afloat, but in the absence of any prime ministerial willingness for such work to continue, the Committee was all but doomed: the government's reply to the April report made clear that the government was committed only to removing the hereditary peers and establishing an independent Appointments Commission. The Joint Committee thereafter slipped into oblivion.

The government resolved to proceed with a bill to remove the remaining hereditary peers and redesign the Appointments Commission. Bizarrely, in light of the possible defeat of the bill in both Houses, the government, in February 2004, indicated it might well proceed with direct elections to the reformed chamber (*The Guardian*, 9 February 2004). In March 2004, the prime minister was advised against proceeding with the bill on account of mounting divisions amongst MPs and ministers, and it was abandoned, although the government pressed ahead with its plans to establish a Supreme Court, and thereby remove the Law Lords from the second chamber.

Yet, despite the apparent disarray into which the government's plans for Lords reform had seemingly fallen, the Labour Party's 2005 election manifesto nonetheless contained a commitment to another free vote in parliament on the composition of a reformed second chamber. Crucially, however, the new parliament did not begin with any attempt to fulfil that commitment, but instead once more to lay the groundwork for reform. In late spring 2006, a Joint Committee on Conventions was established with the very specific task of examining the vast range of conventions which structured the relationship between the two Houses of Parliament, in the particular context of House of Commons primacy, in order to determine the practicality of codifying those conventions (HC 1151, 2005–6). The Joint Committee comprised twenty-two members, eleven from each House, with Lord Cunningham in the chair, who had previously chaired the Joint Committee on Reform of the House of Lords. The Committee published its lengthy 125-page report in November 2006 (HC 1212, 2005–6). One of its most crucial statements came early on, and cast doubt on its role in firming up the ground for reforming the composition of the second chamber:

> If the Lords acquired an electoral mandate, then in our view their role as the revising chamber, and their relationship with the Commons, would inevitably be called into question, codified or not. Should any firm proposals come forward to change the composition of the House of Lords, the conventions between the Houses would have to be examined again. (HC 1212, para. 63)

The report nevertheless sought to make clear the specific powers of the House of Lords, particularly with reference to government legislation, and the capacity of the second chamber to interfere with and/or delay such legislation. In addition, the Joint Committee reached its conclusions without the need for division.

However, although the Joint Committee emphasised that those conclusions might change in the context of the introduction of elections into the second chamber, the government nevertheless proceeded to situate its subsequent white paper on Lords reform, published in February 2007 (Cm 7027, 2007), against the background of the Joint Committee's work. Crucially, though, unlike the 2001 white paper, which emerged from cabinet with very little, if any, consultation with anyone at all, the 2007 white paper emerged following a series of meetings of the Cross-Party Working Group on Lords Reform, chaired by the Leader of the House of Commons, Jack Straw, and incorporating many senior figures from both Houses, including the Conservative and Liberal Democrat Leaders of both Houses, and the convenor of the cross-bench peers. It met eight times between its creation in the summer of 2006 and the publication of the white paper, and successfully located 'a significant degree of consensus' across a range of issues, if not all of them. Key to the agreements found within the Working Group was the important stipulation that reform of the composition of the second chamber should proceed from the basis of a 'long transition period, with new members phased in over time'. In addition, given the differences between the parties, no specific composition option was supported by the Working Group, although the notion that reform would produce a hybrid House was broadly accepted. It was on this basis that the government once more pledged to provide a free vote in parliament in order to produce a 'clear answer' to the composition question (Cm 7027, 2007, paras 2.3–2.12). While the 2007 white paper simply restated much of the same discussion about what kind of second chamber is required – the merits of a hybrid chamber, the nature of an elected second chamber, the plans for the transitional House – the government did state its own preference for a hybrid option of a 50 per cent elected House (which, significantly, was not even given a formal vote in the Commons in 2003), with elections run on a partially open list system in European constituencies at the same time as European elections. However, one of the most interesting aspects of the white paper was its attempt to avoid another spectacular catastrophe such as that of 2003, by forcing a clear decision from the House by way of an alternative vote process. This clear departure from House of Commons procedure, which has never before entertained any voting system other than that of the majority wins in any division, provoked immense backlash from across the chamber, and Jack Straw was subsequently forced to abandon this experiment in procedural innovation.

Much of the subsequent focus on the government's proposals was therefore on the nature of the direct elections proposed, and the extent to which they would hand untold power to political parties because of the nature of the list system proposed. Yet, despite the plans mapped out by the white paper, and despite the government's stated preference for a half-elected, half-appointed House, the discussion about House of Lords reform had become couched in the context of the imminent change in prime minister, and the impending hand-over from Tony Blair to Gordon Brown. The Conservative leadership in the House of Lords made it clear that, in the event that Gordon Brown pushed on with the plans once prime minister, they would be blocked in the second chamber along with the rest of the government's legislative programme (*The Guardian*, 7 February 2007). Furthermore, no one in the House was under any illusion that there were significant differences between Blair and Brown with regards to their views on Lords reform, and that the government's stated preference for a 50 per cent elected House would likely be abandoned in the Brown premiership. It was against this background of speculation about the future path of reform, and the preferred choices of a future prime minister, that parliament once more voted on 7 March 2007 on House of Lords reform, with options for a 100 per cent and an 80 per cent elected House receiving majorities of 113 and 38 respectively. Crucially, the 60 per cent elected option, which had been promoted as a 'centre of gravity' by the Public Administration Committee in 2002, was defeated by a staggering majority of 214. The government's preferred option of a 50 per cent elected option was defeated even more convincingly by a majority of 263. Yet, we must be cautious about assuming that the majority support for both the 100 per cent and the 80 per cent options meant that the House of Commons had, collectively, come around to the idea of a democratically elected House of Lords. The vote also involved a division on whether to keep the second chamber at all, and although it was defeated by a majority of 253, 163 MPs voted against the motion. The role played by the unicameralists in distorting the vote cannot therefore be ignored. As one Labour MP in favour of a unicameral parliament explained:

> I voted for the 100 per cent elected option just to bugger the whole thing up. Once the 80 per cent [option] went through, there were nods around the chamber to say, 'Bugger it, we'll just vote for the 100 per cent too'. And so that fudged it all, but it was spontaneous. (Interview, 19 June 2007)

The government's reform plans were therefore almost immediately in doubt, with the Commons stating a clear preference for a wholly or very substantially elected second chamber, regardless of the motivations behind it. The imminent exit of Tony Blair from 10 Downing Street also meant that there was clearly little appetite for engagement in a constitutional battle that had never particularly interested the prime minister anyway. Furthermore, with the House of Commons seemingly becoming collectively *more* attached to an at least very substantially elected second chamber (the activities of the unicameralists aside), it was clear that the game might well be up for those who continued to argue in favour of a predominantly nominated House of Lords. Indeed, as the prospect of Tony Blair's departure from 10 Downing Street approached, it became apparent that House of Lords reform might be postponed until after a general election, so as not to weigh down the first portion of the Brown premiership with mighty constitutional struggles. This was confirmed in July 2007, when Jack Straw stated that Lords reform was once more on ice. Another white paper was promised, that would again outline the shifting position of the government by abandoning the 'half-and-half' option in favour of a wholly or very substantially elected second chamber, an option that was apparently favoured by Gordon Brown, and which, it was promised, would appear as a clear statement of preference in the next Labour election manifesto.

Conclusion

In February 2003, the House of Commons came close to securing a solid basis on which to reform the composition of the House of Lords. However, as with the attempt at substantial select committee reform in March 2002, that particular endeavour ended in disappointment. It might be countered, of course, that with most of the hereditary peers removed, and with a party balance more in evidence, significant steps had already been taken towards a reformed House of Lords, and that the second chamber considered itself more legitimate since its membership basis has been altered (Russell 2003). The whole question of what counts as a 'more legitimate' House, and how legitimacy is measured, is however a far from straightforward matter. The term 'legitimacy' was utilised in many different ways throughout the recent House of Lords reform episode, and the criteria for what would make the House 'more' legitimate changed constantly (Kelso 2006).

However, in the rush to judge the success of the House of Lords endeavour, and whether or not the resulting chamber was 'more' legitimate, it is easy to overlook the quite profound constitutional change which did take place. The vast majority of the hereditary peers were removed successfully from the second chamber, and no other single attempt at House of Lords reform in the previous century came even close to securing that kind of overwhelming change. Pointing to this remarkable reform is not, however, the same as suggesting that the Labour government approached reform from a particularly principled position. The government's main motivation following its election in 1997 was to remove Conservative dominance from the second chamber, not to usher in an age of democratic renewal simply for the sake of it, despite what the rhetoric may have indicated to the contrary. It was a measure motivated by political expediency and by the desire of the incoming government to ensure that it could secure its legislative programme without excessive interference from and delay by the second chamber. Despite the manifesto claims regarding the need to create a more democratic House of Lords, it remains the case that removing the hereditary peers was a proposal that was difficult to argue against. The time taken to embark on 'stage two' of reform is testament not only to the trickiness of the issue, but to the nature of the motivations of the executive as the dominant actor at Westminster.

Ultimately, the Labour Party was never really sure what it wanted to secure following the removal of the hereditary peers, and possessed no clear rationale along which to reform the composition of the second chamber (Dorey 2006: 617). Yet, despite the Labour government's constitutional conservatism, it was nevertheless forced to proceed with a more radical 'stage two' than it would have liked as a result of the comprehensive rejection of the white paper of 2001. In analysing those events, it is obvious that a window of opportunity and political leadership were in place as important preconditions required for reform to proceed. What is less obvious is that there was a clear reform agenda behind which reformers could unite, and the House of Commons was ultimately unable to choose one particular option for composition over others. It is also clear that, because MPs were unable to make a clear choice, there was a distinct lack of political will to secure reform – had there been such will, one option would have been triumphant. The overwhelming support for a substantially elected chamber amongst MPs was fatally weakened by party political considerations, which consistently constrain political will for reform. What the episode demonstrates, as did the select committee reform episode in 2002, is an inherent problem with the whole notion of political will, not only in terms of the difficulties associated with actually generating it, but also in terms of how we analyse and conceptualise it.

The struggles between the Leader of the House, Robin Cook, and his government colleagues, notably the Lord Chancellor but also the prime minister, demonstrate the restricted capabilities of individual actors when seeking to challenge established institutional norms. Cook's efforts to build consensus for Lords reform, and to consolidate the support of a significant portion of the PLP in support of change, were extensive, but ultimately insufficient for breaking down the institutional norm of the pre-eminent Commons. The language of historical institutionalism helps to determine the specifics of this apparent change of heart amongst a sufficient number of MPs. Institutional change, as Hay and Wincott (1998: 955) explain, must first filter through the perceptions that are determined by the structured institutional context that favours certain strategies for change over others. The structured institutional context at Westminster creates a 'logic of appropriateness' that MPs use as a reference point in order to perceive events around them and to determine their goals and actions. The logic of appropriateness at Westminster encourages MPs to rank their party commitments above their parliamentary ones, and also to ensure that a strong government in a pre-eminent Commons is preserved. It was the practical impact of this logic of appropriateness which helps account for why MPs collectively failed to support any one single option for Lords reform. The ideas forwarded in favour of an elected second chamber ultimately failed in 2003 to destabilise the dominant set of shared beliefs about the need to preserve a pre-eminent Commons.

The discourse adopted by those who were against an elected element in the Lords, including the prime minister, that it would lead to a 'rival' chamber, served to bring to centre stage the idea that, above all, the House of Commons had to remain pre-eminent and that elected members in the second chamber might undermine that pre-eminence. This has long been a vital weapon in the armoury of executives and other actors who wish to ensure that the government-dominated House of Commons should not be frustrated by the second chamber. The debate has been cast in terms of one house attempting to usurp the other, yet the fault-line is not really between the House of Commons and the House of Lords, but is in fact between parliament and the executive. The argument that the pre-eminence of the House of Commons must be preserved has itself become a norm derived from the structured institutional context of Westminster, and which has become a part of the parliamentary fabric. It was used by the Liberal and Labour governments respectively in order to secure the Parliament Acts, and it was used in

1968–69 by backbenchers as a way of thwarting reform. In 2003, the core beliefs held by MPs that the pre-eminence of the Commons was paramount served to persuade sufficient numbers of MPs not to vote for elections to the second chamber. The months after the mauling of the government white paper in 2001 may have appeared to be a critical juncture that could have jolted the pre-eminent Commons norm and facilitated more radical reform. This historical longevity of the pre-eminence argument, however, meant that it was ultimately reinforced, despite the episode being a close-run thing in the end. Despite initial consensus on the need for change, and the possibility of utilising that political will in order to secure it, the assertion of the norms and values of the Westminster institutional infrastructure served to muddy the waters and prevent reform from proceeding. It was the eventual absence of political will for reform that was the undoing of this particular House of Lords reform episode.

However, while reform may well have been undone in 2003, the entire episode nevertheless had a profound effect on the political context in which reform was discussed, and it altered the institutional path within which reform had thus far been contained. Once more, as was the case with the issue of effectiveness reform in the House of Commons, process mattered more than outcome. Parliamentary discussion and, crucially, voting on the question of reforming the composition of the House of Lords had never before been so extensive as it was in 2003. The Commons may well have been unable to reach a clear decision, but the voting patterns revealed an underlying preference amongst MPs for a substantially elected House, and thereafter it was increasingly unthinkable that the issue would simply recede into the background. The institutional context in which Lords reform was discussed was significantly altered by the various dialogues which took place in the lead-up to the 2003 votes, and by the emerging Commons view that a predominantly nominated second chamber was not a feasible option in the longer term. In other words, the events of 2003 may well have ended in short-term failure, but they also facilitated a small shift in the institutional pathway, which was sufficient to keep the matter on the political agenda. Whether that shift was the result of partisan manoeuvrings or of genuine commitments to the principle of election, the fact remains that the air was sufficiently stirred to prevent the return of stale impasse. In the final analysis, the failure of the 2003 reform endeavour, rather than mark the end of the attempt to re-establish the House of Lords on a democratic basis, instead underpinned its continuation, because the failed attempt itself altered the institutional context in which the reform discussion took place. The initial outcome may not have been what reformers wished for, but the process of that reform episode did affect the context in which reform was discussed subsequently.

Of course, these events do not spontaneously emerge out of the ether, and key individuals have been highly significant throughout in driving reform. Robin Cook's presence and contribution was not sufficient to consolidate reform in 2003, but it nevertheless helped structure the role later played by Jack Straw in keeping the question of House of Lords composition very firmly on the agenda. Yet, in the entire Blair era, the prime minister's preference for a significantly nominated chamber, and his underlying ambivalence about the need for reform in the first place, structured the reform debate. However, the desire of the new prime minister, Gordon Brown, to resolve the House of Lords issue, and his apparent predisposition to an elected solution, along with Brown's decision to retain Jack Straw in a crucial position in the reform landscape, are testimony to the importance of individuals in the tapestry of parliamentary development, and to the profound effect of the preferences of key elites on the likelihood and nature of reform. Institutional norms and values matter with respect to the course of parliamentary reform, but so too do the individuals who inhabit that institution, not just for the plainly obvious reason that individuals affect institutions, but for the more subtle one that some individuals can *choose* to affect institutions in particular ways at particular times, while others can only attempt to do so, with each scenario in turn structured by the predilections of the institutional context in existence. The stop-start pattern of House of Lords reform in the period after 1997 is, if nothing else, testament to this fact. In this respect, then, political will is an important condition, but it is not sufficient. As the Blair era reached its end in the summer of 2007, the institutional context had been considerably altered by the very process of House of Lords reform undertaken up to that point, making it far more malleable in the hands of those government elites who were by then committed to taking reform forward. Once more, whether we judge the efforts at House of Lords reform in the post-1997 era as successful or unsuccessful, the lesson uncovered here is that the process of reform matters more than the outcome.

9

Understanding parliamentary reform

Parliamentary reform in perspective

There have been several different arguments pursued in this book, but one in particular has served to link all the others together, which is that institutions are characterised both by persistence and by change, and we must have devices in our conceptual toolkit that are capable of analysing, and perhaps even explaining, both. Historical institutionalism has been used here because it not only forces us to take the long-term view of an institution's development, but also gives us insights into norms and values, institutional contexts, agents and ideas, path dependency and critical junctures, all of which assist in the analysis of institutional persistence and change. It is in facilitating consideration of the context in which parliament, and its reform, exists that the application of the historical institutionalist lens provides the most value. Historical analysis coupled with the conceptual framework provided by institutional theory structured this inquiry into parliamentary reform, and has helped us provide a richer analysis of what does, and does not, take place.

As Chapter 2 illustrated, 'institutions provide the context in which political actors define their strategies and pursue their interests' (Thelen and Steinmo 1992: 7). As a formal institution, parliament provides 'systems of meaning' for the actors who reside therein (Peters 1999: 26), and structures their construction of a 'logic of appropriateness' to which they refer when considering the various courses of action open to them in different situations (March and Olsen 1989: 23). This logic of appropriateness guides actors as they negotiate the dominant value system that operates within their institution. Historical institutional theory builds on normative institutionalism by suggesting that institutions constrain politics and 'structure political interactions and in this way affect political outcomes' (Thelen and Steinmo 1992: 13). Both the strategies and the goals that actors pursue are shaped by the institutional context in which they exist (Thelen and Steinmo 1992: 8). Path process. The reforms of 1911 and 1949 were pursued because the executive did not want the House of Lords to constrain its governing capability. Yet there has also been another line of thought with respect to House of Lords reform, which maintains that the purpose of reform should be to secure an altogether new kind of upper house, and which has focused first and foremost on the issue of composition. This approach has only been tangentially couched in discussions about effectiveness, and has instead been a discourse couched far more in the language of legitimacy. From this perspective, reform has been championed because the main problem with the second chamber is said to be its unacceptable composition. However, despite the removal of the majority of the hereditary peers in 1999, the specific basis on which the second chamber should be composed was not rationalised during the first decade of the Labour government's term of office. The structured institutional context at Westminster therefore favours those reforms which are designed to preserve and extend the pre-eminence of the House of Commons – by removing and curtailing the powers of the House of Lords – while also facilitating resistance to those other reforms that would conceivably undermine that pre-eminence. Path dependency has therefore precluded a sustained focus on the issue of composition, at least until recently.

That said, it is necessary to restate the claim made here that the relationship between efficiency reforms and effectiveness reforms is not zero-sum: the two kinds of reform can complement each other, and can be mutually reinforcing. Nonetheless, the various reform tales told here makes plain the lack of harmony that has characterised these two different streams of reform in the past century, particularly with respect to the House of Commons. That such tensions exist serves to demonstrate the quite different perspectives that are adopted by different parliamentary actors in terms of the role and function of parliament. We may, from an academic perspective, claim that effectiveness reforms and efficiency reforms do not necessarily relate to each other in a zero-sum way, but the dominant parliamentary elites do not, on the whole, see it that way at all.

Why now?

While it is important to understand why different actors want to reform parliament in different ways, it is also necessary to understand why demands for parliamentary reform seem to peak at particular times. Again, the distinction between effectiveness and efficiency can be useful here. As Chapters 3 and 4 illustrated, executives are almost always interested in reforms that can help them secure their legislation speedily. The 1902 package of efficiency reforms, which altered parliamentary procedure so as to expand executive capabilities, came in the wake of those changes that had occurred at the end of the nineteenth century in response to Irish obstructionism, and were geared towards building on those changes while conditions remained favourable. The 1906–7 procedural reforms occurred because the Liberal government wanted to ensure it could pass its broad package of legislation, some of which was fairly radical, without undue interference from Commons opponents. The 1945–46 reforms were a response to the need to reconstruct the nation after the Second World War, and to the desires of the Labour government to implement its welfare legislation, and so were also aimed at ensuring that parliamentary procedure would help with the expeditious despatch of executive business, rather than hinder it. Similarly, the various efficiency reforms pursued after 1997 were the result of the new Labour government, after almost twenty years in opposition, wishing to ensure that its vast legislative package would not be unduly delayed as it progressed through the Commons. With respect to efficiency reforms, therefore, the most important changes have taken place at times when governments have perceived parliamentary procedure as either a real or potential constraint on the capabilities of the executive to legislate in the way it intends. However, while there have been particular times when considerable changes have been made to the efficiency of the House of Commons, there has also been an on-going process of efficiency adaptations, which was particularly marked in the years after 1960 when the Procedure Committee regularly examined ways to enhance the efficiency of the Commons, most notably in terms of improvements designed to streamline its working practices.

Demands for efficiency reforms peak at times when governments have a particularly pressing wish to enhance the expeditious dispatch of business, and their emergence onto the agenda at different times is therefore largely dependent on the executive. In contrast, the emergence onto the agenda of demands for effectiveness reforms requires more careful explanation. Chapter 5 charted the progress of effectiveness reforms throughout the twentieth century, and demonstrated that there was a peak in demand for comprehensive reform of parliament in the early 1930s, the early to mid 1960s, and the mid to late 1970s. Of course, there were calls for effectiveness reforms at other times: for example, the continued call for the creation of investigative committees persisted at various levels for much of the post-1945 era. Yet there is no question that demand reached a crescendo in the three periods noted. There were significant political and economic concerns in the early 1930s and 1960s, and the late 1970s, which help us contextualise the introspection which occurred and the consequent questioning of the political institutions in existence. Parliament was only one of several different institutions that were examined and found wanting during these episodes. Calls for reform to enhance the effectiveness of the House of Commons gained such apparently broad support amongst various commentators at those specific times because the political and economic crises that Britain then endured led many people to conclude that only considerable institutional innovation could remedy the situation.

So, exogenous pressures can cause internal institutional change, this much is clear. But the historical institutional perspective does not mean that endogenous pressures for change do not also exist. One of the key conclusions drawn about the creation of the specialised committees and then the departmental select committees in the House of Commons is that pressures for these changes emerged as a result of a growing awareness amongst parliamentary actors themselves that the executive was too strong – in other words, the institution itself sought to address the problems which had resulted from its own particular pathway of historical development. This process took time – almost two decades from when serious talk began regarding committees in the early 1960s to their creation in the late 1970s. New ideas about new institutional configurations required time to gain acceptance, and time was also required to reach a basic consensus about the 'best' format of those new configurations.

Accounting for why there were demands for effective Commons reform in the post-1997 era requires somewhat more careful consideration. The calls for select committee reform that reached a crescendo in 2001 cannot be accounted for with reference to widespread concerns about the political or economic systems in which parliament operated, for the simple fact that there were few such explicit concerns. Instead, these demands for reform were the product of analysis of the functioning of the Commons by parliamentarians themselves, analysis that culminated in the conclusion that the select committee system had to be strengthened significantly in its relationship with the executive, and which was an extension of the same conclusions reached in the late 1970s. The calls for reform in the 1930s and 1960s were prompted largely (although not exclusively) by specifically exogenous events – political and economic crises. In contrast, the calls for reform from 1999 onwards were prompted by events endogenous to parliament, mainly the long-standing strife between the select committees and the executive. The move to embark upon reform was greatly aided by the role of the Leader of the House, Robin Cook, which underlines the significant role played by agency in the course of institutional development. This was also demonstrated in Chapter 5, with reference to the role of Richard Crossman as Leader of the House when the specialist select committee system was instituted, and also of Norman St John-Stevas when the departmental select committees were created. Chapter 6 demonstrated the role of extra-parliamentary organisations in framing the reform debate after 1999. However, it remains the case that the demand to reform the select committee system after 1999 was the result of internal Commons pressure on the executive for change, aided considerably by the existence of a 'network of reformers'. Groups such as the Hansard Society served to promote and facilitate the demand, rather than initiate it. In this respect, the post-1997 evidence casts doubt on the claim that institutional change can only proceed as a result of the impact of exogenous forces.

The demand for reform of the select committee system after 1999 was prompted by developments that were endogenous to parliament, and this means that those developments were very clearly shaped by the structured institutional context in which parliament exists. Indeed, the political system of which parliament is a part remained the integral reason why the effectiveness of the House of Commons was thought to need enhancing in the first place. The calls for reform made in the period after 1997 largely questioned the nature of executive-legislative relations, and the dominance of the executive within the political system. Consequently, the reasons why demands for reform reach a crescendo at certain times may be the result of either exogenous or endogenous events (and both may occur simultaneously). However, regardless of whether the 'crisis' is external or internal to parliament, the root cause of both types of crisis always stems from discontent about the nature of the political system, and the operation of the norms and values that provide the structured institutional context from which dominant elites benefit.

Similar reasons help explain why calls for reform of the House of Lords peak at certain times. The two major reforms of the twentieth century which curbed the powers of the second chamber were both initiated at the behest of government. On the first occasion, in 1909–11, the reforms occurred at that particular time because the second chamber was interfering with the ability of the government to secure its legislation. On the second occasion, in 1948–49, the reforms occurred because the government was anxious that the second chamber might interfere with controversial legislation it planned to introduce late in the parliament. On both occasions, therefore, the timing of the reforms was the direct result of political expediency. The attempted reforms of 1968–69 are a little harder to account for in terms of timing, as Chapter 7 illustrated. They came after much of the concern about the functioning of parliament had begun to recede, and were not a response to any substantial obstructionism from the upper house. Nonetheless, the reasons why the attempted reform occurred when it did is partly accounted for by the continued desire of the government to restrict further the powers of the Lords, which then led to an expansion of analysis to include the issue of composition, and which was largely an accidental outcome of the political circumstances of the time.

The situation was somewhat turned on its head in 1997. The Labour Party committed to the removal of the hereditary peers from the House of Lords primarily because it would remove the dominance of the Conservative Party there, and because it seemed, at face value at least, an easy task, and one which would demonstrate the party's professed commitment to democratic renewal. The various attempts at reform which followed the removal of the bulk of the hereditary peers in 1999 can be attributed to the desire of reformers to move on to the 'second stage' of reform, and to the unintended consequences of removing a significant proportion of the second chamber's membership without knowing in advance what would replace it. Of course, whether these unintended consequences were quite as unintended as they may seem remains a moot point. At any rate, the post-1999 House of Lords reform story underlines perfectly the extent to which process matters much more than outcome with respect to institutional change at Westminster: regardless of the timing of the reforms, the process itself opened up discussion about the future of the second chamber, and the weighing of respective ideas about what that future should look like.

Why have some reforms been more successful than others?

We have talked throughout about the 'success' of parliamentary reform. Making a judgement about success depends, first, on what kind of parliamentary reform we are referring to, and, second, on what we mean by 'success.' Efficiency reforms have enjoyed profound success over the past century, at least if they are measured in terms of the extent to which they have strengthened the position of the executive inside parliament, enhanced its procedural dominance in the House of Commons, and increased the speed with which it secures its legislation. The executive has managed this rate of success because, as the dominant actor at Westminster, it possesses the resources required to secure changes in its own interests. Path dependency has privileged the position of the executive at Westminster, and this position has consequently been used to ever greater effect. However, discussing the 'success' of reform is arguably far more interesting when we focus instead on what we defined as effectiveness reforms.

A range of different kinds of effectiveness reforms have been promoted during the past one hundred years. Electoral reforms were proposed early in the last century as a way to redress the imbalance in executive-legislative relations, and thereby contribute to a more effective House of Commons. Proposals for parliamentary devolution were suggested around the same time as a way to assist parliament in refocusing its energies so as to operate more effectively. However, in terms of the way effectiveness has been defined here, there was very little progress made with respect to improvements pursued by institutional means until the 1960s, when the specialist committee system was formed, a development which was consolidated in 1979 with the creation of the departmental select committee system. This system itself became the focus of reform attempts after 1999, in a flurry of parliamentary analysis that sought to pinpoint the problems the system faced, accompanied by attempts to locate and implement remedies. Yet, at each critical stage in the development of a House of Commons scrutiny committee system, reform endeavours fell short of securing the full breadth of institutional change pursued, and the system, in its various manifestations, has consistently lacked the kind of influence and oversight that reformers wished to establish.

In accounting for the disparity between aims and outcomes, it is necessary, and not at all surprising, to take into account the political and institutional context in which reform is pursued. The attitudinal approach to parliamentary reform indicates that substantial and effective reform can be achieved only when certain conditions have been fulfilled. However, although these conditions were largely met in 2001–2 with respect to the select committee system, the substantial reforms pursued failed to find complete approval and implementation. Effectiveness reforms are infrequently implemented in the way their advocates argue they should be, and their success is consequently qualified. For example, when the select committee system was established in 1979, its potential success was limited because of restrictions placed on its powers of inquiry and on its institutional capabilities. Similarly, the select committee reforms approved in 2002 excluded the important proposal to remove the power of the whips from the nomination process.

Reforms which are aimed at enhancing the effectiveness of the House of Commons are, by their very nature, in diametrical opposition to the norms and values that comprise the structured institutional context in which parliament exists. The dominant elites at Westminster who benefit from those norms and values will consistently resist the implementation of effectiveness reforms, and work to dilute the impact of those reforms that do proceed. The select committee system was proposed as a means to realign the ministerial responsibility convention, and restrain the influence of partisanship in the House. In its implemented form, the select committee system has not succeeded in fully achieving either of these goals.

The picture is somewhat more complicated as far as the House of Lords is concerned, because the issue of effectiveness is tied intimately to whether we are discussing functional legitimacy or democratic legitimacy. On the one hand, the House of Lords adapted its institutional configuration during the latter half of the twentieth century in a way which greatly enhanced its functional effectiveness in terms of scrutiny. In addition, the removal of the hereditary peers in 1999 seemingly had the consequence of enhancing the perception of the remaining peers that they were 'entitled' to obstruct the government when appropriate, thus enhancing the effectiveness of the second chamber in terms of its functional performance. Yet, the effectiveness issue has been repeatedly complicated by the question of democratic legitimacy. Ostensibly, the reason given for opposing the introduction of democratic legitimacy in the Lords has been the need to preserve the democratic legitimacy, and pre-eminence, of the Commons, or more specifically, the sovereignty of the executive that resides in the Commons. The long-standing argument against a democratically composed second chamber is that it would impact on the norm of executive sovereignty and restrict the governing capabilities of the executive. Yet, the apparent functional effectiveness of the House of Lords in its post-1999 manifestation simply underlines the complexity of the assumptions involved: while some argue against an elected House because it would undermine parliamentary effectiveness by producing gridlock between the two Houses, others argue against election because it would remove the quality that has produced the effectiveness that is now championed, that is, independence and expertise. Consequently, although we define effectiveness reforms as those which seek to rebalance executive-legislative relations, discussions about House of Lords reform highlight perfectly just how varied are the interpretations of how that rebalancing might be achieved.

The attitudinal approach to parliamentary reform suggests a seductive remedy to the imbalance in executive-legislative relations: once the three prerequisite conditions for reform have been met, parliamentarians must summon the political will to secure change. Yet, effectiveness reforms are designed as a remedy to the problem of an over-dominant executive, but also require that problem to absent itself temporarily in order for them to be successful. In advocating changes to the operation of executive sovereignty, inverted ministerial responsibility, and skewed partisanship, parliamentary reformers successfully locate the 'problem' of parliament in terms of the structured institutional context in which it exists. However, at the point of prescription and remedy, reformers plead the case that a strong executive needs a strong parliament, a rationale that simply ignores the norms and values of the structured institutional context they seek to alter.

The structured institutional context at Westminster favours some strategies for change over others. The nature of the institutional norms and values of that context means that changes designed to enhance the efficiency of parliament are favoured over those designed to enhance its effectiveness. Efficiency reforms benefit the dominant elites at Westminster in a number of ways: they shore up the operation of executive sovereignty by securing the expeditious dispatch of legislation through both Houses of Parliament with the expenditure of the minimum of resources, and they promote strategies that impede parliament's ability to secure ministerial responsibility. These efficiency reforms are procured by means of the partisan structures that underpin political life at Westminster, and which provide MPs with the logic of appropriateness they need in order to justify their actions and goals. Simultaneously, the structured institutional context at Westminster is biased against effectiveness reforms, because such reforms are detrimental to the dominant elites in as much as they seek to alter the norms and values on which their dominance is based. They aim to temper the operation of executive sovereignty by involving parliament more fully in legislative scrutiny, and secure more comprehensive parliamentary accountability through the convention of ministerial responsibility. To secure such reforms, MPs are required to abandon their logic of appropriateness based on partisanship, and replace it with one based on the merits of parliamentarianism. Time and time again, MPs fail to do this, and thus fail to assert the political will required to achieve effective change, because the norms and values in operation at Westminster support executive dominance and strong government. Those norms and values maintain a bifurcated parliament, not a corporate one. Reformers therefore acknowledge the structured institutional context that favours some kinds of reform over others, but fail adequately to engineer strategies that accommodate that context sufficiently to allow their frequently expansive reform programmes to proceed. At the point of action, reformers revert to an almost idealistic vision of parliament and the political system, one in which it would be true to claim that a strong government can benefit from a strong parliament.

The paradox of parliamentary reform

The central basis on which parliamentary reform has been advocated in the past century is that the executive is too strong and too dominant at Westminster, and, consequently, that parliament is marginalised and unable to hold the executive effectively to account. These diagnoses stem directly from the nature of the Westminster political system, which has evolved in a way that favours strong and responsible government. They are, in essence, criticisms of the remarkable success of the political system in maintaining the principle of strong government during the many centuries of change that have passed since it was first established.

The diagnosis that the executive is too strong is a comment on the political system, and it may be a convincing one. But reformers have proceeded nevertheless from that diagnosis to produce two particular paradoxes in the defence of parliamentary reform. The first concerns the basis on which effective parliamentary reform is promoted, and in particular, the basis on which it is promoted to the dominant elites in parliament, both of which are distinct from the basis on which the need for reform is originally diagnosed. The second concerns the way in which reformers reconcile the potential outcomes of parliamentary reform with the practical implications of the operation of the political system.

Despite the diagnosis that reform must proceed because the executive is too strong and overbearing, reformers have consistently made the case that effective parliamentary reform would actually contribute to *better* government. This argument threaded through much of the advocacy of devolution in the early twentieth century, and comprised a considerable part of the supporting evidence in favour of a specialist Commons committee system. Those who backed the creation of committees in the 1930s partly based their case on the extent to which they would assist departments in making better policy choices. This approach was prominent in the 1960s, when reform advocates, Bernard Crick in particular, argued that strong government needs a strong parliament. In the late 1970s, select committees were countenanced as a mechanism to restrain departments and improve policy making. Similarly, the parliamentary reforms advocated in the post-1997 era, particularly those relating to the select committee system, were also based on the argument that strong government needs a strong parliament, and that good scrutiny contributes to good government, with such rhetoric proving to be a staple for the Hansard Society Commission, the Norton Commission, the Liaison Committee and Robin Cook. The Norton Commission argued that 'government, ultimately, benefits from an effective Parliament' (Conservative Party 2000: 9), and Robin Cook repeatedly used the phrase 'good scrutiny makes for good government'. The idea of a strong parliament implies the reinvigoration of both Houses of Parliament, working together through complementary mechanisms of scrutiny and accountability in order effectively to check the executive and thus contribute to better government.

In strictly conceptual terms, 'strong' government does not necessarily equate with 'good' government. Similarly, a 'strong' parliament does not equate with 'good' scrutiny or an 'effective' parliament. Nevertheless, there has been a degree of conflation of these terms, which may perhaps be justified, to the extent that good and effective scrutiny cannot be achieved unless there is a strengthening of parliament's capabilities. Furthermore, the desire to strengthen parliament has been justified because it will mean that the government is better able to govern effectively. This approach demonstrates the extent to which parliamentary reform has been rationalised as a means to modernise government and improve public policy making. It has been made more palatable to the dominant elites by means of the argument that the ultimate outputs of government will be improved as a result of enhanced parliamentary involvement in legislative and scrutiny processes. One Conservative member of the Modernisation Committee, for example, commented that 'if you have a government which is being held effectively to account by the legislature, you're going to get better, more accountable government' (interview, 23 May 2002). A Labour member of the Modernisation Committee corroborated this view, arguing that 'strong parliamentary scrutiny makes better laws; it's in the government's interest to have strong scrutiny' (interview, 15 May 2002). Another Labour Modernisation Committee member also utilised this justification for parliamentary reform, stating that:

> We want the quality of legislation to be good, we want the quality of decision-making by the government to be good. And that means good quality scrutiny

too, and a good government shouldn't be afraid of good scrutiny by parliament. (Interview, 13 May 2002)

Similarly, a Hansard Society Commission member explained that 'good scrutiny keeps government on its toes, ensures that government learns from its mistakes, and ensures that government is a learning organisation' (interview, 28 November 2001). More succinctly, a Norton Commission member commented that 'a batsman becomes a better batsman, the better the bowler is' (interview, 23 April 2002). Therefore, while those who advocate effective parliamentary reform do so on the basis that the executive is too strong, they nevertheless justify their reform proposals on the grounds that executive dominance would, to all intents and purposes, be continued.

The second paradox of parliamentary reform involves the way in which advocates of reform accommodate the potential outcomes of parliamentary reform with the nature of the political system. Much of the reformist discourse has been based on the idea that a strong government and a strong parliament are not mutually exclusive in the Westminster context. This was a point defended by many of the interviewees involved in promoting parliamentary reform. One Liberal Democrat member of the Modernisation Committee, for example, argued that the creation of a strong parliament in the context of a strong government should be 'the ultimate goal' of parliamentary reform (interview, 23 April 2002). However, one Conservative member of the All-Party Group for Parliamentary Reform accepted that it was 'very difficult to achieve both' (interview, 14 May 2002). A member of the Hansard Society Commission explained that the co-existence of a strong government and a strong parliament depended on a change in behaviour, and that there needed to be an element of realism 'about the attitude of working politicians' (interview, 17 April 2002). Yet, the point is a delicate one, and a member of the Norton Commission qualified the matter by explaining that the aim was 'to facilitate strong government, not over-strong government' (interview, 29 November 2001).

However, these ideas that strong government needs a strong parliament and that good scrutiny makes for good government share the same weakness, in that they largely ignore the practical implications of the Westminster political system. Parliamentary reformers have argued that reform is required because the executive is too strong, but defend their reforms on the grounds that the strength of the executive would not be detrimentally reduced by them. As one Labour member of the Modernisation Committee remarked, despite talk of the attractiveness of a strong legislature, 'parliament has to ensure that the executive gets its way in the end' (interview, 13 May 2002). The British political system is based on the principle of strong government legitimated by a representative parliament that exists to reflect the wishes of the political community. The political system first and foremost facilitates a strong executive, not a strong parliament. The extent to which reformers have felt compelled to justify reform on the basis that it would enhance governing capabilities is itself testament to the predilections of the Westminster political system and the institutional context it has fostered.

The logic of parliamentary reform

These paradoxes of parliamentary reform help uncover one important truism about its focus and its success over the past one hundred years. Parliamentary reformers have located the central problem that reform seeks to address in the way in which government dominates the political system. However, that identification has not led to changes designed to alter the political system that propagates that dominance. Reforms have focused on institutional innovations and adaptations, such as the introduction of committee systems, and in so doing, have focused on the consequences of executive dominance, not the cause. Reformers have proposed institutional changes, rather than changes to the wider context in which those institutions operate. Reformers frequently argue for parliamentary reforms of one kind or another, when their own diagnosis actually requires the reform of the system of party government, which is itself dependent on the accepted merits of parliamentary government. The logical prescription to the diagnosis of a dominant executive underpinned by partisanship is a reform solution that alters that partisanship. Consequently, the logic of the reform argument is that external reform of the political system is in order, rather than internal reform of parliament.

Of course, one of the most obvious ways to achieve the kind of external reform that would impact upon the partisan underpinnings of the political system is to embark upon a process of electoral reform. As with most propositions in the realm of parliamentary reform, this is by no means a novel suggestion. Contemporary discussions of electoral reform normally defend it primarily because it might secure a fairer system of representation, with a reduction in partisanship and executive dominance largely being viewed as a welcome by-product. Nonetheless, some academic observers have promoted electoral reform precisely because of its likely impact on the norms and values of the political system (Johnson 1977; Walkland 1983). The aim here is not to embark upon an analysis of the merits of electoral reform as a cure for the failings of parliamentary government. However, it is illuminating to note the attitudes of those involved in contemporary parliamentary reform endeavours towards this claim about the ultimate logic of parliamentary reform and the potential of electoral reform. For example, while Liberal Democrat members of the Modernisation Committee displayed sympathy to this proposition, as a result of their party's position on the matter, they nevertheless maintained that effective parliamentary reform could also be secured by internal reforms (interviews, 23 April 2002). One Liberal Democrat member of the All-Party Group for Parliamentary Reform noted that electoral reform would bring about a change in the 'culture' of parliament, but also insisted that there could be such a change 'if there was the will to make it happen amongst existing colleagues' (interview, 14 May 2002). One Conservative member of the Group insisted that electoral reform would produce a less effective parliament, because of the profound changes to the 'culture and dynamics' of the place (interview, 23 April 2002). Some Labour members of both the Group and the Modernisation Committee argued that, while electoral change was necessary, it was such a long way off that parliament simply had to proceed with its own internal changes in the interim (interviews, 18 April 2002, 14 and 15 May 2002). One Labour Modernisation Committee member stated that 'external factors are always the ones that promote internal change' and argued that 'big bangs', such as electoral reform, are often required to bring about meaningful change (interview, 15 May 2002). One Conservative member of the Modernisation Committee, who was extremely critical of the way in which adversary politics undermined the capabilities of parliament and the functioning of parliamentary government, nevertheless described the proposition regarding electoral reform as 'absolute rubbish' (interview, 23 May 2002).

Executive dominance at Westminster is underpinned and supported by the norms and values of partisanship, and the adversary politics that it propagates. The logic of parliamentary reform is, therefore, to reform the political system that facilitates this partisanship, and thus to engage with electoral reform. That logic itself produces yet another paradox of parliamentary reform: electoral reform can only be achieved if the dominant elites at Westminster possess the political will to secure such reform. As they ultimately benefit from present electoral arrangements, political will for such reforms is unlikely to be forthcoming. More proportional systems may have been introduced for the devolved legislatures, but as Tony Blair remarked, 'that does not mean that that system is right for the House of Commons' (HC Debs, 13 July 2000, col. 1099).

Parliamentary reform is paradoxical in its logic. It is proposed as a means to realign the norms and values that structure parliament's institutional context. Yet those inverted norms and values structure the institutional context, favouring some reforms over others, and ultimately make it extremely difficult to secure effectiveness reforms. However, strong government is legitimated with reference to the principle of parliamentary representation. The continued undermining of that principle may at some stage force the kind of reforms required in order to stave off the sort of 'legitimation crisis' that some commentators argue is endemic in the British political system (Judge 2004: 700). Indeed, this book began by noting some of the concerns which have been voiced about the operation of representative democracy in Britain, concerns which have gradually begun to encourage parliament itself to rethink how it engages with both the government and the governed. It would indeed be a considerable irony if the most recent principle on which the political system at Westminster is founded, that of parliamentary democracy, played midwife to the reforms required to salvage the oldest, that of parliamentary government.

The realities of parliamentary reform

Thankfully, we do not live in a political system where our institutions are perfect: they can never be so, and rather than persistently berate parliament for its shortcomings, we should perhaps be happy that we can reflect on how to refine and improve it, even if perfection is unattainable. Too much of what is said about parliamentary reform is seemingly predicated on the need to create an institution that is faultless. Simultaneously, a great deal of what is said about parliamentary reform is based on a desire to pursue a big-bang approach which will, in the blink of an eye, significantly overhaul the way that parliament functions. And of course the traditional assumption about how things work at Westminster is that big-bang approaches are eschewed, and that incremental, almost unnoticeable, change is in fact how reform takes place. Yet, the creation of the departmental select committee system in 1979 and the removal of the bulk of the hereditary peers in 1999 were hardly incremental in nature.

It is too easy to become absorbed in various ways to *describe* the nature of change at Westminster, and to indulge in the language of evolution and incrementalism, when it is far more interesting, and challenging, to *explain* change. In the final analysis, there must be certain pre-conditions in place before parliamentary reform – that is, institutional change – can proceed. The most difficult condition to secure is that of political will, which is also the most problematic from an analytical perspective. Key political elites must be in favour of, or at least acquiescent in, reform, and backbench political will for reform will not by itself be sufficient – that is the inference made from our understanding of the institutional context in which reform would take place. Yet, by looking at parliamentary reform through the lens of historical institutional theory, we have analysed both institutional persistence and institutional change. The perspective is generally accepted as well-placed to account for institutional persistence, as we discovered – path dependency makes it incredibly difficult for substantial institutional change to take place. However, as the post-1997 chapters illustrated, we can accommodate processes of change within a historical institutional framework, because institutions themselves provide the necessary corrections to the faults in their own path dependencies. Dominant norms and values have successfully preserved strong government at Westminster. However, new ideas about institutional configurations – such as select committees – do sometimes succeed in upsetting the dominant institutional frame of reference. Furthermore, while structures are important, so too are agents – none of the successful effectiveness reforms examined in this book would have happened had it not been for the key political actors who supported them. Furthermore, all of the reforms examined here were accompanied by considerable political conflict and disagreement about their purpose and impact, and that conflict itself helped structure the extent to which institutional persistence or change won the day. Consequently, historical institutional analyses must in future give more attention to the role of ideas, agency and political conflict when it comes to analysing, and attempting to explain, institutional change.

But there is more to it that this. Ultimately, process matters more than outcome when we try to understand the story of parliamentary reform. Reform efforts may fail, and they do fall short very often. However, the very process of attempting to secure reform can, and often does, change the institutional path along which parliament travels, and the more extensively the reform pre-conditions have been met in advance, the greater will be the divergence from the existing institutional path. Focusing too much on the substantive outcome of reform episodes might be detrimental to enhanced understanding of how reform dynamics change and develop over time. Outcome matters from the perspective of building institutional capacity, but process matters more in facilitating the maximisation of those outcomes.

This is particularly the case at the end of the Blair era in British politics, an era that was characterised by significant constitutional reforms in the UK. The process of devolution has led to the creation of a Scottish Parliament and a Welsh Assembly, both of which Westminster is increasingly likely to look to for lessons as it proceeds along its own path of institutional development. The prime minister appointed in June 2007, Gordon Brown, initiated a process of examining the Governance of Britain (Cm 7170, 2007), which explicitly addressed the need to rebalance executive-legislative relations in Britain. The process of existing alongside devolved institutions, and the process of fresh analyses of governance relationships, will have implications for the generation of new parliamentary procedures and their outcomes.

It has become common-place to describe devolution in Britain as a process, not an event. This too must become the mantra of Westminster parliamentary reform. The process does not just facilitate an outcome – the process more often than not is the outcome.

Bibliography

Adonis, A. (1993), *Making Aristocracty Work: The Peerage and the Political System in Britain 1884–1914*, Clarendon Press, London.

Aspinwall, M.D. and Schneider, G. (2000), 'Same menu, separate tables: the institutionalist turn in political science and the study of European integration', *European Journal of Political Research*, 38:1, 1–36.

Bagehot, W. (1867), *The English Constitution*, Oxford University Press, Oxford.

Bailey, S.D. (1954a), 'Introduction', in S.D. Bailey (ed.), *The Future of the House of Lords*, Hansard Society, London.

Bailey, S.D. (1954b), 'Life Peerages', in S.D. Bailey (ed.), *The Future of the House of Lords*, Hansard Society, London.

Baines, P. (1985), 'History and rationale of the 1979 reforms', in G. Drewry (ed.), *The New Select Committees: A Study of the 1979 Reforms*, Clarendon Press, Oxford.

Baldwin, N. (1999), 'The membership and work of the House of Lords', in P. Carmichael and B. Dickson (eds), *The House of Lords: Its Parliamentary and Judicial Roles*, Hart Publishing, Oxford.

Beattie, A. (1995), 'Ministerial responsibility and the theory of the British state', in R.A.W. Rhodes and P. Dunleavy (eds), *Prime Minister, Cabinet and Core Executive*, Macmillan, London.

Beer, S. (1974), *The British Political System*, Random House, New York.

Beetham, D., Byrne, I., Ngan, P. and Weir, S. (eds) (2002), *Democracy Under Blair: A Democratic Audit of the United Kingdom*, Politico's, London.

Berrington, H. (1968), 'Partisanship and dissidence in the nineteenth century House of Commons', *Parliamentary Affairs*, 21:4, 338–74.

Birch, A.H. (1964), *Representative and Responsible Government*, George Allen and Unwin, London.

Blackburn, R. and Kennon, A. (2003), *Parliament: Functions, Practices and Procedures*, Sweet and Maxwell, London.

Blank, S. (1979), 'Britain's economic problems: lies and damn lies', in I. Kramnick (ed.), *Is Britain Dying? Perspectives on the Current Crisis*, Cornell University Press, London.

Borthwick, R. (1979), 'Questions and Debates', in S.A. Walkland (ed.), *The House of Commons in the Twentieth Century*, Clarendon Press, Oxford.

Boulton, C.J. (1969), 'Recent developments in House of Commons procedure', *Parliamentary Affairs*, 23:1, 61–71.

Bowler, S., Farrell, D.M. and Katz, R.S. (1999), 'Party cohesion, party discipline and parliaments', in S. Bowler, D.M. Farrell and R.S. Katz (eds), *Party Discipline and Parliamentary Government*, Ohio State University Press, Columbus.

Bradley, A. (2007), 'The sovereignty of parliament: form or substance', in J. Jowell and D. Oliver (eds), *The Changing Constitution*, Oxford University Press, Oxford.

Bromhead, P.A. (1958), *The House of Lords and Contemporary Politics 1911–1957*, Routledge, London.

Bromhead, P.A. (1959), 'How should parliament be reformed?', *Political Quarterly*, 30:3, 272–82.

Bromhead, P.A. and Shell, D. (1967), 'The Lords and their House', *Parliamentary Affairs*, 20:4, 337–49.

Brown, G. (1992), 'The servant state: towards a new constitutional settlement', *Political Quarterly*, 63:4, 394–403.

Buller, J. (1999), 'Britain's relations with the European Union in historical perspective', in D. Marsh et al, *Postwar British Politics in Perspective*, Polity Press, Cambridge.

Butler, D. (1963), *The Electoral System in Britain Since 1918*, Clarendon, Oxford.

Butt, R. (1969), *The Power of Parliament*, Constable, London.

Cairncross, A. (1994), *The British Economy Since 1945*, Blackwell, Oxford.

Catterall, P. (2000), 'The British electoral system, 1885–1970', *Historical Research*, 73:181, 156–74.

Cd 9038 (1918), *Report of the Conference on the Reform of the Second Chamber*, HMSO, London.

Chapman, R.A. (1963), 'The significance of parliamentary procedure', *Parliamentary Affairs*, 16:2, 179–87.

Charter 88 (1998), 'Parliamentary briefing on the Modernisation of the House of Commons', July 1998.

Chester, D.N. (1966), 'The British Parliament, 1939–66', *Parliamentary Affairs*, 19:4, 417–45.

Close, D.H. (1977), 'The collapse of resistance to democracy: Conservatives, adult suffrage and second chamber reform, 1911–1928', *The Historical Journal*, 20:4, 893–918.

Cm 78 (1986), *Government Response to the First Report from the Treasury and Civil Service Committee (HC 62) and to the First Report from the Liaison Committee (HC 100)*, HMSO, London.

Cm 4183 (1999), *Modernising Parliament – Reforming the House of Lords*, HMSO, London.

Cm 4534 (2000), *A House for the Future: Report from the Royal Commission on the Reform of the House of Lords*, HMSO, London.

Cm 4737 (2000), *Government Response to the Liaison Committee Report, Shifting the Balance*, HMSO, London.

Cm 5291 (2001), *The House of Lords: Completing the Reform*, HMSO, London.

Cm 5628 (2002), *Government Response to the Procedure Committee Report on Parliamentary Questions (HC 622)*, HMSO, London.

Cm 7027 (2007), *House of Lords: Reform*, HMSO, London.

Cm 7170 (2007), *The Governance of Britain*, HMSO, London.

Cmnd 3799 (1968), *House of Lords Reform*, HMSO, London.

Cmnd 4507 (1970), *Select Committees of the House of Commons*, HMSO, London.

Cmnd 9841 (1986), *Government Response to the Seventh Report from the Treasury and Civil Service Committee*, HMSO, London.

Cmnd 9916 (1986), *Government Response to the Third and Fourth Reports from the Defence Committee*, HMSO, London.

Cockerell, M. (2001), 'The politics of second chamber reform: a case study of the House of Lords and the passage of the House of Lords Act 1999', *Journal of Legislative Studies*, 7:1, 119–34.

Collier, R.B. and Collier, D. (1991), *Shaping the Political Arena: Critical Junctures, the Labor Movement and Regime Dynamics in Latin America*, Princeton University Press, Princeton.

Conservative Party (1999a), *Commission to Strengthen Parliament: Consultation Paper*, Conservative Party, London.

Conservative Party (1999b), *Report of the Constitutional Commission on Options for a New Second Chamber*, Douglas Slater, London.

Conservative Party (2000), *Strengthening Parliament: The Report of the Commission to Strengthen Parliament*, Conservative Party, London.

Conservative Party (2002), 'The case for a stronger parliament', Press release, 11 December 2002.

Cook, R. (2003a), 'A modern parliament in a modern democracy', *Political Quarterly*, 74:1, 76–82.

Cook, R. (2003b), *The Point of Departure*, Simon and Schuster, London.

Cowley, P. (2005), *The Rebels*, Politico's, London.

Cowley, P. and Stuart, M. (2001), 'Parliament: a few headaches and a dose of modernisation', *Parliamentary Affairs*, 54:2, 238–56.

Crick, B. (1963), 'What should the Lords be doing?', *Political Quarterly*, 34:2, 174–84.

Crick, B. (1965), 'The prospects for parliamentary reform', *Political Quarterly*, 36:3, 333–46.

Crick, B. (1970), *The Reform of Parliament*, Weidenfeld and Nicholson, London.

Dicey, A.V. ([1885] 1959), *An Introduction to the Study of the Law of the Constitution*, Macmillan, London.

DiMaggio, P.J. and Powell, W.W. (1991), 'Introduction', in W.W. Powell and P.J. DiMaggio (eds), *The New Institutionalism in Organisational Analysis*, University of Chicago Press, London.

Donnelly, K. (1997), 'Parliamentary reform: paving the way for constitutional change', *Parliamentary Affairs*, 50:2, 246–62.

Dorey, P. (2006), '1949, 1969, 1999: the Labour Party and House of Lords reform', *Parliamentary Affairs*, 59:4, 599–620.

Dorfman, G.A. (1979), 'The Heath years: some further thoughts about union influence', in I. Kramnick (ed.), *Is Britain Dying? Perspectives on the Current Crisis*, Cornell University Press, London.

Douglas, R. (1986), *World Crisis and British Decline, 1929–56*, Macmillan, Basingstoke.

Douglas, R. (2002), *Liquidation of Empire*, Palgrave, Basingstoke.

Drewry, G. (1972), 'Reform of the legislative process: some neglected questions', *Parliamentary Affairs*, 25:4, 286–99.

Drewry, G. (1985a), 'Scenes from committee life – the new committees in action', in G. Drewry (ed.), *The New Select Committees: A Study of the 1979 Reforms*, Clarendon Press, Oxford.

Drewry, G. (1985b), 'The 1979 reforms – new labels on old bottles?', in G. Drewry (ed.), *The New Select Committees: A Study of the 1979 Reforms*, Clarendon Press, Oxford.

Drewry, G. (2000), 'The new public management', in J. Jowell and D. Oliver (eds), *The Changing Constitution*, Oxford University Press, Oxford.

Eurobarometer 68 (2007), *Public Opinion in the European Union*, European Commission, Brussels.

Evans, E.J. (1985), *Political Parties in Britain, 1783–1867*, Methuen, London.

Flinders, M. (2000), 'The enduring centrality of individual ministerial responsibility within the British constitution', *The Journal of Legislative Studies*, 6:3, 73–92.

Flinders, M. (2002), 'Shifting the balance? Parliament, the executive and the British constitution', *Political Studies*, 50:1, 23–42.

Flinders, M. (2007), 'Analysing reform: the House of Commons, 2001–5', *Political Studies*, 55:1, 174–200.

Foley, M. (1999), *The Politics of the British Constitution*, Manchester University Press, Manchester.

Garrard, J. (2002), *Democratisation in Britain*, Palgrave, Basingstoke.

Giddings, P. (1985), 'What has been achieved?', in G. Drewry (ed.), *The New Select Committees: A Study of the 1979 Reforms*, Clarendon Press, Oxford.

Giddings, P. (1994), 'Select committees and parliamentary scrutiny: plus ca change', *Parliamentary Affairs*, 47:4, 669–86.

Giddings, P. (1997), 'Parliament and the executive', *Parliamentary Affairs*, 50:1, 84–96.

Gilbert, M. (1976), *Winston S. Churchill: Volume 5 1922–1939*, Heinemann, London.

Goldsworthy, J. (1999), *The Sovereignty of Parliament*, Oxford University Press, Oxford.

Gorges, M.J. (2001), 'New institutionalist explanations for institutional change: a note of caution', *Politics*, 21:2, 137–45.

Grant, M. (2003), 'Historians, the Penguin Specials and the 'state-of-the-nation' literature, 1958–64', *Contemporary British History*, 17:3, 29–54.

Grantham, C. (1992), 'Select committees', in D. Shell and D. Beamish (eds), *The House of Lords at Work*, Clarendon Press, Oxford.

Griffith, J.A.G. (1977), 'Standing committees in the House of Commons', in S.A. Walkland and M. Ryle (eds), *The Commons in the Seventies*, Fontana/Collins, Glasgow.

Group of Conservatives (1946), *Some Proposals for Constitutional Reform*, Eyre and Spottiswoode, London.

Hall, P.A. (1986), *Governing the Economy: The Politics of State Intervention in Britain and France*, Oxford University Press, New York.

Hall, P.A. and Taylor, R.C.R. (1996), 'Political science and the three new institutionalisms', *Political Studies*, 44:5, 936–57.

Hansard Society (1967), *Parliamentary Reform: A Survey of Recent Proposals for the Commons*, Cassell and Company, London.

Hansard Society (1993), *Making the Law: The Report of the Hansard Society Commission on the Legislative Process*, Vacher Dod, London.

Hansard Society (2001), *The Challenge for Parliament: Making Government Accountable*, Vacher Dod, London.

Hansard Society (2005), *Members Only? Parliament in the Public Eye*, Vacher Dod, London.

Hanson, A.H. (1957), 'The Labour Party and House of Commons reform – I', *Parliamentary Affairs*, 10:4, 454–68.

Hanson, A.H. (1964), 'The purpose of parliament', *Parliamentary Affairs*, 17:3, 279–95.

Hanson, A.H. (1970), 'The House of Commons and Finance', in A.H. Hanson and B. Crick (eds), *The Commons in Transition*, Fontana, London.

Harling, P. (2001), *The Modern British State*, Polity, Oxford.

Harrop, M. (2001), 'An apathetic landslide: the british general election of 2001', *Government and Opposition*, 36:3, 295–313.

Hart, J. (1992), Proportional Representation: Critics of the British Electoral System 1820–1945, Clarendon Press, Oxford.

Hay, C. (1999), 'Crisis and political development in postwar Britain', in D. Marsh et al, Postwar British Politics in Perspective, Polity Press, Cambridge.

Hay, C. (2007), Why We Hate Politics, Polity Press, Cambridge.

Hay, C. and Wincott, D. (1998), 'Structure, agency and historical institutionalism', Political Studies, 46:5, 951–7.

HC 9 (1945–46), First Report from the Select Committee on Procedure, HMSO, London.

HC 19 (1989–90), The Working of the Select Committee System, Second Report from the Select Committee on Procedure, HMSO, London.

HC 20 (1991–92), Report from the Select Committee on Sittings of the House, HMSO, London.

HC 49 (1984–85), Public Bill Procedure, Second Report from the Select Committee on Procedure, HMSO, London.

HC 58 (1945–46), Second Report from the Select Committee on Procedure, HMSO, London.

HC 60 (1998–99), The Parliamentary Calendar: Initial Proposals, First Report from the Select Committee on Modernisation of the House of Commons, HMSO, London.

HC 61 (2000–1), Ministerial Accountability and Parliamentary Questions, Second Report from the Select Committee on Public Administration, HMSO, London.

HC 62 (1986–87), Ministers and Civil Servants, First Report from the Treasury and Civil Service Committee, HMSO, London.

HC 87 (1995–96), Third Report from the Trade and Industry Committee, HMSO, London.

HC 89 (1906), First Report from the Select Committee on House of Commons Procedure, HMSO, London.

HC 92 (1958–59), Report from the Select Committee on Procedure, HMSO, London.

HC 92 (1985–86), Civil Servants and Ministers: Duties and Responsibilities, Seventh Report from the Treasury and Civil Service Committee, HMSO, London.

HC 100 (1986–87), Accountability of Ministers and Civil Servants to Select Committees of the House of Commons, First Report from the Liaison Committee, HMSO, London.

HC 129 (1931–32), Report from the Select Committee on Procedure, HMSO, London.

HC 153 (1966–67), The Times of Sittings of the House, First Report from the Select Committee on Procedure, HMSO, London.

HC 157 (1986–87), A Parliamentary Calendar, First Report from the Select Committee on Procedure, HMSO, London.

HC 161 (1930–31), Special Report from the Select Committee on Procedure on Public Business, HMSO, London.

HC 171 (2002–3), House of Lords Reform, First Report from the Joint Committee on House of Lords Reform, HMSO, London.

HC 178 (1990–91), Parliamentary Questions, Third Report from the Select Committee on Procedure, HMSO, London.

HC 188 (1964–65), Question Time, Second Report from the Select Committee on Procedure, HMSO, London.

HC 189 (1945–46), Third Report from the Select Committee on Procedure, HMSO, London.

HC 190 (1962–63), Expediting the Finance Bill, Second Report from the Select Committee on Procedure, HMSO, London.

HC 190 (1997–98), The Legislative Process, First Report from the Select Committee on Modernisation of the House of Commons, HMSO, London.

HC 194 (1998–99), Sittings of the House in Westminster Hall, Second Report from the Select Committee on Modernisation of the House of Commons, HMSO, London.

HC 198 (1969–70), Question Time, Second Report from the Select Committee on Procedure, HMSO, London.

HC 224-I and II (2001–2), Select Committees, First Report from the Select Committee on Modernisation of the House of Commons, HMSO, London.

HC 225 (1985–86), The Government's Reply to the Committee's First Report, Session 1984–1985, First Special Report from the Liaison Committee, HMSO, London.

HC 276 (1964–65), Expediting the Finance Bill, Third Report from the Select Committee on Procedure, HMSO, London.

HC 300 (1999–2000), Shifting the Balance: Select Committees and the Executive, First Report from the Liaison Select Committee, HMSO, London.

HC 303 (1964–65), Fourth Report from the Select Committee on Procedure, HMSO, London.

HC 313 (1995–96), Second Report from the Public Service Committee, HMSO, London.

HC 321 (2000–01), Shifting the Balance: Unfinished Business, First Report from the Liaison Select Committee, HMSO, London.

HC 323-I (1996–97), The Work of the Select Committees, First Report from the Liaison Select Committee, HMSO, London.

HC 324 (1985–86), Allocation of Time to Government Bills in Standing Committee, Second Report from the Select Committee on Procedure, HMSO, London.

HC 325 (2003–4), Programming of Legislation, Fourth Report from the Select Committee on Procedure, HMSO, London.

HC 337 (2006–7), Revitalising the Chamber: The Role of the Backbencher, First Report from the Select Committee on Modernisation of the House of Commons, HMSO, London.

HC 350 (1986–87), The Use of Time on the Floor of the House, Second Report from the Select Committee on Procedure, HMSO, London.

HC 356 (1967–68), Dates of the Session and the Financial Year, Report from the Select Committee on Procedure, HMSO, London.

HC 363 (1984–85), The Select Committee System, First Report from the Liaison Select Committee, HMSO, London.

HC 368 (2003–4), Connecting Parliament with the Public, First Report from the Select Committee on Modernisation of the House of Commons, HMSO, London.

HC 382 (2000–1), Programming of Legislation, First Report from the Select Committee on Modernisation of the House of Commons, HMSO, London.

HC 389 (1997–98), Explanatory Material for Bills, Second Report from the Select Committee on Modernisation of the House of Commons, HMSO, London.

HC 393 (1971–72), Report from the Select Committee on Parliamentary Questions, HMSO, London.

HC 410 (1968–69), Scrutiny of Public Expenditure and Administration, Report from the Select Committee on Procedure, HMSO, London.

HC 440 (2001–2), Modernisation of the House of Commons: A Reform Programme for Consultation, Memorandum submitted by the Leader of the House of Commons, HMSO, London.

HC 446 (2003–4), Annual Report for 2003, First Report from the Liaison Select Committee, HMSO, London.

HC 465 (2004–5), Scrutiny of European Business, Second Report from the Select Committee on Modernisation of the House of Commons, HMSO, London.

HC 491 (1974–75), Late Sittings, Third Report from the Select Committee on Procedure, HMSO, London.

HC 491 (2003–4), Results of Sitting Hours Questionnaire, Second Report from the Select Committee on Procedure, HMSO, London.

HC 494-I and II (2001–2), *The Second Chamber: Continuing the Reform*, Fifth Report from the Select Committee on Public Administration, HMSO, London.

HC 513 (2006–7), *Public Petitions and Early Day Motions*, First Report from the Select Committee on Procedure, HMSO, London.

HC 519 (1985–86), *Westland plc: The Government's Decision-Making*, Fourth Report from the Select Committee on Defence, HMSO, London.

HC 538 (1970–71), *The Process of Legislation*, Second Report from the Select Committee on Procedure, HMSO, London.

HC 539 (1966–67), *Public Bill Procedure, Etc.*, Sixth Report from the Select Committee on Procedure, HMSO, London.

HC 543 (1997–98), *Carry-Over of Public Bills*, Third Report from the Select Committee on Modernisation of the House of Commons, HMSO, London.

HC 558 (2002–3), *Annual Report for 2002*, First Report from the Liaison Select Committee, HMSO, London.

HC 569 (1990–91), *Short Speeches*, Fourth Report from the Select Committee on Procedure, HMSO, London.

HC 570 (1983–84), *Short Speeches*, First Report from the Select Committee on Procedure, HMSO, London.

HC 588 (1977–78), *First Report from the Select Committee on Procedure*, HMSO, London.

HC 589 (1999–00), *Programming of Legislation and Timing of Votes*, Second Report from the Select Committee on Modernisation of the House of Commons, HMSO, London.

HC 590 (2001–2), *The Work of Select Committees 2001*, First Report from the Liaison Select Committee, HMSO, London.

HC 592 (1985–86), *Short Speeches*, Third Report from the Select Committee on Procedure, HMSO, London.

HC 622 (2001–2), *Parliamentary Questions*, Third Report from the Select Committee on Procedure, HMSO, London.

HC 623 (1984–85), *Short Speeches*, Fourth Report from the Select Committee on Procedure, HMSO, London.

HC 668 (2002–3), *House of Lords Reform*, Second Report from the Joint Committee on House of Lords Reform, HMSO, London.

HC 671 (1974–75), *Restrictions on the Length of Speeches*, Fourth Report from the Select Committee on Procedure, HMSO, London.

HC 687 (1992–93), *Parliamentary Questions*, First Report from the Select Committee on Procedure, HMSO, London.

HC 692 (2001–02), *Select Committees: Modernisation Proposals*, Second Report from the Liaison Select Committee, HMSO, London.

HC 719 (1998–99), *Thursday Sittings*, Third Report from the Select Committee on Modernisation of the House of Commons, HMSO, London.

HC 748 (1999–2000), *Independence or Control?*, Second Report from the Liaison Select Committee, HMSO, London.

HC 791 (1997–98), *Scrutiny of European Business*, Seventh Report from the Select Committee on Modernisation of the House of Commons, HMSO, London.

HC 820 (1997–98), *Ministerial Accountability and Parliamentary Questions*, Fourth Report from the Select Committee on Public Administration, HMSO, London.

HC 821 (1998–99), *Ministerial Accountability and Parliamentary Questions*, Fourth Report from the Select Committe on Public Administration, HMSO, London.

HC 865 (1998–99), *Work of the Committee: Second Progress Report*, First Special Report from the Select Committee on Modernisation of the House of Commons, HMSO, London.

HC 906 (1999–2000), *Sittings in Westminster Hall*, Fourth Report from the Select Committee on Modernisation of the House of Commons, HMSO, London.

HC 954 (1999–2000), *Thursday Sittings*, Third Report from the Select Committee on Modernisation of the House of Commons, HMSO, London.

HC 1027 (2002–3), *House of Lords Reform: Government Reply to the Committee's Second Report*, Second Special Report from the Joint Committee on House of Lords Reform, HMSO, London.

HC 1086 (2001–2), *Ministerial Accountability and Parliamentary Questions*, Ninth Report from the Select Committee on Public Administration, HMSO, London.

HC 1097 (2005–6), *The Legislative Process*, First Report from the Select Committee on Modernisation of the House of Commons, HMSO, London.

HC 1109 (2001–2), *House of Lords Reform*, Special Report from the Joint Committee on House of Lords Reform, HMSO, London.

HC 1168 (2001–2), *Modernisation of the House of Commons: A Reform Programme*, Second Report from the Select Committee on Modernisation of the House of Commons, HMSO, London.

HC 1222 (2002–3), *Programming of Bills*, First Report from the Select Committee on Modernisation of the House of Commons, HMSO, London.

HC 1248 (2003–4), *Public Petitions*, Fifth Report from the Select Committee on Procedure, HMSO, London.

HC 2121 (2005–6), *Conventions of the UK Parliament*, Report from the Joint Committe on Conventions, HMSO, London.

Hill, A. and Whichelow, A. (1964), *What's Wrong with Parliament?*, Penguin, London.

HL 81 (1998–99), *Election of Hereditary Peers*, Third Report from the Select Committee on Procedure, HMSO, London.

Hollis, C. (1949), *Can Parliament Survive?*, Hollis and Carter, London.

Humphreys, J.H. (1911), *Proportional Representation*, Methuen and Co., London.

James, R.R. (ed.) (1974), *Winston S. Churchill: His Complete Speeches, 1897–1963*, Chelsea House Publishers, London.

Jefferys, K. (1997), *Retreat from New Jerusalem: British Politics, 1951–64*, Macmillan, Basingstoke.

Jenkins, R. (1989), *Mr Balfour's Poodle*, Collins, London.

Jennings, I. (1934), *Parliamentary Reform*, Victor Gollancz, London.

Jennings, I. (1957), *Parliament*, Cambridge University Press, Cambridge.

Jogerst, M. (1993), *Reform in the House of Commons: The Select Committee System*, The University Press of Kentucky, Lexington, Kentucky.

Johnson, J. (1999), 'Britain's economic decline: cultural versus structural explanations', in D. Marsh et al, *Postwar British Politics in Perspective*, Polity Press, Cambridge.

Johnson, N. (1970), 'Select committees as tools of parliamentary reform', in A.H. Hanson and B. Crick (eds), *The Commons in Transition*, Fontana, London.

Johnson, N. (1975), 'Adversary politics and electoral reform: need we be afraid?', in S.E. Finer (ed.), *Adversary Politics and Electoral Reform*, Anthony Wigman, London.

Johnson, N. (1977), *In Search of the Constitution*, Pergamon Press, Oxford.

Johnson, N. (1979), 'Select committees and administration', in S.A. Walkland (ed.), *The House of Commons in the Twentieth Century*, Clarendon Press, Oxford.

Judge, D. (1981), *Backbench Specialisation in the House of Commons*, Heinemann, London.

Judge, D. (1983a), 'Introduction', in D. Judge (ed.), *The Politics of Parliamentary Reform*, Heinemann, London.

Judge, D. (1983b), 'Why reform? Parliamentary reform since 1832: an interpretation', in D. Judge (ed.), *The Politics of Parliamentary Reform*, Heinemann, London.

Judge, D. (1989), 'Parliament in the 1980s', *Political Quarterly*, 60:4, 400–12.

Judge, D. (1992), 'The 'effectiveness' of the post-1979 select committee system: the verdict of the 1990 procedure committee', *Political Quarterly*, 63:1, 91–100.

Judge, D. (1993), *The Parliamentary State*, Sage, London.

Judge, D. (2004), 'Whatever happened to parliamentary democracy in the United Kingdom?', *Parliamentary Affairs*, 57:3, 682–701.

Judge, D. (2005), *Political Institutions in the United Kingdom*, Oxford University Press, Oxford.

Kam, C. (2000), 'Not just parliamentary cowboys and indians: ministerial responsibility and bureaucratic drift', *Governance*, 13:3, 365–92.

Keeton, G.W. (1952), *The Passing of Parliament*, Benn, London.

Kelso, A. (2003), '"Where were the massed ranks of parliamentary reformers?" "Attitudinal" and "contextual" approaches to parliamentary reform', *Journal of Legislative Studies*, 9:1, 57–76.

Kelso, A. (2006), 'Reforming the House of Lords: navigating representation, democracy and legitimacy at Westminster', *Parliamentary Affairs*, 59:4, 563–81.

Kelso, A. (2007a), 'Parliament and political disengagement: neither waving nor drowning', *Political Quarterly*, 78:3, 364–73.

Kelso, A. (2007b), 'The House of Commons Modernisation Committee: who needs it?', *British Journal of Politics and International Relations*, 9:1, 138–57.

King-Hall, S. (1962), 'What is parliamentary democracy?', *Parliamentary Affairs*, 16:1, 13–21.

Koelble, T.A. (1995), 'The new institutionalism in political science and sociology', *Comparative Politics*, 27:2, 231–43.

Kramnick, I. (1979), 'Introduction: the making of a crisis', in I. Kramnick (ed.), *Is Britain Dying? Perspectives on the Current Crisis*, Cornell University Press, London.

Krasner, S. (1984), 'Approaches to the state: alternative conceptions and historical dynamics', *Comparative Politics*, 16:2, 223–46.

Labour Party (1992), *It's Time to Get Britain Working Again*, Labour Party, London.

Labour Party (1997), *New Labour: Because Britain Deserves Better*, Labour Party, London.

Lascelles, F.W. (1952), 'A second chamber', in Lord Campion et al, *Parliament: A Survey*, George Allen and Unwin, London.

Laski, H. (1938), *Parliamentary Government in England*, George Allen and Unwin, London.

Lenman, B. (1992), *The Eclipse of Parliament*, Edward Arnold, London.

Leonard, D. (1995), 'Replacing the Lords', *Political Quarterly*, 66:4, 287–98.

Levi, M. (1997), 'A model, a method and a map: rational choice in comparative and historical analysis', in M. Lichbach and A. Zuckerman (eds), *Comparative Politics: Rationality, Culture and Structure*, Cambridge University Press, Cambridge.

Liberal Democrat Party (2002), 'Legitimacy, accountability and freedom for the 21st century second chamber', Press release, 12 December 2002.

Lindner, J. and Rittberger, B. (2003), 'The creation, interpretation and contestation of institutions – revisiting historical institutionalism', *Journal of Commons Market Studies*, 41:3, 445–73.

Longford, Lord (1999), *A History of the House of Lords*, Sutton Publishing, Gloucestershire.

Low, S. (1906), *The Governance of England*, T. Fisher Unwin, London.

Lowell, A.L. (1912), *The Government of England*, Volume 1, Macmillan, New York.

Macdonald, R. (1920), *Parliament and Democracy*, National Labour Press, London.

March, J.G. and Olsen, J.P. (1984), 'The new institutionalism: organisational factors in political life', *American Political Science Review*, 78:2, 738–49.

March, J.G. and Olsen, J.P. (1989), *Rediscovering Institutions*, Free Press, New York.

Marshall, G. (1965), 'Parliament and the constitution', *Political Quarterly*, 36:3, 255–66.

May, T. (1995), *An Economic and Social History of Britain, 1760–1990*, Longman, Harlow.

McKechnie, W.S. (1909), *The Reform of the House of Lords*, James MacLehose and Sons, Glasgow.

McLean, I., Spirling, A. and Russell, M. (2003), 'None of the above: the UK House of Commons votes on reforming the House of Lords, February 2003', *Political Quarterly*, 74:3, 298–310.

More, C. (1997), *The Industrial Age: Economy and Society in Britain 1750–1995*, Longman, Harlow.

Morgan, J.P. (1975), *The House of Lords and the Labour Government 1964–1970*, Clarendon Press, Oxford.

Morgan, K.O. (1990), *The People's Peace: British History, 1945–1990*, Oxford University Press, Oxford.

Morrison, H. (1964), *Government and Parliament*, Oxford University Press, London.

Muir, R. (1930), *How Britain is Governed*, Constable, London.

Nairn, T. (1979), 'The future of Britain's crisis: a political analysis', in I. Kramnick (ed.), *Is Britain Dying? Perspectives on the Current Crisis*, Cornell University Press, London.

Norton, P. (1981), *The Commons in Perspective*, Martin Robertson, Oxford.

Norton, P. (1982), *The Constitution in Flux*, Martin Robertson, Oxford.

Norton, P. (1983), 'The Norton view', in D. Judge (ed.), *The Politics of Parliamentary Reform*, Heinemann, London.

Norton, P. (1985), 'Parliamentary reform: where to from here?', in P. Norton, *Parliament in the 1980s*, Basil Blackwell, Oxford.

Norton, P. (2000), 'Reforming parliament in the United Kingdom: the report of the Commission to Strengthen Parliament', *The Journal of Legislative Studies*, 6:3, 1–14.

Norton, P. (2001), *The British Polity*, Longman, London.

Ostrogorski, M. (1902), *Democracy and the Organisation of Political Parties*, Quadrangle, Chicago.

Palmer, J. (1970), 'Allocation of time: the guillotine and voluntary timetabling', *Parliamentary Affairs*, 23:3, 232–47.

Parliament First (2003), *Parliament's Last Chance*, Parliament First, London.

Peters, B.G. (1999), *Institutional Theory in Political Science*, Pinter, London.

Peters, B.G., Pierre, J. and King, D.S. (2005), 'The politics of path dependency: political conflict in historical institutionalism', *The Journal of Politics*, 67:4, 1275–300.

Pierson, P. (1996), 'The path to European Integration: a historical institutional perspective', *Comparative Political Studies*, 29:1, 123–63.

Pierson, P. (2000a), 'Increasing returns, path dependence and the study of politics', *American Political Science Review*, 94:2, 251–67.

Pierson, P. (2000b), 'The limits of design: explaining institutional origins and change', *Governance*, 13:4, 475–99.

Polidano, C. (1999), 'The bureaucrat who fell under a bus: ministerial responsibility, executive agencies and the Derek Lewis affair in Britain', *Governance*, 12:2, 201–29.

Polidano, C. (2000), 'The bureaucrats who almost fell under a bus: a reassertion of ministerial responsibility?', *Political Quarterly*, 71:2, 177–83.

Political Quarterly (1963), 'The decline of parliament', *Political Quarterly*, 34:3, 233–39.

Political Quarterly (1965), 'Parliament today and tomorrow', *Political Quarterly*, 36:3, 251–5.

Poole, K.P. (1979), 'The powers of select committees of the House of Commons to send for persons, papers and records', *Parliamentary Affairs*, 32:3, 268–78.

Power Commission (2006), *Power to the People, The Power Inquiry*, London.

Power, G. (2001), 'Making government accountable – the report of the Hansard Society Commission on Parliamentary Scrutiny', *Journal of Legislative Studies*, 7:2, 1–12.

Pugh, M. (1978), *Electoral Reform in War and Peace, 1906–18*, Routledge and Kegan Paul, London.

Pugh, M. (2002), *The Making of Modern British Politics, 1867–1945*, Blackwell, Oxford.

Punnett, R.M. (1965), 'The House of Lords and Conservative governments 1951–1964', *Political Studies*, 13:1, 85–8.

Redlich, J. (1908), *The Procedure of the House of Commons*, Volumes 1, 2 and 3, Constable, London.

Richard, I. and Welfare, D. (1999), *Unfinished Business: Reforming the House of Lords*, Vintage, London.

Richards, P.G. (1979), 'Private Members' Legislation', in S.A. Walkland (ed.), *The House of Commons in the Twentieth Century*, Clarendon Press, Oxford.

Robbins, K. (1994), *The Eclipse of a Great Power: Modern Britain 1870–1992*, Longman, Harlow.

Robinson, A. (1985), 'The financial work of the new select committees', in G. Drewry, *The New Select Committees: A Study of the 1979 Reforms*, Clarendon Press, Oxford.

Robson, W. (1964), 'The reform of government', *Political Quarterly*, 35:3, 193–211.

Rush, M (1979), 'The Members of Parliament', in S.A. Walkland (ed.), *The House of Commons in the Twentieth Century*, Clarendon Press, Oxford.

Rush, M. (1981), *Parliamentary Government in Britain*, Pitman, London.

Rush, M. (1999), 'The House of Lords: the political context', in P. Carmichael and B. Dickson (eds), *The House of Lords: Its Parliamentary and Judicial Roles*, Hart Publishing, Oxford.

Rush, M. (2001), *The Role of the Member of Parliament Since 1868*, Oxford University Press, Oxford.

Rush, M. and Ettinghausen, C. (2002), *Opening Up the Usual Channels*, Hansard Society, London.

Russell, M. (2003), 'Is the House of Lords already reformed?', *Political Quarterly*, 74:3, 311–8.

Ryle, M. (1965), 'Committees of the House of Commons', *Political Quarterly*, 36:3, 295–308.

Samuel, H. (1931), 'Defects and reforms of parliament', *Political Quarterly*, 2:3, 305–18.

Searing, D. (1994), *Westminster's World: Understanding Political Roles*, Harvard University Press, Massachusetts.

Seaward, P. and Silk, P. (2004), 'The House of Commons', in V. Bogdanor (ed.), *The British Constitution in the Twentieth Century*, Oxford University Press, Oxford.

Self, R. (2000), *The Evolution of the British Party System, 1885–1940*, Longman, London.

Shanks, M. (1961), *The Stagnant Society*, Harmondsworth, Penguin.

Shell, D. (1988), *The House of Lords*, Philip Allan, Oxford.

Shell, D. (1992a), 'The European Communities Committee', in D. Shell and D. Beamish (eds), *The House of Lords at Work*, Clarendon Press, Oxford.

Shell, D. (1992b), 'Conclusion', in D. Shell and D. Beamish (eds), *The House of Lords at Work*, Clarendon Press, Oxford.

Shell, D. (1999), 'To revise and deliberate: the British House of Lords', in S.C. Patterson and A. Mughan (eds), *Senates: Bicameralism in the Contemporary World*, Ohio State University Press, Columbus.

Shell, D. (2000), 'Labour and the House of Lords: a case study in constitutional reform', *Parliamentary Affairs*, 52:2, 290–310.

Simon, H. (1985), 'Human nature and politics: the dialogue of psychology with political science', *American Political Science Review*, 79:1, 293–304.

Skocpol, T. (1985), 'Bringing the state back in: strategies of analysis in current research', in P.B. Evans, D. Rueschemeyer and T. Skocpol (eds), *Bringing the State Back In*, Cambridge University Press, Cambridge.

Smith, E.A. (1992), *The House of Lords in British Politics and Society 1815–1911*, Longman, London.

Southern, D. (1986), 'Lord Newton, the Conservative Peers and the Parliament Act of 1911', in C. Jones and D.L. Jones (eds), *Peers, Politics and Power: The House of Lords, 1603–1911*, Hambledon Press, London.

Strachey, J. and Joad, C.E.M. (1931), 'Parliamentary reform: the New Party's proposals', *Political Quarterly*, 2:3, 319–36.

Stoker, G. (2006), *Why Politics Matters*, Palgrave, Basingstoke.

Study of Parliament Group (1969), 'Parliament and legislation', *Parliamentary Affairs*, 22:3, 210–15.

Theakston, K. (2004), *Winston Churchill and the British Constitution*, Politico's, London.

Thelen, K. and Steinmo, S. (1992), 'Historical institutionalism in comparative politics', in S. Steinmo, K. Thelen and F. Longstreth (eds), *Structuring Politics: Historical Institutionalism in Comparative Analysis*, Cambridge University Press, Cambridge.

Thorpe, A. (1992), *Britain in the 1930s*, Blackwell, Oxford.

Thorpe, A. (2001), *A History of the British Labour Party*, Palgrave, Basingstoke.

Tivey, L. (1995), 'Constitutional reform: a modest proposal', *Political Quarterly*, 66:4, 278–86.

Tomlinson, J. (2001), *The Politics of Decline: Understanding Post-War Britain*, Longman, Harlow.

Tomlinson, J. (2003), 'The decline of the empire and the economic 'decline' of Britain', *Twentieth Century British History*, 14:3, 201–21.

Torfing, J. (2001), 'Path-dependent Danish welfare reforms: the contribution of the new institutionalisms to understanding evolutionary change', *Scandinavian Political Studies*, 24:4, 277–309.

Vincent, J.R. (1966), 'The House of Lords', *Parliamentary Affairs*, 19:4, 475–85.

Walkland, S.A. (1960), 'The House of Commons and the estimates', *Parliamentary Affairs*, 13:4, 477–88.

Walkland, S.A. (1964), 'Science and Parliament – the origin and influence of the parliamentary and scientific committee', *Parliamentary Affairs*, 17:3, 308–20.

Walkland, S.A. (1976), 'The politics of parliamentary reform', Parliamentary Affairs, 29:2, 190–200.

Walkland, S.A. (1979), 'Government legislation in the House of Commons', in S.A. Walkland (ed.), The House of Commons in the Twentieth Century, Clarendon Press, Oxford.

Walkland, S.A. (1983), 'Parliamentary reform, party realignment and electoral reform', in D. Judge (ed.), The Politics of Parliamentary Reform, Heinemann, London.

Walters, R. (2004), 'The House of Lords', in V. Bogdanor (ed.), The British Constitution in the Twentieth Century, Oxford University Press, Oxford.

Weare, V. (1965), 'The House of Lords – prophecy and fulfilment', Parliamentary Affairs, 18:4, 422–33.

Webb, S. and B. (1975), A Constitution for the Socialist Commonwealth of Great Britain, Cambridge University Press, Cambridge.

Weir, S. and Beetham, D. (1999), Political Power and Democratic Control in Britain, Routledge, London.

Wells, J. (1997), The House of Lords: From Saxon Wargods to a Modern Senate, Hodder and Stoughton, London.

Weston, C.C. and Kelvin, P. (1986), 'The 'Judas Group' and the Parliament Bill of 1911', in C. Jones and D.L. Jones (eds), Peers, Politics and Power: The House of Lords, 1603–1911, Hambledon Press, London.

Wheeler-Booth, M. (2003), 'The House of Lords', in R. Blackburn and A. Kennon, Parliament: Functions, Practice and Procedures, Sweet and Maxwell, London.

Wiseman, H.V. (1959), 'Parliamentary reform', Parliamentary Affairs, 12:2, 240–54.

Wiseman, H.V. (1960), 'Procedure: The House of Commons and the select committee', Parliamentary Affairs, 13:2, 236–47.

Wiseman, H.V. (1970a), 'Standing committees', in A.H. Hanson and B.Crick (eds), The Commons in Transition, Fontana, London.

Wiseman, H.V. (1970b), 'The new specialised committees', in A.H. Hanson and B.Crick (eds), The Commons in Transition, Fontana, London.

Woodhouse, D. (1994), Ministers and Parliament, Clarendon Press, Oxford.

Woodhouse, D. (2001), 'The role of ministerial responsibility in motivating ministers to morality', in J. Fleming and I. Holland (eds), Motivating Ministers to Reality, Ashgate, Dartmouth.

Woodhouse, D. (2004a), 'UK ministerial responsibility in 2002: the tale of two resignations', Public Administration, 82:1, 1–19.

Woodhouse, D. (2004b), 'Ministerial responsibility', in V. Bogdanor (ed.), The British Constitution in the Twentieth Century, Oxford University Press, Oxford.

Index

CPSIA information can be obtained at www.ICGtesting.com
Printed in the USA
LVOW09s0327301014

3753LVUK00004B/65/P